CAMILO TORRES

CAMILO TORRES

by German Guzman

translated by John D. Ring

Sheed and Ward, Inc., New York

Library of Congress Catalog Card Number 69-16991

Manufactured in the United States of America

Contents

CAMILO TORRES

Chapter 1

Symbol Rather than Myth

Jorge Camilo Restrepo Torres came into the world in Bogotá on the 3rd of February, 1929. He was born into the home of Calixto Torres* Umaña, a doctor of medicine, and Isabel Restrepo Gaviria, both of the upper urban class. In my search for details on his life, I have spoken with his friends and relatives and with classmates in high school, the university, and the seminary. But it is from his mother that we receive the best information regarding her son:

"When he was two years old, we took him to Europe, where he

* Isabel Restrepo Gaviria was married twice: the first time, to a German citizen, Carl Westendorf. Carlos Edgardo (today living in Chile) and Gerda Maria were born of this union. From the second marriage came Luis Fernando (a doctor now living in Illinois) and Jorge Camilo.—Author's note.

lived for three years in Belgium and Barcelona. While there he contracted scarlet fever and his father, worried about his health, took many precautions. This is why he hired a tutor who taught him to read and write.

"When he was eight he entered the German school in Bogotá, where he took his first classes until the school was closed because of the war. It was the time of the Second World War, and I remember that on the very first day of school, a German boy was speaking against Colombia in front of Camilo, and Camilo's immediate reaction was to sock him. From that day on he became the most respected boy in his class.

"As a small child, he was very quarrelsome. Upon entering high school he was initiated into the Quinta Mutis, a branch of the Colegio del Rosario, but because he was involved in so many other activities, he failed the fourth year. At that time he was inclined towards newspaper reporting and he wrote, edited, financed, and sold a very nice little periodical which he printed at first on a mimeograph machine a friend had given him. It was called *El Puma* and the explanatory note said, 'A weekly daily paper appearing each month.' In the periodical he was very critical of the professors, but then, he was always a rebel.

"He repeated the fourth year in the Liceo Cervantes, which was then a lay institute, where he continued editing *El Puma*. At the beginning of the sixth year of school and in the face of the reproaches of his father and me, he solemnly promised to be a better student, and in fact he far exceeded our hopes. He took all the first prizes, including a book which the French Embassy gave to the best student; he won it unanimously. All the professors congratulated him, including Dr. Manuel Mosquera Garcés.

"He was always an excellent athlete; I don't think there was a game he didn't play. In the school he was president of all the sport clubs. He also belonged to the Boy Scouts and went on several excursions down the Magdalena River on rafts of plantain shoots. On one occasion he arrived at Honda in such a pitiful state that they confused him with a fugitive.

"He entered the National University to study law, but he was only there one semester. In that period he collaborated as an editor of *La Razon,* a periodical which Juan Lozano directed.

"He became friendly with the family of Dr. José Antonio Montalvo, whose daughter became his girl friend for a time. They introduced him to the Dominican Fathers, and Camilo resolved to become a member of that order. In the train station itself, I stopped him when he was going off to the monastery of Chiquinquira, and I almost had to use force to make him return. I preferred that he enter the diocesan seminary, and even though the courses had already begun, the rector, Monsignor José Manuel Diaz, accepted him. I believe it was a mistake for me to do that, but then the other boys who went with the Dominicans returned within three months and the only one to become a priest was Camilo.

"In the seminary he was a brilliant student and was singled out for his education to such a point that Cardinal Luque advanced his ordination so that he might go to Louvain to study sociology.

"In Louvain he lived one year with me and was Vice-Rector of the Latin American College. He lived after that in a very humble little village where he had to prepare his own meals and wash his own clothes.

"While at Louvain he took advantage of the opportunity to travel throughout Europe, even to Prague where he celebrated a Mass. In Paris he worked with Abbé Pierre collecting rags, dressed like a laborer. He lived very poorly.

"On his return to Colombia he was appointed chaplain of the National University, where he endeared himself to all the students. He built a chapel there and was one of the founders of the Department of Sociology. But he was relieved of the chaplaincy after defending two students who had been unjustly expelled. He then went to the parish of Vera Cruz as an assistant and to the School of Public Administration (ESAP) as dean. He began various cooperatives in Tunjuelito and belonged to the Board of Directors of Incora. While in Esap he founded at Yopal an experimental farm for the preparation of technicians.

"He was a voracious reader. From childhood he displayed his

solidarity with the exploited. While still a child he would take the medical samples of his father and give them away to the poor. Even the money which he received for the movies was always given to the children in the poor neighborhoods.

"That deep love of his for the poor convinced him that only by seizing power could the common people effectively change their situation."[1]

In order to understand Camilo it is necessary to get inside him. This demands total honesty of us and a mind free of stereotypes and prejudices. It is also necessary to place him in the proper context so that we shall not sever the connection between his ideas and his witness.

Starting from these premises, we will proceed to enter the world of his multiple activities. We will feel that we cannot return unperturbed to our own lives because he will have aroused within us excitement, compassion, confusion, admiration, respect, and affection. For many the effect will be remorse. He was a man of such a compelling and challenging appearance that his extraordinary message becomes tremendously overpowering. He does not send us others with his message. He confronts us with it himself.

We cannot consider the Colombian situation or the problem of Latin America as an accidental and momentary episode, because both have an historical dimension and transcendency. One must start with the present before he can enter into the future.

It is an understatement to say that it is a difficult task to interpret a man of such contradictions—both priest and guerilla—of such surprising decisions, such obstinate impulses, such magnificent honesty, such enduring loyalty, such giving of himself without limit. "He is known for his generosity, love, noble heart, courage, sincerity, loyalty, frankness, integrity, heroism, friendship, nobility, hospitality, courtesy, openness, gratitude, decency, culture, and all those qualities of the just and perfect gentleman."[2]

An analysis of Camilo is very difficult because so many factors, which appear and cross one another, form his personality. And we understand personality in Ribot's sense of the individual in his totality, continuity, and psychosomatic unity.[3]

Heredity and constitutional tendencies, the influence of environment and education, bursting energy, psychic variables, affective-active predispositions—all of them could be used as a point of reference in order to construct the personality of Camilo. Nevertheless, I wish to disentangle myself from preestablished standards in order to discover the man and, through this, to study what he was, what he longed for and dreamed of and what he wanted to accomplish. It is a useless pretense at understanding him or capturing him, if we omit his human dimension. We must start with the real man in order to uncover completely the hidden thread of his triumph and his sorrow.

As is the case with every complex personality, we run the risk of having a unilateral and simple outlook, of ignoring for reasons of sympathy or aversion what he really was in order to present him in a neat little package for those who are anxious to know him.

For some, he could be the protean martyr, heroic, inimitable, unique, intangible, far beyond any attempt at analysis; for others he could turn out to be the pitiful fool, the terrifying lunatic, the rebel without a cause, the frustrated individual whose name must be pronounced in a whisper, the anti-social type who has degenerated into a malicious archetype of common delinquency.

One can also fall into the trap of having Camilo say things which he never said or thought, or having him express things which he thought but not in the same way.

Those are not to be forgiven who picture him in a simple parable and treat him with pity, tears, evasions, like a Turkish genie whose sacrifice would be diluted to the point of evaporation into the air where his memory will barely float.

The question is exactly where do we place him? Between hero and myth, deification and insignificance, genius and stupidity, overpowering greatness and flighty childishness, determined warrior and flash in the pan. Between authentic witness and irreverent apostasy, the truth in broad daylight and fatal hallucination, proud rebelliousness enlightened by sincerity and vain egocentric gesture.

How will we interpret him? Dreamer or creator, visionary of today, messianic destiny, the spreading flame, deplorable frustration? Rallying standard, bold champion of the impoverished, magnificent or ridiculous, tormented or deluded, the complete answer to the hope of a people who could crown him with opprobrium or with praise?

We lived together for almost five years. I assisted at the overflowing of his early unrest; I knew his every mood; I saw how he was propelled towards the goals he had set for himself. Basing my case on this and on many other valid reasons, I wish to present a Camilo purified of arbitrary mixtures: the true Camilo, the real Camilo, the human Camilo, the authentic Camilo.

We also rebel against that caravan of mercenary grave diggers and historical grave robbers. The first try to hide him, to blot him out, to erase him from the conscience of Colombia and America, proposing to show that he was "killed in time." The second reclaim him in order to pay him the homage of courteous and useless memorials. And there we have the error: all of these, both the grave diggers and the grave robbers, are obsessed with the corpse of Camilo: the frustrated Camilo, the emotional Camilo who remained on the mountain in hope that "his mouth would be filled with flowers and wheat."[4]

I do not support those who adopt extremist attitudes regarding him: of condemnation in order to bury him under the leaden headstone of silence; of diluting him, alleging that he should not even be mentioned; of exalting him, so that he is upheld as a hero and martyr without the permission of the historical event; of exploiting him, in order to submit him to personal or group interests; of demeaning him, publicly proclaiming him a demagogue, lunatic, thief, and criminal.

We owe it to all the generations who are fighting throughout the Americas for liberty and authentic democracy, to penetrate deeply into the meaning of the purpose and the sacrifice of Camilo.

By what right do some egotists claim him for their own property, convinced that they are the exclusive interpreters of his ideas and his life? They nauseate us. Camilo does not fit into easy categories.

Out of respect for Camilo, those who do not want to be disturbed should not read this book; nor should those with a hypocritical spirit, a Manichean conscience, or a malicious personality. And much less those who are always genuflecting before the God of fear, the God of mathematics, the God of convenience. No! They should not open these pages! The masters of wheeling and dealing, the suspicious, the prudent who are easily scandalized; nor should those with a bourgeois mentality; the Christians who do not witness, the soldiers of honor, the puritanical critics, the opportunists who never commit themselves. Don't even look at him, you who long to live your lives uncontaminated, unpolluted, unshaken, and satisfied.

Camilo has a unique heritage in the dimensions of the temporal and of history—the people. The people will keep him as he was. It is up to the poor people, the peasant and worker of America, because he is the response to the hunger, the helplessness, the widespread sickness, the clamor which comes from the jungle. He is the voice of the exploited class, of the serf, of the anonymous man destined to be cleverly broken; of the blood which accuses, of silent immolation, the profaned dead, the body left unburied, the carrion on the road. He is a shout of hope and of the certainty of an immeasurable destiny.

Camilo attempted things which the people understood. As a result of this it can be said that he brought the revolution to everyone. He revived nonconformity and defeated conformity. Because of that some follow him while others curse him.

But there is something more: there is the synthesis. He captures the heritage of all those who have sacrificed for the true liberty of Latin America and of all those who have sincerely believed in the urgency of a revolutionary change. Because of that it can be said that he epitomizes the anxiety of all those who fell in battle with the conviction that the political system against which they rebelled was unjust, cruel, monstrous, bloodthirsty, and intolerable.

This book is a message for the people. It is written so that the common people might understand him. It is direct, abrupt, disturbing, and challenging.

It is difficult for me to speak of Camilo in any other way. This book is neither scientific nor written for the pseudo-intellectuals who, beforehand, will brand it as emotional and founded on apriori judgments, as a tribute to bandits, whitewashers of hatred and violence, apologists of crime, disturbers of the public order, communists, irreverent, tendentious, heretics. I am not deserving of the mercenary criticism of such critics nor of their hypocrisy. In their conscience they are frightened. Camilo terrifies them. He dreamed, he lived, he rebelled, he fought, he fell with the grandeur of one who never betrayed his principles. This faithfulness to his principles determined his death.

He gambled everything because he was completely committed. At all times he maintained a vital attitude of commitment to the people as a priest, as a Christian, and as a revolutinary. He believed it was his duty to be on the side of the poor, and for this he sacrificed his life without stint or any desire for praise.

Because of that the people will defend him against every attack, against every possible exploitation. With the death of Camilo something is started. His sacrifice breathes hope into the people of America for a new day. Camilo is spirit and life, movement, honesty and threat. He is the future, destiny. He is destined to be a great prophet of the new world, a symbol of the deep hope of all those men in the Americas who want to be free—a hope which grows and is translated into living, thinking, and working for freedom. He is the guaranty of the authenticity which America needs without foreign or mixed influences, because the revolution of this continent either is America's revolution or it is nothing. No one will be able to promote this revolution if it is not placed at the service of the dispossessed. The dynamic symbolism of Camilo is rooted in this. Symbol rather than myth. Reality rather than a legend.

This revolutionary and guerilla priest should be considered an unusual and unique case in the Americas today.

In order to proceed with dialectical rigor it is necessary to ask: What are the elements which go into the "act of Camilo Torres"? In my understanding the following can be considered as helps because they give us the key to this human riddle and they make an integral interpretation much more possible.

1. He conceives of existence as love and he searches in Christianity and in the priesthood for the best way to accomplish this love in the service of man.

2. He knows the problems of Colombia as a result of his studies

(of scientific character) and by being in contact with socio-economic realities (application of objective methods).

3. As a Christian, as a priest, as a scientist, he concludes that the solution to these problems is the seizure of power by the people through a revolution.

4. He judges that the only effective way to bring about the revolution is through armed rebellion.

This is his plan of action. Sad and brilliant. He realizes it without messianism and without vain presumption but with unswerving decisiveness and loyalty.

Chapter 2

Christian and Priest

Basically, Camilo was a man in continual search of the transcendent. He discovered that the best way to find it was as a believer in Christianity and, as a Christian, in the priesthood. His decision was categorical: "I chose Christianity because I found in it the best way to serve my neighbor. I was chosen by Christ to be a priest forever, motivated by the desire to devote myself completely to the love of my brothers."[1] It is impossible to understand him unless we see him as both believer and priest.

Going a little further, his question to "two-dimensional" man, as formulated by himself, reads thus: "The Christian in a pluralistic society finds himself in situations which mire him in perplexity: Should he, then, continue to theorize or should he act?"[2] He found his answer in the theology of charity, according to which the temporal commitment of the Christian is exercised in the love of God and neighbor.

He emphasized this thesis in the statement which he read at the

Second International Congress of Pro Mundi Vita in September of 1964. "You cannot have supernatural life without charity, and that charity must be effective charity. Actions performed for the benefit of our neighbor are indispensable if that charity is going to be meaningful. At the same time, ineffective charity is not charity."[3] For Camilo, the man who is truly integrated from the point of view of the material and the spiritual, the natural and the supernatural, can only live out of love.

In the temporal world the Christian extends Christ's witness of love by continuing the work of creating a world where every man can develop himself completely. Wherefore, the work of building temporal structures which will be fitting for the divine plan constitutes the responsibility of the Christian.

This is why Camilo interprets Christianity as a life of action, dedication, and justice.[4] His life will necessarily be one of service, witness, and proclamation. His Christianity is open to the problems hidden in every man and to the society in which human values must be developed. It is a Christianity which is free of all that is exclusive and Manichean.

His attitude and his actions come into immediate conflict with those of many Catholics who reduce Christianity to a sentimental "devotionalism" which would not hesitate to burn Protestants and Communists alive; to a political-religious zeal which would render the Church subject to political parties and national sentiments; to a "providentialism" in which God is conceived as just another force in the natural universe working on the level of other secondary causes; to an "angelism" according to which each man must ignore the real world; to a conformism expressed in resignation, which is the religious form of escape from responsibility. All of these pictures carry with them attitudes of "for or against" for the pseudo-Christian because they do not take man in his existential condition or in his social circumstances.

Since Camilo judged that the best way to express charity as effective service of man is through the priesthood, it can be said that the priesthood—in his case—is a consequence of his search for Christianity. Thus we are led to speculate about the development of his priestly vocation.

Some Dominican priests, Blanchet among others, were preaching spiritual retreats in which Camilo participated. He said that he found in the discussions of the French priests something new, a different language, an honest approach to man and to the world. For him the absence of God was converted into presence; in his own words, he finally began to think.

"Why did you go to the seminary?" I asked him one day when we were both working in the office; "family circumstances, a disappointing love affair, interior emptiness, a religious awakening?"

"A little bit of all that," he told me. "Actually what happened was the following. During one of my vacations I went to Llano. The immensity of that place, the silence, the tropical explosion of life, of sun, impressed me very much. I began to be disturbed. I wanted to be alone. I realized that life as I understood it, as I was living it, lacked meaning. I thought I could be more useful socially. I was faced then with the great problem: where and how could I be more useful? I analyzed the professions, one by one: medicine, law, engineering, chemistry . . . ? None of those. What about the seminary? I told myself that the immensity of Llano had helped me find God. It was the solution. It seemed to me a total solution. The most logical. I returned to Bogotá determined to enter the monastery of the Dominicans."

"Why?" Camilo was silent. Then he went on.

"There was an explosion. My mother was fiercely opposed. Finally, we compromised on the diocesan seminary, and so I entered. What do you think of the police detaining me at the train on my way to Chiquinquira!"

"But why were you attracted to the Dominicans?"

"Perhaps because I connected the silence of Llano with the silence of the cloisters. I wanted silence, meditation, tranquility. Then too, the talks of the French priests had fired me up."

"And in the seminary?"

"Well, you might say that they put up with me. A friend of ours said they spoiled me there, that I always got my own way. With some classmates I founded *Los Caimanes*. We certainly had some uneasy moments, but in the end they ordained me."

Nevertheless, his aptitude for the priestly life has been called into question. That is what appears from these words of a priest: "If there was any failure on the part of Camilo's superiors in the seminary, it was an excess of kindness and tolerance. His whole way of life did not recommend him for the priestly life; but his extraordinary gift of understanding always compensated for the faults which had already begun to appear. His intelligence, more quick than profound, made his superiors decide that it was not necessary for him to take a complete philosophy course; they thought that those early studies which he had taken in law could replace it."[5]

This statement prompted the following comment: ". . . the superiors of Camilo, you say, in the face of his quick intelligence, did not make him study, and in the place of philosophy, they accepted a few months of study in the School of Law. How ignorant you must be of our Archdiocesan Seminary today and, in fact, always. Only thus can I understand how you can affirm such falsehoods. I ask you to examine the process which the seminary uses and has always used, following the norms set down by the Holy See for the ordination of a student, and check the books for those courses which Camilo took and you will see that he completed them with every academic requirement fulfilled."[6]

The Belgian Canon François Houtart, Director of the Center of Socio-Religious Studies and professor at the Institute of Pastoral Theology at Louvain, in speaking of Camilo as a priest, holds that "from the beginning, the priesthood of Camilo was a reflective priesthood. If he had doubts, it was not about his priesthood but whether or not he should choose the life of a religious or a secular priest, moved precisely by a deep desire for faithfulness to his vocation."[7]

It should not cause surprise that in dealing with Camilo, everything is called into doubt, even his priesthood. For those who knew him well there is no doubt about the honesty of Camilo when he entered the seminary. Dishonesty finds no place in a man who had no guile. He was an open and sincere man.

Cardinal Luque sent him to Louvain to study sociology so that, upon his return, he might work in the social organizations of the Archdiocese of Bogotá. Camilo always spoke to me of the Cardinal as a very human prelate, understanding, simple, fatherly.

At Louvain his social concern and his nonconformity increased. He now began to speak of the urgency of preparing young men to bring about a change in the prevailing situation in Colombia. Even more, he demanded the necessity of a structural change through revolutionary means. This attitude became evident to some bishops after speaking to a few Louvain professors when they were returning in December, 1965, from the last session of the Council. One example, among others, was the Bishop of Ibaque, Monsignor José Joaquin Florez.

Did this attitude in Camilo arise from defects in his own academic training or from his connections with Marxists? "He was sent to special studies at Louvain, the center of much ideological agitation. This is always unfortunate for those who do not have a sound philosophical foundation. He was caught up with a group of Marxist students; or better, he had permitted the Colombian group to become strongly infiltrated with Marxism, because of which his superiors, informed of the direction which his activities had taken, recalled him before he finished his studies in Sociology."[8]

Fr. Enrique Acosta Rincon remarks on the foregoing statement: "I find very interesting the paragraph in which you say that Camilo knew very well that there already existed a powerful Catholic social movement which he did not want to follow because he already had a Marxist mentality. Your statement is too simplistic. That he had little confidence in such a movement is true, but for other reasons, whether they were correct or not. Sometimes because he saw it was very clerical; other times because it had a very paternalistic direction or because its important positions had to be controlled by the hierarchy or technically its methods did not convince him, etc., but not because Camilo was a Marxist. Vincente, don't you believe that we should have more tolerance when judging those who do not think as we do?"[9]

Canon François Houtart, writing from Brussels, comments on the article of Fr. Andrade in a letter to the editor of the magazine *America:*

"When I was in New York I had the opportunity to read the article in *America* on Camilo Torres. Having been an intimate friend of Camilo Torres, this article deeply saddened me. Therefore I must point out that I consider it tendentious.

"It is very easy to present Camilo Torres as a man overcome

with Marxist ideas from the time he was studying in Louvain and to say he was not a true priest. It is much too big a task to explain in one letter the story of Camilo but, if I can, I wish to show that what the article says is, in great part, inexact, or at least that it is incomplete. To do that I will give some few examples.

"It was said that Camilo was called home from Louvain before finishing his degree in sociology. This is not true. Camilo obtained the M.A. in Social Science and remained a long time after that in Louvain (for at least one year) as vice-rector of the Latin American College, a seminary founded by the Belgian bishops for the formation of priests for Latin America. He had planned to return to Louvain in order to present his doctoral thesis, but not without having first completed his research in Colombia.

"I don't know who were the Marxists or pro-Marxists in Louvain, except perhaps persons such as Jacques Leclerq. Charles Moeller, Jean Ladriere, and myself. It would have been very strange if the Belgian bishops had accepted as rector of the Latin American College a priest who 'was sent to Louvain for advanced studies in sociology where he was immediately contaminated with the ferment of those ideologies.' Contrary to what was said in the article, Camilo was never chosen to conduct research at the Center of Socio-Religious Studies in Bogotá instead of performing the 'exhausting but apostolic work of the typical young priest.' He was named chaplain of the university, and during this time he conducted research on the radio schools of Colombia. I suppose this is not apostolic or exhausting work.

"If I cite these examples it is only to demonstrate how unfounded are some of the assertions in the article. Many friends of Camilo did not agree with him on several points, and I was one of them. But all of them had a very real respect for him and knew him to be a real man and priest. They were witnesses of his true (and not Marxist or abnormal) generosity and love for the poor.

"If Camilo went too far, that is explained by the structural situation of the country and by the fact that the majority of the leaders of the Church are deeply conservative, and even reactionary in many cases. Without this knowledge it is impossible to explain his situation. In this sense, even when we cannot prove it, the gesture of Camilo Torres holds a prophetic significance: to remind the people of their sins. We hope that at least some of them will understand it."

The Jesuit Renato Poblete, writing from Santiago, Chile, made the following comments on this article: "I was in Berkeley with Father Gustavo Perez who studied Sociology in Louvain with Camilo and was an intimate friend of his. Father Perez complained that the article of Fr. Andrade was very prejudicial. Various priests I met at the Theology Conference at Notre Dame reacted very strongly against the article of Fr. Andrade. Our opinion here, where many knew Camilo very well, is one of regret that *America* has published such an article.

"We do not justify the acts of Camilo Torres, as can be seen in the last issue of *Mensaje*, but no Christian could say that 'he did not have a vocation': or that he was exploited by Marxist extremists at Louvain and was immediately captivated by them from the moment of his arrival in that city; or that 'his temperament and family background would hardly recommend him for the priestly life.' I believe that this last statement is completely false and lacking in charity."

There is in addition, the following document, kept by Camilo in his personal files, which gives us a glimpse of his relationship with his hierarchical superior:

"Archdiocese of Bogotá
Chancery Office
Bogotá, July 28, 1958

Camilo Torres
Louvain

Dear Camilo,

It gives me pleasure to reply, even briefly, to your letter of July 15th. I agree that the doctorate should not be lost sight of because of the advantage which it contains and especially when you can come here to work on your thesis.

You have permission to remain in Europe until the beginning of October and then to stop in the United States. Your project there, as you have pointed out, can constitute an important part of your formation and prepare you better for your future apostolate.

Crisanto Cardinal Luque
Archbishop of Bogotá"

The priesthood, for Camilo, even though he had not endured the "exhausting but apostolic work of the typical parish priest," as Father Andrade writes, could never be distinct from a love which was always in evidence. Such a concept would have been a barrier for him with the poor, with those in misery.

For Camilo the priesthood should be, above all else, "a profession of love at all times." It must be a love that has as its chosen, though not exclusive, object the poor. The priesthood is either directed to the poor or it is not an authentic priesthood. In this orientation to the poor a severe lack of social justice is discovered when one analyzes the causes of their misery. Social justice, according to the social encyclicals of the Church, should prevail over kindness as an expression of the true sense of Christian love.

Camilo held that the mission of the priest should not be limited to a routine administration of the sacraments but that it should demand the holding of definite positions regarding social justice. Such an attitude demanded freedom from temporal pressures, so that he might strike with equal force at the conscience of the exploiters and the exploited.

It was a conviction of his that the priest is obliged to involve himself deeply in the battle against every human disorder which is injurious to the interests of the community. Therefore, he pointed out that it was urgent that the ecclesiastical hierarchy speak out in a courageous way, less hesitantly and more explicitly, regarding the abusive situations caused by the minorities who enjoyed the use of power.

Following his conscience he repeated before the crowd: "I am not here as an overseer of the people but as their servant."

The essence of the apostolate rests in working so that everyone might have supernatural life and have it abundantly. Nevertheless, there are various signs of the existence of the supernatural life which condition apostolic activity. It is important that apostolic activity is directed towards producing those signs as means and not as ends: "There is an external element which is at the same time the sign and the necessary condition of apostolic action. It is the manifestation of love for one's neighbor."[10] Camilo drew his conviction of service and dedication from the New Testament: Mt. V, VI, VII, 16; Jn. X, XVIII, 3; Rom. XII, 10, 11, 15, 16, etc. I do not think he can be accused of a lack of New Testament principles. At the same time, he did not go to the people out of opportunism nor to exploit their religious devotion.

A natural religiosity prevails in Colombia as in many other areas of the Americas. It is easy to see that apostolic efforts have continually and very evidently been oriented towards conserving that religiosity, thus giving predominance to the ritualism of Christianity. As a result of this the priesthood is converted into a vehicle of cultural devotionalism far removed from authentic Christianity.

Perhaps here we can examine why the role of the great magician in the community is attributed to the priest and is in turn the origin of the confusion of Christianity with clericalism. It is from this confusion that we get this unorthodox maxim: Christianity is genuine in the proportion to which it is fanatically clerical. From such great inanity, which no one can deny, came three historical consequences diligently preached, defended, and guarded: (1) the predominance of a feudal clerical structure; (2) the unassailable position of privilege; and (3) obsequious relationship with temporal structures, oligarchies, minorities, and the powerful.

Camilo was one priest who went before public opinion without compromising himself with a pre-determined culture. He exercised a priesthood without privileges, without fanaticism and pious businesses, without agreements with the powerful who exploit the Church and the clergy, while serving them in order to maintain their own interests or to achieve dubious ends.

He was completely devoted to the practice of effective love for everyone of every condition, race, origin, family, opinions, ideology or belief. His great merit was that he lived his love.

Notwithstanding all of this, many have based the authenticity of Camilo's message on the fact that he was a priest. We can understand this because in our culture great importance is given to symbols. They are elevated by virtue of a sacral-emotional interpretation to the point where human values and the message itself pass over to a secondary place.

Camilo the man, Camilo the idea, Camilo the priest, remains subordinate to the symbol which is, in this case, the religious habit. it is this which gives him respectability, value and force.

Men consecrated to God and to the religious habit constitute in Colombia a union in which, until very recently, no possible dichotomy could fit. The common belief seems to be that a person is a priest by the fact that he puts on the religious habit. Among almost all people, whether cultured or not, you cannot succeed in establishing the distinction between the priest and the external symbol.

This is why Camilo was not spoken of as a new event in America, nor was his significance in opening up minds discussed, nor the value of his message, but rather his activity was referred to as the rebellion against the clerical habit.

Such an attitude is easy to explain: it obeys the laws of ancestral fanaticism. Camilo was praised because he wore the habit. Or, he was condemned because, wearing the habit, he caused scandal when he habitually undertook to destroy traditions and structures which were considered untouchable, and acted as if he had the right to adopt such "wild" positions.

Because of that, one arrived at this position: The theses of Camilo had validity as long as he didn't take off his habit; but without it the Levite and his doctrines come to nothing. Logical! The fact is that for us priests the habit confers prestige, demands submission, guarantees reverence, opens the doors of the great and the powerful, preserves respect, marks us for adulation, wins praise, promises tribute, overcomes obstacles and solves difficulties, makes our counsel infallible, gives authority, accomplishes the impossible—all of which, along with many other perquisites, is lost when one takes off the habit, whether for valid reasons or not.

Camilo did not escape the pressure of the conventional, even though he had a very advanced mentality and important achievements in every order. It is sufficient to follow the thread of his own personal case attentively.

The Primate declared on June 18, 1965, that "the activities of Father Camilo Torres are incompatible with his sacerdotal character and with his religious habit itself. It can happen that these two circumstances induce some Catholics to follow the erroneous and pernicious doctrines which Father Torres proposes in his program."

In a letter of March 10, 1965, Camilo writes: "After more than ten years in the priestly ministry I realize that, in the particular historical circumstances of the Church in Colombia and my own proper circumstances, I can pursue our objectives more effectively as a layman." That is to say, precisely by taking off the religious habit.

In a letter of June 24th, Camilo petitioned the Cardinal for reduction to the lay state. On the 26th of June the Cardinal granted that request.

On June 27th *El Tiempo* comments: "The decision of Father Camilo Torres to leave the priesthood to better emphasize a profound ideological conviction and a greater loyalty to his followers will offer popular psychology the opportunity to study one of the weakest points of the Colombian people. We are referring to their capacity for conviction and to the attraction which the external features of persons possess.

". . . We will have to see . . . if the political platforms, the interviews, the angry letters, the appearance on the first page in the national press, the obstinacy in the course of debate, were a phenomenon provoked by the habit or by the monk."

The humorist Klim called Camilo "his ex-reverend Camilo Torres," and he adds: "The actual dilemma then, as far as these curates who speak like Camilo are concerned, is to know if the habit makes the monk or if a hog in disguise is still a hog for all of that."[11]

In *El Tiempo* on September 2nd, Klim once again takes aim on Camilo: "Since resolving to take off the cassock, which gave him the respectability which he lacks today, he is a man without direction. Whatever he says now does not have the endorsement which it had before when he belonged to the Church. Today the extremist theses which he preaches, not from the pulpit but from the rostrum, are the simple demagogical slogans which revolutionaries with a more political bite than his have made of them. . . . He is not a structural man, as ex-general Alberto Ruiz Novoa, who took off his uniform just as Camilo took off his habit, has said. No one knows where he is going. It is as if, when he took off the habit, instead of putting it in the closet, he had wrapped it up within reach."[12]

In another paper we could read commentaries of the same kind: "Camilo Torres without his habit is being reduced to less of a personality each day. He is more of an agitator, a disorientated, difficult child, floating around in politics until such time as the diarrhea of the novelty passes. After that, oblivion, indifference, and loathing will come."[13]

And for even more elaboration: "Don't be taken in by the extraordinary spectacle of a priest without his habit preaching revolution; it will not last long."

Camilo considered the problem from three points of view.

The Sociologist. "The suppression of the habit, the clothes worn by university students in the street during the Middle Ages, has been left to the discretion of each bishop," he writes. "In my opinion it would be necessary to make a thorough study in each diocese of the social impact which this suppression would produce. We could then determine in each social sphere to what proportion the use of the habit encourages magic ideas of religion and to what proportion it destroys authentic religious understanding.

"The pastoral tendency is to diminish the distances (without suppressing the differences) between the clergy and the faithful. It is possible that this tendency will end up in the suppression of the religious habit by considering it a pastoral element unfavorable in a determined diocese, in a particular society, or in the world."[14]

The Instructor. His involvement in the political arena conflicted with the external exercise of the priestly ministry and with the religious habit which was a demonstrable sign of his condition as a man consecrated to God. He felt he had to ask for a corresponding release from the obligations of his state and so he did it.

The Man. In his political work the religious habit kept him at a distance from the people, erected barriers, created misunderstandings. Also, in accord with the demands of the revolution, he knew he had to go all the way, and so he asked for reduction to the lay state so that he might give his witness as a simple Christian.

Considering only this secondary focus, Camilo broke with conventional symbol, with the accidental—understood in its multiple aspects—with the medieval, in order to be tuned into the circumstances which led to his promise to fight for the rights of the people. Did he win or lose?

In Colombia, which is dominated by ancestral fanaticism and conventional ultraconservatism, we must confess that he lost ground in the eyes of the pious old ladies and the sanctimonious hypocrites. But not with the masses. For the people he continued to be Father Camilo! They interpreted his gesture as an irrefutable demonstration of his decision to fight. Simply speaking, Camilo gave up all the privileges which came from wearing clerical garb and the people saw in that an evidence of honesty.

Many ask if Camilo's revolutionary activity and rejection of the habit lessened in him his opinion of the priesthood.

Two episodes should be brought to light.

One day we were talking alone intimately. I asked him: "How was your interview with the Cardinal on June 22nd?"

"It was like this," he replied. "We said hello to one another. I told him I wanted to ask him to tell me which were my erroneous theses and which were the points irreconcilable with the doctrine of the Church.

"He told me: 'My answer was given in my statement of the eighteenth of June.'

" 'But what I wanted,' I argued with him, 'for the tranquility of my conscience, is that Your Eminence should show where my error is.' "

"It is in my statement. The priest should not get mixed up in politics."

"I believed, Your Eminence, that both as a priest and as a simple Christian, I could look for dialogue."

"No, I have nothing more to add. Everything was said in my statement."

"The Cardinal stood up. I left. The interview could not have lasted more than five minutes. If I had believed that I had parted from the doctrines of the Church, I would not have gone to the Cardinal."

On Thursday, June 24th, Camilo asked the Cardinal to relieve him of the external exercise of the priestly ministry.

On Monday, June 28th, in the afternoon, I had another long talk with Camilo. It led to a discussion of his priesthood.

"Are you thinking of giving up the priesthood?"

"No, that never. I asked, precisely, that I be allowed to celebrate Mass on Sundays. They told me no. I am a priest. . . . I did not invent my priesthood but they won't let me say Mass.* I would have said it in private. My priesthood is Christ's and belongs to the people. I cannot betray my conscience."

He then began to cry. He couldn't stop crying. Certainly, he didn't do it from weakness. For me his attitude was very respectable. It was an intimate scene between two priests. He then asked me to hear his confession.

What a noble soul he had!

"I could know Camilo as a priest," writes one of his students, "I should note that my 'conversion' and my discovery of the Christian life are owed to him. His religious habit never gave me the impression of being something exterior to himself, something that separated him from me and from the others.

"I was impressed and delighted with the way he said Mass. One time he asked me to serve him. I told him I had forgotten how to serve Mass. He told me: 'Don't worry. It is very simple; apply this principle: in case of doubt, genuflect!' That day I could see from close to him how he valued the Mass when he was officiating. He was transfigured and completely taken up in it.

"His homilies were always current and simple. Camilo began to translate the text of the Mass, to dialog with the faithful, and to turn the altar around before the others did it. The prayers which he wrote on small papers to be read at the Offertory had a lot of meaning for him. He always told us, 'Don't ask for yourselves. Ask for others.'

"In the confessional he was demanding. He asked for an expla-

* Camilo offered his last Mass in the Church of San Diego June 26, 1965.

nation for everything, and you had to tell a lot about yourself in order to receive absolution. After that the certainty of pardon would fill me with happiness. I have never had a spiritual peace as great as when I confessed to Camilo.

"In the groups of Christians or in the pluralist groups with whom we met once or twice a week, we found him a person who spoke with the same interest both of the necessity of putting into effect the Christian message and of the reality of the country. He had one idea which he insistently repeated: The Christian of today must give a pluralistic testimony and his commitment to the world, especially in the Latin American world, is to the revolution. He was not satisfied simply with revolutionary rhetoric but he gave meaning to his affirmations.

"He never doubted God, and his faith in 'El Patrón,' as he called Him, was contagious."[15]

Should these comments be interpreted as partial because of the friendship between this young student and Camilo? I don't think so. I find in his testimony a deep sense of sincerity and truth; it contains such validity that it deserves full acceptance.

Chapter 3

The National Reality

This chapter raises the question of whether Camilo was able to understand our historical crisis, belonging, as he did, to the middle class.

It is accepted by the social sciences that it is impossible to disavow the influence of the class or the group over the activity of those individuals who comprise those groups. To be free of those influences demands an exceptional case. Camilo taught that this is achieved only through discipline, scientific formation, moral courage and professional attitudes as well as self-criticism and the recognition of proper value judgments. All this is required in order to be preserved from class influences in the objective examination of facts. For him, to constitute that exception is the necessary foundation for a scientific outlook.[1]

This was exactly the case with Camilo and the course which he followed. When you carefully analyze his sociological writings, you discover in them a sustained anxiety to interpret reality according to scientific norms.

His position contradicts the focus which was given by us until very recently to a sociology which concentrated on the purely philosophical, descriptive, and folkloric, or which placed great emphasis on terminology without applying scientific criteria to the reality. Also, the schools of sociology in the United States and Europe had followers in Latin America who were imitators rather than interpreters of their sociology.[2]

Professor Orlando Fals Borda asserts that it is possible to distinguish three stages in the development of sociology in Colombia: the philosophical or European phase; the transitional or Euro–North American phase; the present stage which involves an elaboration of the other two.[3]

Personally, I agree with Alberto Prades, who distinguishes four stages in the intellectual evolution of Camilo. He began with empirical research at the time of his studies in Louvain (1958 on), and this continued until 1961, when he published his last works of sociological research. From 1961 to 1964 he dedicated himself to the synthesis of a social theory. From the beginning of 1964 to the middle of 1965 Camilo gradually abandoned his activities as a sociologist and prepared himself for direct political action. During 1965 and 1966, finally, he left the field of scientific analysis in order to seek concrete solutions to Colombian social problems.

In the first stage he was influenced by Leclerq, Moeller, Ladriere, and François Houtart, just to cite a few who held professors' chairs at the University of Louvain.

In 1959 he was one of the founders of the faculty of Sociology at the National University. With the first dean, Dr. Fals Borda, they were determined to orient the program to a modern empiricism, applying scientific methods to the investigation and interpretation of the local realities.

Secondly, he came into contact in the National University of Bogotá with the anti-conformist intellectual sector, and he discussed the human problems of the country at numerous round tables, complementing theoretical information with direct observation thanks to numerous trips to the various districts of Colombia.

He began to operate from a threefold base: science, technology and reality.

In order to increase his active participation he organized community action in the suburban neighborhood of Tunjuelito, utilizing objective methods in the promotion of the community. There he could apply the formula which he had followed since Louvain in 1957: "It is indispensable that every social action be based, in its doctrinal foundation, on the positive investigation of reality."[4]

The experience of Tunjuelito was born of NUNIPROC, a group founded by Camilo. It consisted of university students and professionals in order to give the necessary push to the process of change in the community with thoughts of being converted into a powerful movement later.

In 1962 he left the National University. The cause was a strike organized because of the expulsion of ten students without fair hearing or a previous investigation. Camilo, in association with the Dean of Sociology and almost all the professors of that Faculty, proposed an intelligent solution which did not discard the application of sanctions but had an objective basis and avoided ideological persecution. The Rector called them clowns and announced, as a possible measure, the "definite closing of the university." In answer the students demanded that Camilo be made Rector. For this, Cardinal Concha Cordoba ordered him to renounce his position as chaplain and professor.

It was at this point that he wrote: "By desire of my Ordinary, from February of this year I am fulfilling the functions of Dean of the Institute of Social Administration which belongs to the School of Public Administration, an official autonomous entity directed by Doctor William Nonnetti."[5]

In the School of Public Administration (ESAP), Camilo's activity unfolded on four levels. (1) the organization and direction of a seminar on social administration, in which the most qualified professionals in the socio-economic sciences participated; (2) the creation of the Institute of Social Administration.

In a report given by Camilo May 15, 1965, we see its general objectives.

Objectives of the Institute of Social Administration

Social politics is that part of governmental politics which is related to the social welfare of the citizens. Social administration is an application of social politics. In the underdeveloped countries in general, and in Colombia in particular, agrarian reform is considered as the center of social reform. Nevertheless, for an accelerated social development, the displacement of the economic activity of the rural sector by the other sectors appears to be not only inevitable but indispensable to increase the effective demand for agricultural products and to industrialize the country. Social Politics in Colombia must then consider the problems of the rural sectors in conjunction with those of the urban sectors.

The Institute, in order to obtain the personnel for the necessities noted above and in order to accomplish the corresponding studies, oriented its activities towards the acquisition of contracts with those government institutions which execute programs for rural or urban welfare. This was especially true whenever these institutions had a vision of the connection (rural-urban) of the Colombian social problem.

For the rural sector, the Institute develops its programs with the direct cooperation and the collaboration of the Colombian Institute of Agrarian Social Reform, of the Ministries of Government, Agriculture, and Public Health.

For the urban sector, the Institute works with the Ministry of Justice, the Special District of Bogotá and the Ministry of Education. Neither should we forget the support of these two sectors from the international organizations such as Inter-American Center for Living (CINVA), UNICEF, the OMS, and the Office of Social Affairs of the United Nations.[6]

The organization of the Institute was in two sectors: training and research. In the latter, considerable work was accomplished on the migration of the peasants to the large metropolis, based on materials developed and revised by Camilo in his capacity as Dean of the Institute.

(3) Organization of mobile schools to impart information on agrarian reform. Camilo thought up a very specific methodology, adaptable to distinct levels, which embraced peasants, rural lead-

ers, students, pre-professionals and professionals. They were given in Bogotá, Medellín, Popayán, Palmira, Manizales, Ibagué, Cartagena, Pasto, Montería, Yopal, Paipa, Pamplona, and Cali.

The International Seminar on Agrarian Reform and the course which was given for three months to promoters of community action came from this program. There was also cooperation in personnel with three official organizations.

(4) Organization of the Union of Rural Action of Yopal (UARY), in the eastern plains. Section K of the 2nd article of law #135 of 1961 creating the Institute of Agrarian Reform enumerated its functions: "To promote the formation of the units of rural action! . . ."

In the report to which reference has been made, we read:

> This program is executed as a result of a contract subscribed to by the Minister of Agriculture, for an annual sum of $487,000.00. The program is set up in a farm-school close to Yopal (Boyaca) basically for community development. The objectives of the project are the following:
>
> 1. Organization of the community in a geographic zone fifteen kilometers in radius, with a population of 286 families.
> 2. Employment of young peasants as directors and instructors with a quota of 60 students.
> 3. Granting of technical assistance in farming, cooperatives, and community development for the communities of Siribana, Palomas, El Pedregal, and Tacarimena and the extension of the same to other communities, following the results of the first experiences.
> 4. Establishment of cooperatives for the small and medium farm-owners in the communities cited. These cooperatives can be transformed into multiple-function cooperatives (production, transport, credit, and consumer).
> 5. Technical improvement and diversification of agriculture for the farmer and eventually for the market.
> 6. Organization of the communities to solve immediate local necessities (paved roads, schools, latrines, churches, health centers) in collaboration with governing bodies already established there or to be established.
> 7. Study of the functioning of public services in order to plan their coordination and improvement in the future.

The personnel of the Institute who were responsible for this contract, with the exception of the secretary, resided in Yopal. They included: the director, one agronomist, one agricultural instructor, a home economist, a professor of general culture, a paymaster, a supervisor, an economist, two general assistants and one secretary. They also considered naming a second agronomist and an additional agricultural instructor. The director of the project was responsible to the Dean of the Institute, who in turn was responsible to the Director of ESAP.

The farm school was proposed in order to form a new type of rural educator who would be able to work for the advancement of the peasant community. In fact, sixty peasants between the ages of fifteen and twenty were sent by community action committees in the nearby towns. They received free training in such general subjects as geography, history and mathematics, as well as in agricultural methods and cattle breeding. In addition they were trained in the formation of rural cooperatives and trade union activity.

UARY promoted the establishment of the "Cooperatives of Community Development of Yopal" with a basic capital of $15,000 and a prospect of sales of $1,000 daily.[7]

Camilo put his heart and soul into the project. He thought up new operational procedures, worked out study plans, held meetings for young farmers, presided over the towns and facilitated the contact of the university students and the technicians with the people.

Camilo already spoke a very advanced language, but one which was constructive and realistic. Even the simplest people understood him.

Notwithstanding all this, in secret meetings he was accused of having established in Yopal a center camouflaged for guerilla purposes, and immediately the directors of ESAP, the rural Administrative Department of Security (DAS) of Llanos and many petty officials descended on them. Also some individuals (the custodians, as Camilo called them) went there, and these, from within, made injurious reports which led to adverse suspicions against the project UARY (Unit of Rural Action of Yopal).

One day Camilo returned from Llano humming.

"What is that?" I asked him.

"It is the music for the hymn of the revolution," he answered with a sly, boyish smile. When he was feeling lighthearted he used to improvise couplets, musical poems and strophes, which he jotted down on paper, entertaining all of us with his own music.

Suddenly he exclaimed, "I have it. This is the hymn of the revolution with my music and the lyrics of the people":

Colombia, be brave, wake up
To battle for our liberty.
Look at the people before you
who don't want to suffer anymore.

The revolution is begun
Against the assassin State.
It will succeed triumphantly
For workers and peasants.

The riches of Colombia
Are not only for one class.

We will obtain victory
For the workers in the country.
We support those from below
Who have heroically suffered violence
But now it comes in turn
To the ruling class.

Victims of the violence
Were always peasants.
The ruling structure
Was pledged to the assassins.

God rules in heaven
And only in heaven does He rule.
In this land of ours must rule
The Colombian People.

Another strophe was added when Camilo promoted the Movement of the Peoples' United Front:

The poor in our country
Have been divided in their fight
But now they are resolved
To form a United Front.

As poetry, a disaster! But it occurred to someone to make copies of it. As a result the copies were distributed and consequently came into the hands of the superiors. No need to say more. Camilo, without doubt, was a dangerous instrument of explosive ideas contrary to democratic theses, norms, and methods. Proofs? The hymn. It could easily be brought forward as an irrefutable document to institute proceedings against him.

As Dean of the Institute of Social Administration, he was assigned as the representative of the Catholic Social Action organization, privately named by the Cardinal according to Art. 7, letter *a* of law 135 of 1961, on the governing board of the Institute of Agrarian Reform (INCORA). A terrific fight was unleashed there to introduce scientific social criteria and to apply legal norms without exceptions which favored the privileges of the large landowners.

A demonstration of his attitude is found in the two documents which follow. The first is a letter:

"Bogotá, D. E.
March 22, 1964

Dear Eugenio:

I appeal to you as a Catholic, as a friend and as the principal representative of the workers before the Governing Board to ask you the favor of interceding with the President of the Board that he might reserve time in the schedule of the meeting of October 2, 1964, in order to give Dr. Alvaro Gómez Hurtado an opportunity to make a presentation.

Dr. Gómez manifested a desire in the last meeting to prove to me that I had voted in accordance with the law but against my conscience and the natural law. This solemn affirmation makes me suppose that the motion will have a very personal character and be of the highest theoretical significance. Such circumstances force me to insist once again on clarifying my points of view.

With many thanks for your attention in this matter, I remain,

Sincerely yours,
Camilo Torres Restrepo"[8]

The second document is a memorandum, signed by Camilo:

The undersigned member of the Board of Directors of the Colombian Institute of Agrarian Reform was allowed to make the following motion at its sessions of February 10, 1964, which ended in the approbation, on the part of the Board, of the suppression of the "El Gobernador" estate, located in the township of Los Venados, in the jurisdiction of the municipality of Valledupar, department of Magdalena: That the decision of the Board is a very dangerous precedent, but even more dangerous are the reasons for their decision. There are three principal reasons:

1. Because the application of a legal norm is subjected to such criteria as "reasons of State" and opportunity. When the application of a legal norm is submitted to the discretion of those who should apply it, it depends on the arbitrary will of those governing and subjects the authority of the legislators totally to the personal judgment of those applying the law. This procedure carries within itself the seed of State Totalitarianism contrary to the spirit and the letter of the Colombian Constitution. Because of this, persons can use legal procedures to which they can recur when a law is considered inconvenient or anti-constitutional.

Additionally, the Colombian Institute of Agrarian Reform has, by means of its Governing Board, institutional links with the legislative branch of Public Power through which it enjoys a greater facility for intervening in Colombian legislation.

2. Because it is presumed that our agrarian legislation does not sanction the suppression of ownership except for totally unexploited or uncultivated farms, forgetting the action introduced in our legislation on "Economic Exploitation."

In a country like Colombia, when we should use to the greatest advantage our natural and human resources, it would constitute a luxury of anti-social character to restrict the suppression of ownership only to uncultivated lands, tolerating the right of private property over farms which, in accord with an objective norm, have an anti-economic and even, in the case of our country, an anti-social exploitation.

While rejecting the proposition on the suppression of ownership which is based on the argument that the lands in question are uncultivated, we are going back several years in our agrarian legislation.

3. Because one returns to the procedure which made impossible the application of law 100 to 1936 in the matter of the suppression of ownership demanding of the National Government that it prove that the property which is presented for suppression has not been exploited during the past ten years. This procedure to which they wish to return is contrary to article 24 of law 135 of 1961 according to which "the burden of proof regarding the exploitation of an estate or of one part of it falls to the proprietor or the proprietors of the same."

The previous motion does not have as its object to raise a new discussion on the decision taken, but to place for the consideration of the members of the Governing Board some points of view which should be taken into account for future decisions which could constitute precedents of the most grave consequence to the detriment of our democratic institutions, the socio-economic development of the country and the future of agrarian reform in Colombia.[9]

The position which Camilo occupied in the Governing Board of Incora gave him a direct and profound knowledge of the subhuman conditions in which the rural sectors live. I can remember now the reactions which the misery of the peasants produced in him. He spoke with them in such a way that all the aspects of their tragedy came out without holding back or fears. Camilo indicated solutions to them and gave them a message. After each contact with the agrarian community he was filled with growing rebellion and an intense desire to do something positive for the people.

It was evident that as a sociologist he had not renounced his commitment to speculation, but that the intense living experiences he had made it more human, for he felt the sorrow of the dispossessed and the exploited. Now it is not the evidence of the facts in statistics and inquiries which made him determined but an existential motive, oriented towards reasonably effective solutions. This led him to go beyond the hypothesis of the North American economists. As Prades puts it, he subordinated the economic explanation to the political explanation which scorched his conscience. The analysis of the political origins led him to look for solutions of a political type. [10]

In this way he arrived at a conclusion:

It is not possible to create a Colombian sociology without taking into account universal sociology. However, it is necessary to develop a Colombian sociology in two senses: (1) applying the theory and the general sociological methods to our concrete and specific reality; and (2) contributing to this theory and to these methods the analysis of unpublished situations which our situation can suggest.

Since this is not the case, Colombian sociology has been frustrated in its structures as much by the absence of empirical investigation as by the lack of theoretical generalization. Therefore, our study tries to effect, above all, a contribution to this second aspect.[11]

What Camilo had detected by direct observation he complemented with data supplied by many priests with whom he came into contact. He found some of them convinced of the necessity of looking for a way out; others remained anchored in their conformity to the village rulers, satisfied and jealous guardians of the status quo, in a rut, distant from the problems of the people.

The accumulating of all these factors here described inflamed in him the decision to give himself in an immediate and effective action. The roads, the plazas, and the streets, filled with human agony and injustice, waited for him. He felt the command to go even to the ultimate consequence burning in his soul like a fire. Camilo entered the third stage of which Prades speaks, and he took his place in the movement of the people.

Chapter 4

The Movement Cannot Be Stopped

At the broad base of the Colombian social pyramid, there has evolved a phenomenon of expanded consciousness, that is, the substructure is more conscious each day that it is a class with a right to participate in the activity of the country.

This phenomenon follows a gradual process. It begins with the entrenchment of specific subhuman conditions, along with their continuance to the point that they appear to be permanent. A second stage is reached with the appearance and gradual assimilation of new ideas among this social group. This leads to the realization that the social order is seriously defective. A growing unwillingness to accept these disorders in society occasions attempts to discover their underlying causes. The subsequent stage is characterized by a widespread desire for social change and the felt need for unity among all those of like mind. Finally, a decision is taken to overcome the prevailing social injustices.

The more conscious of their situation the masses become, the more open they are to a revolutionary ideology. Failure to grasp this fact on the part of the upper levels of society does not destroy the strong popular tendency toward social change. This unrest becomes constantly more fearless and more anxious as the people's consciousness grows more able to express itself. This does not only occur in the cities. In most sections the peasants and workers also want to observe and experience the new as it breaks through cultural inertia characterized by the persistence of antiquated social forms. In addition, as the deterioration of the paternalistic and semi-sacred relationship between employer and worker becomes more generally known, the collapse of regional bossism increases and the traditional patterns of the distribution of power are changed.

Doctor Alberto Lleras wrote, "The shackled aspirations of the people overflow, aspirations which are in the majority of cases legitimate. A tremendous scarcity of food, houses, schools, hospital beds, drugs, services and even graves in the cemeteries, pushes our people to shake off their poverty and with it their traditional acceptance of pain, hunger and injustice." [1]

This phenomenon of expanding consciousness raises up continuously more and more groups which exhibit a surprising capacity for acute criticism. With rigorous logic they express opinions of the highest interest and evaluate all of us in their judgments: government and Congress, the military and judiciary, the professional associations and organizations of workers and peasants; they weigh capitalism, the landowners and intellectuals, Communism and the old as well as the new political parties and tendencies; the university students, artists, the Peace Corps, the United States, Russia, China, Cuba and Vietnam—indeed, all the elements of contemporary society.

This phenomenon differs in intensity and audacity according to the psychology of the distinct cultural regions as it denounces feudal submission in favor of self-determination. The people discover the aspiration to advance from traditional passivity towards a very definite attitude of intransigent opposition to the subhuman conditions of their existence. They are not given to illusions, for they realize that negative and innocuous measures will hinder the progress of the people. The movement towards justice and liberty cannot be stopped by recurring to old handy "sophisms." It may be useful to state some of these.

The first "sophism" is religion. Religion should be an essential element of the social order as our constitution recognizes. The "sophism" is that the Church may make the believer a conformist, submissive in terms of temporal reality, dominated solely by a preoccupation with the eternal. Consistent with this, the Church can disregard the apostolate which is orientated towards obtaining changes in those earthly structures which are not in accord with justice. In this way, the Church, in a situation such as ours where its influence is enormous, remains silent and is paralyzed.

All that is a sophism, because it fails to recognize the transcendence of the Church to the present moment, assuming that the last Ecumenical Council set on fire hundreds of stalled motors. Possessed and directed by the truth, the Church is not only a fortress, seated on a rock, but it is a force which moves and directs. It has joined to it a theology of transcendence, a theology of incarnation, the theology of the God-man which has, consequently, interests both on earth and in heaven. [2]

The poor can no longer be assigned a passive role of patiently not protesting, since we recognize the mission of the Church never to condone misery and injustice. This change will deal a blow to complacency, as we realize that each day we come closer to a renovated Church. The great ecclesial change consists in the leap from narrowness to ecumenicity. The post-conciliar period can be much more fruitful than the Council itself. Those who are responsible for the Christian message in all its dimensions cannot be indifferent to the changes of the world.

In Latin America, we are living in an hour of truth and profound authenticity: if we have been nourished since the period of independence with the thinking of western European civilization and fundamentally, with the orientation of French thought, the moment has arrived in which Indo-American man walks his own territory creating his own culture. We see evidence of this in the new vigor of many autonomous manifestations which clearly demonstrate the ascendancy of our own reality. Multiple cultural forms now reasonably assimilated project a second Independence with the outlook that our own culture will be incorporated into the great movements which are disturbing the world today.

In the Americas no one can withdraw from this process of transformation because we find ourselves involved in it as participants and actors. We face a new man who comes out of the prostration of underdevelopment, avid for new horizons and answers; we must believe those who thus interpret the Latin American reality and reject that minority of intellectuals who even now find their inspiration in European winters and the Mediterranean sunsets.

The renewal coming out of the Second Vatican Council and all the new throbbing of continental renewal has an impact upon our priests. Therefore, we must say that in all the sectors of the clergy, but especially the young, there is intense social unrest. New and distinct attitudes are arising. We feel the necessity of new plans for approaching man and the world. We are not treating here a question of generations. It is a tendentious error to call those priests of the new wave liberals and communists, because of their Christian fullness and their human qualities.

These affirmations mean that it is not necessarily virtuous if someone is not accused of divisive tendencies and intentions to sow discord. We are dealing with a fact. What are we going to do with it?

The second "sophism" is collective tranquility. Change is necessary, it is said. But it must not affect the minorities which hold all the tools of power, because the collective tranquility will be disturbed. That is a sophism. They do not realize that it is impossible for tranquility to be born of economic desperation or the discontent of the majority.

Colombians have been suffering a process of growing deception in all areas: hunger, the rising cost of living, the stifling oppression by some foreign powers, the administrative bickering, the anonymity. These are not reasons for the people to be tranquil. There is a defect in the system, and a disorder exists which, so long as it continues, will generate not tranquility but rather nonacceptance.

The repression, in its various forms, to which they are able to appeal in order to stop the free expression of popular nonconformity has not contributed to collective tranquility. The people know that the Colombian oligarchy and their international masters will not be resigned to disappearing peacefully from the stage of history. They will not lose their privileges and their profiting from another's work without furious resistance, appealing to their armed forces, their class justice, their mercenary press and all the means of repression and coercion.

All this, which is tremendously hard but unquestionably certain, cannot be a reason for general tranquility.

The third "sophism" is the public order. This sophism consists in the fact that when protest goes beyond the limits of a single police case and touches the general public it is, ipso facto, placed in the category of an attempt against public order. Basically, what exists is disorder disguised as order or hidden under the sacred trappings of Democracy. This leads inexorably to the search for a solution which cannot be bourgeois reform, for that only offers temporary palliatives without ever arriving at effective results. Moreover, the people's capacity for patience has a limit, the point of desperation. Public order never comes out of collective desperation.

The country hopes for and needs a transformation. If the fulfillment of patriotic pledges comes to nothing, it is possible that social disturbances of the most lamentable consequences will be upon us. The present incumbent said it when taking possession of the Presidency on August 7, 1966:

"The economic and social problems continue with growing complexity, and there is an ever increasing popular pressure for faster development and the better distribution of profits which will guarantee an acceptable level of decent living to a population which has doubled itself in only a quarter of a century, and which is increasing at the rate of a half million inhabitants yearly.

"All of this justifies the general impression that we have reached a critical stage and there is not much time at our disposal before we are overrun by events and they escape dramatically from our control. For me, it is also evident that we must make a great effort now and that any holding back implies a risk of unforeseen gravity."

In his New Year's speech, the President repeated the same warning. Actually, Colombia continues to be a case of public order with a state of siege as a permanent form of government. What has to be sustained by blood and bayonets in order to preserve unacceptable situations can never be accepted public order.

The forth "sophism" is our national pride. We are a democratic and independent country. This is a sophism because we are essentially controlled on every level by the United States to such a point that we are an economic colony of the giant of the North. Because of that we lack the freedom to trade with all nations and are subjected to discriminating procedures which are not justified.[3]

They say that almost every loan is conditional insofar as the plans for investment are developed, directed, and controlled by North American technicians, and paid for with the same money which we receive at high interest and short term.

It is common knowledge that many industries, the army, the police, education, the majority of the businesses, the ministries and not a few of the universities are either directly or indirectly controlled by North American interests.

Under the pretext of helping us to overcome our underdevelopment, they frequenly send us many technical missions. But it is the opinion of many observers that this pretext also serves for establishing webs of espionage and for exerting pressures and threats. Ex-President Valencia felt himself obliged sometimes to speak out against such a situation.

The United States lowers prices for our raw materials. We sell to them cheap and we buy from them at high prices. As a result, we are an underdeveloped and underpaid country. Nevertheless, we never protest because of our traditional nobility and our solidarity with the "free world."

President Dr. Carlos Lleras Restrepo, with patriotic integrity, put things precisely in his speech of November 29, 1966, regarding the recovery of Colombia's integrity.

"I have believed," he said, "that the Colombian government, and I, as president, have the obligation of conserving for the Republic definite rights to guide our own destinies, maintaining those agreements normally accepted from the economic and commercial point of view, but not compromising the right to judge the conditions necessary for the maintenance of social and political peace and normality in the country, because we believe that the government of the nation has been entrusted to us and not to the international organisms. This is true. I think that the international organisms must understand that. We do not pretend to rigidly impose on them our criteria, and we neither wish nor can we accept their imposition of theirs on us so long as we feel we have the obligation to guard the higher interests of the nation and the people whose destinies were entrusted to us by popular will. This government is right in defending definite limits of the national autonomy."

The fifth "sophism" is the harmony of the social classes. The existence of class warfare is undeniable, whether under hidden or obvious forms. To conceal, stop, or delay it is to have recourse to paternalism, and a pseudo-charity, or to simple philanthropy, believing that in this way we eliminate a social conflict which rises from the antagonism between the haves and the have-nots. But inequities do exist. They are a problem not only for Colombia but for all Latin America. There are very profound contrasts which maintain the antagonism in an explosive situation, as the Jesuit sociologist Bigot notes.

John XXIII spoke of "the very sad spectacle of innumerable workers of many nations and entire continents, who receive a salary which subjects them and their families to subhuman conditions of life. In some of those countries the abundance and the extraordinary luxury of the privileged few contrast stridently and offensively with the conditions of extreme misery of many, many people. (*Mater et Magistra, No. 12*)

Among ourselves, monetary devaluations, situations of privilege, official tourism supported by the money of the people, unemployment, liquidation of profits for millions in banks and industry without remedy for the misery and hunger, evasion of taxes by many large companies who resort to subterfuges with the consent and the complicity of mercenary employees, capricious distribution of the national budget, all destroy the harmony between the higher and lower classes of society.

Can you have equilibrium between the defiant opulence of the minority and the ominous misery of the large majority? What is the reality? That the disfavored classes realize these facts, weigh them, become restless and conclude that it is necessary to construct a new order. But they know very well that that order will not be built without them or against them.

There is another undeniable aspect to this reality: We find ourselves before a people who have been moving forward for a long time. Slowly, but nonetheless, moving. A people which appears formidable and admirable. As Le Bon said, "the memorable events of history are always the visible effect of invisible changes in the thinking of men." The movement of our people is determined by ideas, by changes in their manner of thinking, by desire. No sophism will be able to hold it back. We are not treating here of the culture of poverty but of the revolution against poverty.

This movement, this progressive process, can be activated by factors of revolutionary acceleration, in the measure to which the people assimilate them and rebel against unjust situations. It is worthwhile to enumerate them:

1. *POSSESSION OF THE LAND*

3.6% of the landowners possess 64.2% of the farming areas, while 56%—that is to say, the great majority of the peasants—work an area which is scarcely 4.2%. What we see here in very plain language is a lot of land for the few and a little land for the many.

Actually (November, 1966), the President of the Republic, Doctor Carlos Lleras Restrepo, has presented a projected law for the consideration of the Congress, which, in essence, directs that close to 200,000 tenants be declared owners of the land which they are working in an area of approximately 1,200,000 hectares, equivalent to 35% of the land surface actually cultivated in the country. The project, moreover, calls for an increase of 100 to 300 million pesos in the annual budget of the Colombian Institute of

Agrarian Reform; the authorization to declare agriculture bonuses up to 1,800 million pesos; the reduction of exclusive rights which now are vested in those owners of lands adjacent to zones where "districts" of irrigation are administered with state money; the speeding up of the procedure for expropriations and the suppression of the right of domain.

But in the same regions, the peasants have been threatened with jail when they have gone to be registered for their piece of property, because the large landowners tenaciously resist any legal disposition which would modify the ownership of the land.

In the project of President Lleras Restrepo the plans of "Incora," inspired in no small part by the Yankee philosophy of the "Alliance for Progress," are designed to stop that gigantic operation of selling the land at high prices and open up the way to a more complete agrarian reform.

2. *THE NATIONAL INCOME*

While 623,772 individuals receive 8,314,443,400 pesos, 12, 958,828 people receive barely 59% of the national income. That is to say: a very small minority profits from almost half the national income.

3. *HOUSING*

68% of the peasant houses have dirt floors; 92.6% lack water; 88.7% do not have plumbing; 97.4% do not have baths; 95.8% do not have electricity.

4. *MEDICAL ASSISTANCE*

There are only 3 doctors for each 10,000 people. There are 3 beds for each 1,000 people.

5. *EDUCATION*

Out of 1,686,000 peasant children, 1,086,632 were without schools in 1959 and 600,000 were receiving practically no education. In 1965 there was not sufficient space for 50% of the school population in the primary schools, 86% in the secondary and 97% in higher education.[4]

In the distribution of the national budget for 1967, the government gave to the branch of public education a total of 1,037,423,364 pesos out of a total of 6,272,000,000. This is the first time such a large amount (16.5%) has gone to the Ministry of Education.[5]

In 1959, 11,100 teachers without any degree taught in the rural area. The situation (1967) has not appreciably changed. This, if nothing else, places the peasant children in unfavorable conditions of inferiority. What can they do?[6]

6. *THE COST OF LIVING*

Commentaries are not necessary, because there is just not enough money for the middle and lower classes to live on. There is no proportion between the static day's wages and the spiraling cost of living.[7]

7. *UNEMPLOYMENT*

According to the studies of the National Association of Industries (ANDI), in 1966, 225,000 young men should be incorporated into the work force; there were barely 81,000 new jobs, leaving 144,000 unemployed.

An index of unemployment in the three principal cities of Colombia shows the following data:

CITY	*PEOPLE EMPLOYED*	*UNEMPLOYED*
Bogotá	514,300	59,000
Medellín	220,000	26,400
Cali	191,100	25,500[8]
	Total	110,900

The Ministry of Labor recently calculated 500,000 as the total of unemployed. The statistics of ANDI show that in order to absorb such a number, industry should annually employ 230,000 additional persons, but according to the National Department of Statistics (DANE) only 8,467 able workers are newly employed.

8. *INVESTMENTS IN DOLLARS*

Concerning the North American, investments it should be noted:

(a) For each dollar of direct private North American investment in Colombia, annually 2.27 dollars are taken out through profits and dividends.[9]

(b) Between 1951 and 1961, for each dollar which the North Americans brought to the country, they obtained close to four dollars in the monetary exchange.[10]

(c) In 1965 alone, for each dollar which the United States loaned us, Colombia had to pay $1.50 through amortization and interest.[11]

9. *OTHER FACTORS OF REVOLUTIONARY ACCELERATION*

Jacques Chonchol, an economist and a Catholic, author of various projects for the United Nations, points up these factors:

The Economic Factor. The failure of the economic regime which, based on the economy of profit, has led in agriculture "to an enormous subutilization of the land and the people, when labor is a permanent reality for the majority of the populations of our countries." Extensive systems of production, based on the concentration of a lot of land in a few hands and low salaries for those who have neither land nor other opportunities, have increased the riches of the few. Why do we think of intensive agriculture, if the hungry masses can not buy the land?[12]

The Political Factor. There have been political regimes in Colombia which caused the violence whose victims, in an overwhelming majority, are found among the poor. In the political superstructure the fight of the people for liberation will be most difficult because of the cleverness and the great interests of prestige which are at play there. The failure in the political superstructure is rooted, according to Chonchol, "in the fact that, internally, Latin

America sways between personal dictators and oligarchical democracies."

Loss of Confidence among the Ruling Classes. The ruling classes have lost faith in themselves. Their general characteristic, according to Chonchol, is fear and a bad conscience. Fear makes them condemn every change, every equitable adjustment of the socio-economic levels in the people. Their bad conscience prevents them from making the necessary changes in structure. They see them, they preach them, but they don't dare put them into effect. Why? Because they are tied to their personal interests or mortgaged to the imperialist North American financiers.

The Growing Social Awareness of the People. There is a growing realization by the people that the conditions in which they live are unjust. The life of misery is not a natural order desired by God. It is not true to say that Christianity preaches resignation or a hopeless and defeatist attitude in the face of misery and injustice. On the contrary, if Christianity teaches anything forcefully, it is the obligation to fight against all misery and injustice.

The Cuban Revolution. This is a social fact whose influence can not be dismissed. It is important to read what Chonchol writes on this point, for no one doubts his Catholic orthodoxy:

> Latin America is no longer of no importance in North American politics. With the Cuban Revolution and its orientation towards the socialist-Marxist system, the cold war has been installed in the American continent. This war will not be resolved on the military plane even though Cuba should be invaded and its regime destroyed. Sooner or later new focuses would arise, since we are basically talking of a war between different systems which are offered as a solution to the problems of underdeveloped countries.
>
> The Cuban Revolution, just as does every profound social revolution, even though it should not desire it, has considerable international repercussions. Without the Cuban Revolution, for example, it is probable that the Alliance for Progress would not exist; it is also probable that the U. S. would continue supporting the most reactionary political forces on the continent, instead of pressuring them to inaugurate structural changes in society.
>
> Even though some well-intentioned men might not think so, these

pressures fundamentally have a negative character: they tend to stop Communism in spite of everything.

Neither the U. S. nor the other developed countries have yet realized the basic problem: colonial capitalism is not the system which will permit the rapid advance of the underdeveloped countries towards a democratic and progressive society; "free enterprise" is far from being the panacea for backward countries; the only way to obtain rapid development while maintaining a system of political freedom is through tremendous aid from the rich countries, without which rapid economic development is incompatible with representative democracy.

Perhaps they will never understand these truths, or only when it is too late, since rich people are basically conservative and naturally opposed to any kind of revolution.

Whether the great powers like it or not, each day conditions for change are growing more and more powerful in America.[13]

The factors of revolutionary acceleration which have been enumerated, besides others peculiar to Cuba, precipitated the Cuban revolution. That small island, a tropical David against an all-powerful Goliath, is an indication to the underdeveloped countries of Latin America that if a radical change could be obtained there, the same can happen anywhere, if the subhuman conditions of life continue.

On the other hand, the observations of Chonchol are backed up by the facts, since the Cuban revolution, whether we like it or not, continues creating incidents in the politics of the Americas to such a point that the Tri-Continental Conference there is a source of deep worry. The President of Colombia, Doctor Lleras Restrepo, dictated Decree No. 2686 (October 26, 1966), whose article 6 reads: "The passports already issued, or which the Colombian authorities will issue in the future, are not valid for visiting the Republic of Cuba. The Colombian or naturalized foreigner who has visited Cuba after the date of this present decree will have his passport revoked, and he will not be issued a new one without the express written authorization of the Ministry of Foreign Affairs, after previous clearance by the Administrative Department of Security."

The Cuban revolution speeded up the process of liberation in

Latin America. Camilo understood that very well. Because of that he concentrated on projects and activities. He did not theorize excessively but simply produced action. He did not limit his total involvement for one moment.

He serenely went to his crucifixion because the opposition persecute or kill anyone who fights honorably for the people. Priests, authentic Christians, or other individuals can promote the fight. The immediate reaction is always to stigmatize them as Communist.

Camilo, in his very objective style, unmasks these reactionary tactics:

> Every ruling class has a system of defenses, some informal and others formal. When it is the case of an unpopular ruling class, it is necessary for them to look for effective ways to disqualify their adversaries before public opinion. Public opinion is more easily affected by objective than by philosophical disquisitions.
>
> In order to condemn a bridge, it is enough to say it is rotting. In order to condemn a dog, even though it is pedigreed, it is enough to say it has rabies. In the first year of this epoch, to call someone a Christian was to place him outside the law. Afterwards, the enemy of Imperial Rome was called a barbarian in order to be persecuted. Before the French Revolution, the free thinkers, liberals, democrats, and commoners were persecuted. Today the best way for the ruling class to unleash persecution on a dangerous element is to call it "Communist."[14]

If those who defend the people are priests, they brand them intruders, renegades, seditious, opportunists capitalizing on disorders; dangerous, subversive, violent, proud, perverse, deserters, traitors, scandalous, wolves in sheep's clothing. It is inevitable that in today's world nonconformist priests will appear. They will give *good scandal* and not evil scandal, which is unacceptable.

Good scandal consists in daring to seek the acceptance of new values, relating Christianity with reality, an opening to our world; giving to men of today an authentic message; giving testimony to the truth without selling out to injustice, rottenness, compromises, temporal conveniences.

If those who fight for the people are Christians, then don't say they are deviates, misguided, insubordinates, blind, obdurate, schismatics, detestable, faithful to a doubtful orthodoxy.

There are Christians who chatter on proclaiming in theory the excellence of Catholic social doctrine, but when they try to practice it, they don't know how to do it without compromising themselves with the Imperialists who give them money. For such witnesses the doctrine of Christ is good as long as it doesn't touch their own economic interests, involve them too deeply, or lead the people to ultimate conclusions.

This is what makes them afraid. And why? Because they are mortgaged, handcuffed, tied to loans and aids, in concubinage with plotters of exploitation and cheating against the underdeveloped people of Indo-America.

The moment has arrived when it is not feasible to use the name of Christ, his religion, his doctrine, or his Church for temporal necessities which are in conflict with justice, love, or the common good.

Those compliant adulterators of doctrine would want to change the beatitudes of the Master to these:

Blessed are the poor, because they are poor and thus we can continue helping them because they continue to be poor.

Blessed are the submissive because the hour of their rebellion is far away.

Blessed are those who cry, but we will not hear their weeping for a lack of shelter and work.

Blessed are those who hunger, but we will not give them the opportunity to harvest their necessary bread.

Blessed are those in misery, especially when the desperation of the poor does not threaten our economic interests, nor our lands, nor our exorbitantly profitable businesses nor our capital outside the country.

Blessed are the clean of heart, because they will not hate us for our insulting luxury nor for our dissipation in trafficking in all pleasures.

Blessed are the peaceful, because while they remain disunited they will be weak and thus will never rise up against us.

Blessed are those who suffer persecution for justice, for undertaking to relieve the oppressed, the workers, and the peasants. As long as these do not wake up, let them be blessed. . . .

If those who are devoted to the liberation of the people are not Christians, call them foreigners, agents of foreign powers, tricksters, fifth columnists, enemies of democracy, of order, and of the government.

What do you think, man of the people? Some day you will decide. Will you be with those who exploit you or with those who are exploited? With those who fight for your or with the enemies of those who have been sacrificed for you? With those who indoctrinate you so that you continue to be a slave or with those who cry out that you are no longer an outcast? You also have a part in the historic destiny—to build a new country. Are they not speaking in all sectors of the urgency of change? If the people are an essential element in the dynamics of democracy, they will engage in battle. You belong to that people. Enter into your battle. But not in favor of those who frustrate you, of those who oppress you, of those who hold back your movement for justice and liberty.

What has happened? You need land, and many peasants do not have land. You pay taxes, and rural illiteracy continues. You demand work, but you will have to live with hunger in the slums of the big city. You have looked for peace and been given violence. They have promised you marvels, and yet when you vote them in, they continually juggle that promise. Many employers treat you like an idiot in the public offices. You long for equal justice for all, and for you there is no justice. By the very fact that you are a human person you have the right to exist. Ask the priest to be with the people and not against them. Since the priest is the most educated person in the community, the poor hope that he realizes their situation. He should feel it, live it, and not be in conformity with the system which creates it. Ask the authorities to protect your rights. Demand of the employees that they wait on you without your having to tip them. Ask the doctors and the lawyers to charge you what is just so that they do not leave you in misery when they demand usurious fees of you. Denounce the greedy and drunken judges and experts who ruin you in their judicial procedures, obliging you to go into debt in order to pay the price of their salable conscience.

The transformation of which everyone speaks, the impelling force of present-day Colombian government, basically is conditioned on a change of structures. The peacefulness or the violence of this change is subjected, in turn, to three factors: desire and foresight of the ruling class and pressure from the common people. Camilo develops these in the following way:

The pressure to obtain accidental, not structural changes, has generally been the one activity of the principal organized groups. The pressure to obtain reformist changes offers solutions of accommodation. This is to say, solutions which include the common interests of the upper class and the lower class. These solutions do not change the structures, but they adapt them to those interests which exist. On occasion they prepare society for a fundamental change. For example, the laws of agrarian reform serve to prepare the country for industrialization.

The pressure to obtain a revolutionary change is intended to change the structures. It is especially concerned with a change in the structures of property, taxes, investments, consumption, education, and political and administrative organizations. It is equally interested in a change in international relations on the political economic, and cultural levels.

The desire and the foresight of the ruling class are modified by the kind and the intensity of the pressure coming from the common people. In the following chart we see the alternatives which can establish this confrontation of attitudes and forces:

POSSIBLE FORMS OF STRUCTURAL CHANGES

	RULING CLASS		*COMMON PEOPLE*		
Degree	Desire	Foresight	Pressure	Result	Example
a = maximum	b	a	a	Peaceful Revolution	Chile
b = medium c = minimum	c	c	a	Violent Revolution	Cuba
	c	b	b	Reformism	Colombia

RULING CLASS COMMON PEOPLE (*cont.*)

Degree	Desire	Foresight	Pressure	Result	Example
	c	a	b	Rightist Coup d'etat	Brazil
	c	a	c	Repression	Venezuela
	b	b	b	Status quo	Uruguay
	a	a	a	Ideal Peaceful Revolution	?

EXPLANATION OF THE CHART

Degree: Arbitrarily we take three degrees of intensity: maximum, medium, and minimum.

Desire: A traditional or sentimental attitude is not our concern here. Neither is the attitude of isolated persons. Desire can be motivated by economic or group interests. Fear of the danger of not surviving as a class or group is excluded from desire in the picture. This fear is included in the column on foresight. Even if we run the risk of arbitrarily generalizing, it can be said that the degree of desire in the ruling class depends on the number, economic independence, nationalism, and business mentality of the members. A progressive bourgeois can desire structural change. However, the progressivism in the bourgeoisie is also a subproduct of the general development.

Foresight: Foresight is a completely intellectual and rational position. An event can be foreseen even though it may not be desired. The attitude concerning change in structures can vary fundamentally if this change is foreseen. Many decisions can be taken by the ruling class according to that famous principle of "sacrificing something so as not to lose everything." The foresight of the ruling class depends on two factors: the capacity for analysis and information. The capactiy for analysis depends on the qualifications and intelligence of their leaders.

The information depends on the channels of communication. If one of the two factors is weak, the foresight is weak also. Because of that we can trace the discrepancies between the foresight of the ruling class and the pressure of the common people.

Unfortunately, it is possible to find weakness in both in the underdeveloped countries. The average professional qualifications of those ruling can be especially low in those colonized countries where the colonizing countries have impeded the higher education of the nationals. In every way it is probable that the qualifications of the rulers are hurt by the generally low educational level characteristic for underdeveloped countries. This situation is aggravated if the most qualified leave to work in developed countries.

As far as information is concerned, the problem of underdeveloped countries, generally colonized during some particular period of time, is the coexistence of two cultures. Maurice Duverger classifies these two cultures as Modern Population and Antiquated Population.[15]

In general, the ruling minority is identified with the first; and the plebeian majority with the second. The cultural separation is the principal obstacle to information. Each day the communication media are more accessible to the common people. This communication increases the expectations of this class to a degree disproportionately greater than their social and economic progress. The institutions of communication are controlled by the ruling class (press, radio, television, etc.). The common people have few media of communication. This circumstance can lead to relatively good information on the part of the lower class regarding the attitudes of the ruling class, but it can also prevent the ruling class's knowing what is happening in the majority groups. On many occasions it is possible to use the same vocabulary with different meanings because of cultural differences. The language can separate rather than unite. It can happen that very powerful pressure exists on the lower levels which is not foreseen by the ruling class.

Pressure: The different grades of pressure which the lower classes can exert have already been explained. In the chart it was not intended to be precise about which of the three is exerted. The degree of intensity (a,b,c,) refers to the efficacy with which structural change, properly speaking, is sought.

The Result: It can be doubtful, but what we have delineated is considered probable enough.

The Examples: They are taken from Latin American cases which are best known to the author. It may be that they are not totally exact, but they are illustrations.

Conclusions: From the alternatives established the following conclusions can be drawn. In underdeveloped countries, structural changes will not be produced without pressure from the lower class. The peaceful revolution is directly determined by the foresight of the ruling class. Violent revolution is a very probable alternative now that the desire for change on the part of the rulers is difficult to obtain.[16]

The Message to the Oligarchy, published in the weekly *Frente Unido,* is completely explicit.

To address a message to those who do not wish to hear, or are unable to do so, is a painful duty. However, it is a duty, and an historical duty, at the moment in which the Colombian oligarchy is reaching the high point in its iniquity against the country and against the Colombian people.

For more than 150 years, the moneyed caste, the few families who hold almost all the riches of Colombia, have used political power to their own advantage. They have used every artifice and trick to conserve that power swindled from the poor people.

They created the division between the Liberals and Conservatives. This division, which the people did not understand, served well in sowing hatred between the various elements of the lower class. Those ancestral hatreds transmitted from fathers to sons have especially helped the oligarchy.* The people did not understand the politics of the rich, but all the fury which they felt for not being able to eat, to study, for feeling sick, being without a home, without land and work, all that rancor was discharged by the poor in the Liberal Party against the poor in the Conservative Party and the poor in the Conservative Party against the poor in the Liberal Party. The oligarchy, guilty of this pathetic situation of the poor, happily watched the bulls from behind the barrier, making money and ruling the country. The only thing which divided the oligarchy in the Liberal Party from the oligarchy in the Conservative Party was the problem of the distribution of the budget and the public offices. The national budget, the public rents, were not sufficient to satisfy both the Conservative and Liberal oligarchy. Because of that they fought for power; in order to pay off election debts they gave public offices to party hacks and divided up the budget, totally excluding those from the other political party.

For forty years the Liberals did not have positions, and afterwards the same thing happened to the Conservatives for sixteen years. The political and religious differences have now been resolved. Now the oligarchy was not fighting against itself except for government money and public offices. In the meanwhile, the people realized that their fight for the Liberal or Conservative Party each time pulled them further down in their misery. The rich did not realize that the people had had

* While the poor fight, the rich govern for their own benefit.

enough of them. Whem Jorge Eliécer Gaitán appeared campaigning for the moral restoration of the Republic, he did it as much against the Liberal oligarchy as against the Conservative. Because of that the two oligarchies became *Gaitanista* after the Conservative oligarchy had killed him in the streets of Bogotá.

Having started on the path of violence in order to conserve power, the oligarchy would not stop in their use of violence. Liberal peasants were killed along with Conservative ones. When the aggressiveness, the hate, and the rancor of the poor overflowed in a war among all the needy of Colombia, the oligarchy became worried and sought a military coup. The military government did not serve the interest of the oligarchy sufficiently either. Then, the leader of the Liberal oligarchy, Dr. Alberto Lleras, and the leader of the Conservative oligarchy, Dr. Laureano Gómez, said "We have almost lost power for the oligarchy through fighting over the distribution of the budget and the bureaucratic spoils. We must stop fighting over that, making a contract to divide the country between the oligarchies as one would divide a farm in half. Equality and alternating power permit an equal share for both of us, and thus we can form a new party, the party of the oligarchy. And thus the National Front was born as the first class party, as the party of the Colombian oligarchy.

The people are tricked again. They concur in the elections of the plebiscite for Alberto Lleras and for the National Front. The result, naturally, was worse. Now it was the united oligarchy that governed against the people. Because of that all the hopes of Colombians came out the opposite. The National Front offered peace and the peasants continued to be murdered—sugar workers were slaughtered in Santa Bárbara. The universities were invaded and the war budget was increased.

The National Front said that it would correct the financial situation, and doubled the external debt producing three devaluations (up to now) and with them the misery of the Colombian people for many generations. The National Front said that it would put through agrarian reform, and it did not do it but put through a law which guarantees the interests of the rich against the rights of the poor.

It imposed on the country an inept candidate for the Presidency of the Republic. The National Front obtained the greatest electoral abstention in our history, and now, in the face of its total failure, what is the oligarchy doing:

It returns to violence. It declares a state of siege. It rules by decree.

It sells the country to the United States. They meet in a luxurious hotel and decide on the next President. From their rooms they make resolutions for the entire country. They are completely blind.

As a last cry of alarm I wish to tell them: "Sir oligarchs, the people no longer believe anything you say. The people do not want to vote for you. The people are fed up and desperate. The people do not want to go to the elections which you organize. The people do not want Carlos or Alberto Lleras or any of you. The people are suffering and they are very determined. The people know that you, too, are very determined. Because of that I beg of you that you be realistic and that if you wish to trick the people with your new political compromises, don't think that the people will have faith in you. You know that the fight will be to its ultimate conclusion. The experience has been so bitter that the people are already decided to go all out. Unfortunately, the isolated oligarchy, blind, and proud, seems not to want to realize that the revolution of the Colombian masses will not stop now until the people have won power.[17]

Camilo did not direct a message to the people. Camilo himself was a message that scandalized. He obeyed the "naked obligation" of which Bergson spoke.

Chapter 5

Towards the Revolution

My first contact with Camilo was in 1959 during a meeting in the office of the Ministry of Government. His proposals for means to check the effects of the violence were intelligent, bright, exact. They gave us a glimpse of an agile mentality which was looking for a solution. He wanted to think freely, to bring up ideas, and then, in turn, to open up the group present that day to those ideas. He wanted all those who had some thesis to propose it so that through a confrontation of ideas they might arrive at some logical conclusions.

Was he already a rebel? I don't think so. Throughout the dialogue I detected a constructive nonconformity in him.

Nonconformity is the state prior to rebellion. Nonconformity begins when a person does not agree with things which contradict his intelligence or will; he doesn't find these things sufficiently reasonable. At the same time, he seeks arguments, demands answers, and looks for solutions because he is convinced of the possibility of a solution. The nonconformist is more rational than emotional, more theoretical than practical, more one who urges than one who plots. He is a man on the way to radical decisions if he doesn't find a response to his planning. The action of the human spirit, says Silone, is in proportion to the pressure which is exerted on it.[1] The nonconformist rejects the procrastination which the rulers, in a thousand fictitious ways, use to prevent the truth from arriving at its final conclusion, prudence being their main excuse. Their conduct is surrounded by "prudent reasons," forgetting that we honor with such a name only that which passes for unbearable mediocrity.[2]

The nonconformist does not exclude the norm, but he understands when circumstances go beyond the normal and therefore he searches for a development of all that is communitarian, social, and human. Rational nonconformity is a position which is scientifically explained by the philosophical principle of the *battle of contraries.*

In the period of nonconformity, Camilo demanded technical solutions as a rational way out; as we have seen, he acted as a scientist. He expressed himself in such terms as fulfilling a duty. When he passed to the state of rebellion, and entered the sphere of politics, or more exactly, political action, he began to speak in terms of *what must be done*. That is to say, he applied science to objective procedure.

Rebellion is nonconformity translated into act. Nonconformity nourishes rebellion. When rebellion is no longer nonconformist, the way is opened up for the demagogue, the desperado, or the mad megalomaniac, or in other cases the pessimist because of the devaluation of securities. There are as many different kinds of rebellion as there are manifestations of nonconformity.

Rebellion is launched against something, openly, through acts. Camilo was rooted in action and in accord with motivational intensity; he was thrown against the rules which had created in him such painful antagonisms.

The penologist Bernardo Gaitán Mahecha writes:

The problem, basically, is in judging what is true rebellion; it is impossible to judge someone validly by execrating his memory or by pitying him when he, with complete integrity, chooses the heroic life while those responsible for the human shame and the social evils are pharisaically limited to washing their hands and speaking of the "misguided sheep." There must be something wrong in the social component, when we have cases such as that of the priest, Camilo Torres. A society which bears such fruits is necessarily rotten. Because if it is a frequent occurrence that a priest leaves the priesthood for civil life with all its consequences, it is not ordinary, but on the contrary, quite extraordinary, that he does it in order to give living testimony of a profound nonconformity with the entire society, from its ecclesiastical spheres to its socio-economic structures. We are not concerned with judging the procedure for rebellion, but the rebellion itself, as a cultural expression.

What is a rebel? A man who says no. He is also a man who says yes, from his very first move, affirms Camus. But he is something more: he is a man who is completely dedicated to his idea and places it in contradiction to his society and, sacrificing himself for that society, he moves it to renew itself.[3]

And Camilo is that man. The extraordinary and disconcerting aspect of the "Camilo Torres case" is that it treats of a Catholic priest who incites his fellow citizens to revolution, as the only way for the people, the exploited majority, to enter the government and destroy the predominance of the exploiting minority which controls all the tools of power.[4]

In reality, it treats of a universe divided into two camps each day more antagonistic to one another: those who have everything and those who have nothing. The first with plenty; the second in conditions of misery; the first a minority; the second, the great majority. The first constitutes a superstructure which does not take into consideration the common good; the second constitutes a substructure in which the victims of outrages and behavior which destroy the dignity of the human being are gathered.

Ours is a history of the secular domination by an oligarchical class. In effect, once independence had been won, the progressive sector did not come to power, but rather a feudal class which consolidated the feudal structures and put to one side technical and industrial progress. The process of culturation, conditioned to the possession of immense estates with the intangible and social "rights of property," and to the profits from fees, benefices, exemptions, privileges, and riches, never reached the people. Inertia and narrowness characterized the nineteenth century in this section of the world. Commerce basically consisted of products which were sold expensively and a small quantity of imported merchandise.

A great change came with the Second World War. Indo-America entered the era of technology and the atom after a century of backwardness. It experienced a staggering population explosion, growing agitation of the masses in the substructure, large exodus from the country to the city, overpopulation of suburban areas by people living in misery, impoverished and deserted country areas, and a high rate of unemployment in the cities. Services do not grow fast enough. A new social class feels caught between the traditional ruling class and the masses in search of integration into the national life. These strong internal forces are aggravated by the fact that Latin America has fallen into the orbit of international economic imperialism. The invasion of foreign businesses, true leeches of capital, impedes the formation of national businesses. The distance between the rich and the poor, between the developed countries and Latin America, becomes more insuperable each day. Knowledge of this situation, inevitable because of the improved media of communication, has created a pre-revolutionary climate and has brought Latin America to the point where it is considered wrapped up in what Toynbee calls the third revolutionary explosion, the revolution of the Third World.[5]

The development, or rather the full integration of the marginal masses in the life of a nation, and of underdeveloped countries in the community of the nations, as a subject of history, is not possible without a rapid and profound reform of the structures; that is, without what we call social revolution. This one conviction is found in large segments of the Latin American population and, above all, in a notable group of intellectuals. It is impressive to realize how the idea of social revolution has been rapidly extended even among Christians. Without doubt it received a strong push from the Chilean magazine *Mensaje,* which in two special numbers took a very strong position and opted decidedly and clearly for revolution in Latin America. The Catholic theologian Snoeck gives us the same vision in the magazine *Concilium.*[6]

As far as Colombia is concerned, political, economic, cultural, ecclesiastical, and military power have been in the hands of a group which does not represent the interests of the majority of the people, but make decisions on its own regarding the transformation of the country, being able to do this because of a powerful political apparatus.[7]

In the face of this reality, Camilo proclaims the revolution as the only way out. In doing so, he looks at his own position:

> I am a revolutionary [he says] as a Colombian, as a sociologist, as a Christian, and as a priest.
>
> *As a Colombian,* because I cannot be a stranger to my people's battles.
>
> *As a Sociologist,* because, thanks to the scientific knowledge which I have of reality, I have arrived at the realization that technical and effective solutions will not be obtained without a revolution.
>
> *As a Christian,* because the essence of Christianity is love of neighbor and only through the revolution can the welfare of the majority be obtained.
>
> *As a Priest,* because the surrender of oneself to his neighbor, which the revolution demands, is a *requisite of fraternal charity;* it is indispensable for offering the sacrifice of the Mass, which is not an individual offering, but that of the entire people of God through the intercession of Christ.[8]

To what can we ascribe this plan of Camilo's? Above all, to a process of ideological development, his interpretation of Christianity and of the priesthood as service. And secondly, to his profession as a sociologist. Since his days at Louvain, he had thought about teams which would study the Colombian situation with scientific methods and train technical personnel to bring about a great social change.

Other factors were: The direct observation of the reality; contact with thinkers and very advanced minds; participation in the life of both the university and the workers; research in the rural areas; the attitudes of the ecclesiastical hierarchy which would not commit itself to the positive solution of problems, even though it has great influence in our history and undeniable decisive power before our other ruling sectors.

Also it should be added that Camilo exhausted all the means to unite the Leftist groups, without any positive results; he contacted the leaders of worker and peasant organizations; he sounded out possible solutions with those responsible in the government, with many bishops and with the politicians. He explained to them with absolute clarity the urgency of obtaining a radical change. All kept silent. He was convinced once more that the people were the only force capable of accomplishing a meaningful transformation and that there was no other course than the revolution. But what, exactly, is a revolution? Revolution is not a military revolt or an exclusively military blow against the legally constituted authority. It is not merely insurrection or revolt, a violent armed uprising against legal authority with the participation of vast sectors of the population, whose primary objective is to liquidate violently all that is considered a national evil. Revolution can be accompanied by insurrection, but it isn't necessarily an insurrection.

It is not a revolt, mutiny, or rebellion; no, it is not a violent uprising against legitimate authority accomplished through isolated groups in a disorganized way and without prospects of obtaining their objective. It is not subversion, nor is it some action performed for the purpose of stirring up souls against legal authority in a cunning and clandestine way. It is not sedition, nor is it the activity of agitators who provoke disturbances or disorders with the objective of undermining authority and making it difficult for it to fulfill its obligations. It is characterized by disorder, violence, and chaos.

It is not merely that evolution or change which, willy-nilly, is produced in every living organism. Every living organism evolves, and every society is, in a certain sense, an organism. Change through evolution is always gradual, slow, and it does not necessarily imply progress; it may also indicate degeneration and decadence.[9] Snoeck stresses the fact that revolution differs from evolution in the rapidity and the intensity of the process.[10]

It is not reform or change deliberately produced and defined which responds to an idea or a plan. It is different from evolution in so far as it is change which is the fruit of an ideology, deliberately produced, previously planned, rapid, radical and integral. It embraces all basic structures, whether they be political, juridical, social, or economic. It is profound change and also has the character of urgency. Every authentic revolution must contain an ideology, a program for the future, and the will to accomplish it.[11]

In fact, the revolution involves an irrevocable decision to break radically with an "order," which is order for a few but disorder for the majority, with the purpose of constituting a completely new order which will respond to all the just desires of the majority.

In the revolution we should distinguish the momentum and the rate of speed. There is a momentum of radical rupture with prevailing structures which paralyze the development of the nation because they are static, rigid, and ineffective. This involves the development of a new order.

As for the rate of speed, the rupture always comes with rapidity. It is almost a break in history. The development of the new order should be relatively rapid, so that it does not solidify by converting the provisional into the definitive. If this happens, the revolution will have failed as a revolution.[12]

Also, it is necessary to remember that the revolution should be authentic; should constitute in its initial momentum a transitory step; should be just in its proceedings; does not act magically; demands that the men who provoke it be responsible for its success.

It is undeniable, no matter what anyone says, that revolution does not rise up from the Messianism of an adventurer, nor from prefabricated programs to assure greater electoral participation, but from an actual situation which is so oppressive and suffocating that power is needed to unite the people for the irrevocable purpose of liberation.

If we look at its period of incubation, the revolution begins to manifest itself among the common people in the form of uneasiness, social resentments and continual tension.

The young people and some capable elements of the ruling class should be infected with that discontent. Because "the stronger the discontent of the common people, the more riots and disorganized acts of violence they bring about. The fact is that there is no revolution without organized leaders." But those leaders can come from the people.

Camilo presumed that discontent existed in the people and that responsible groups of leaders, capable and coordinated, must be created to work for a significant change, since our history is full of fruitless insurgencies provoked many times by resentments, improvisations or frustrations.

We have more than enough pseudo-leaders, a species of deluded spellbinder, very able in providing insufficient means, in delaying the final result, in juggling and contriving momentary solutions, but with the same undesirable result: the tricking of the people. These confuse the revolution with sophistry.

Would the revolution which Camilo predicted be violent or peaceful? In the report on the Christian apostolate (Congress of *Pro Mundi Vita*), it is stipulated that the possibility of peaceful revolution is directly determined by the foresight of the ruling class, since the desire for change in that class is difficult to obtain. That is to say, those who profit from the tools of power will do everything possible to maintain their positions of privilege, appealing to every kind of palliative and repressive military means. The result of all this is that as the pressure from below grows and the people demand their rights, violent revolution is a probable alternative.

Subsequently, in the discourse to the workers in the Center of the Trade Union of Bavaria, he is more explicit:

They have told me many times that I preach violent revolution; but it is interesting to know why the ruling class portrays me as an advocate of violent revolution. You have realized that my proposals are reduced to this: that the majority exercise power and that governmental decisions be in favor of the majority and not of the minority.

As we all know, this is not easy. I have said that we must be prepared for the eventuality of the minority opposing, through violence, the exercise of power by the majority. And moreover, you see the publications of our great press and the reactions of our ecclesiastical hierarchy which has condemned me, saying that I am defending violent revolution. What is happening then with the ruling class?

It knows who will decide the issue of peace, that is to say, whether the revolution is peaceful or violent. The decision is not in the hands of the lower class but in the hands of the ruling class. And since the lower class is beginning to organize itself courageously, with discipline and decision, and since we are not organizing for the elections, then they assume we are organizing violent revolution.

Because of this, the minority ruling class intends to unleash violence against the majority class; they will oppose by violence the just reforms which the majority lower class demands.

But the violence is accomplished with arms, grenades, tanks and many other costly things which the lower classes do not have; for that reason those who decide on violence are the ones who can afford it. A peasant will not sell a cow which is giving him milk for his children in order to buy a machine gun except in the extreme case where there are persons who will take the life of his children with another machine gun. Therefore, if the peasant arms himself, why will he do it? Against whom is he going to defend himself?

Now that we are organizing around some common ideas, forming a large popular movement and coming close to seizing power, the ruling class tears its garments like the Pharisees; they are hypocrites, because after having practiced violence, they have no right to accuse the majority class of wanting to use violence and much less when the majority class has suffered it for sixteen years and absolutely refuses to allow its continuation.

Therefore, we have to open the eyes of Colombia to these things and show it why we must be determined to fight to the final conclusion and not take one step back; the enemy has shown us that it has a fierce determination, and if we do not have that same determination, we are in a weaker condition. Because of that, we will continue until we have power. The minority class does not permit us to have power, and this is fundamentally antidemocratic if we constitute a majority; if we believe in democracy, we have a right to power. If they are going to profane Colombian democracy by violence, it is important that they know we are ready to meet force with force.[13]

In Colombia they have a fear of the word *Revolution.* In spite of this it is the most appropriate word both linguistically and ideologically for translating the object of our efforts and for expressing the most adequate way to solve the problem.

Cardinal Concha in his pastoral letter of August 12, 1965, condemned the use of such a word because he considered it erroneous, ambiguous, as dangerous as "a two-edged sword,"[14] and he suggested; "Would it not be better to prescind from the word *Revolution* when we wish to understand an evolution, a change, but one which is justifiable, peaceful, and lawful?" But it is revolution, spawned by tremendous injustice, that is being formed in Latin America.

"Please! let us not waste ink, paper, or talent discussing whether or not the use of the word Revolution is fitting," say the Chilean Jesuits, and they continue: "The people do not believe in slow evolutions. They demand a rapid, integral, radical change. Not to call this Revolution is simple blindness."[15]

The Catholic bishop Boza Masvidal, the old auxiliary of Havana, now in exile, declares: "There are many for whom the very word Revolution inspires terror and this is because they have been accustomed to taking it in its worst sense, as a synonym for violence, destruction, injustice, crimes, outrage, oppression, and violation of all rights. Revolution does not have to be anything like that. It means a change which is at once profound and rapid. Profound because the evil is deep and goes even to the roots. Rapid because the remedy is urgent and does not admit delay. There are many who would prefer a slow change, through evolution, like the firm and deliberate steps of an elephant. This, clearly, would be the best. Except that it would arrive a few centuries too late."

There are many, too many, who fear the word but not the situations which produce unbearable conditions. The Colombian economist Diego Majía said that "There is no need to be frightened by the words when they correspond to real and concrete facts. Why deny that we are living a genuine revolution against which neither blessings or exorcisms will work?"

Senator Fulbright in his book *Old Myths and New Realities,* is of the opinion that

> The policy of the United States with respect to Latin America as a whole is predicated on the assumption that social revolution can be accomplished without violent upheaval. This is the guiding principle of the Alliance for Progress and it may in time be vindicated. We are

entitled to hope so, and it is wise and necessary for us to do all that we can to advance the prospects of peaceful and orderly reform.

At the same time, we must be under no illusions as to the extreme difficulty of uprooting long-established ruling oligarchies without disruptions involving lesser or greater degrees of violence. The historical odds are probably against the prospects of peaceful social revolution. There are places, of course, where it has occurred, and others where it seems likely to occur. In Latin America, the chances for such basic change by peaceful means seem bright in Colombia and Venezuela and certain other countries; in Mexico many basic changes have been made by peaceful means, but these came in the wake of a violent revolution. In some other Latin American countries the power of ruling oligarchies is so solidly established and their ignorance so great that the forceful overthrow of established authorities may be unavoidable.

I am not predicting violent revolutions in Latin America or elsewhere. Still less am I advocating them. I wish only to suggest that violent social revolutions are a possibility in countries where feudal oligarchies resist all meaningful change by peaceful means. We must not, in our preference for the democratic procedures envisioned by the Charter of Punta del Este, close our minds to the possibility that democratic procedures may fail in certain countries, and that where democracy does fail violent social convulsions may occur.

We would do well, while continuing our efforts to promote peaceful change through the Alliance for Progress, to consider what our reactions might be in the event of the outbreak of genuine social revolution in one or more Latin American countries. Such a revolution did occur in Bolivia, and we accepted it calmly and sensibly. But what if a violent social revolution were to break out in one of the larger Latin American countries? Would we feel certain that it was Cuban or Soviet inspired? Would we wish to intervene on the side of established authority? Or would we be willing to tolerate or even support a revolution if it was seen to be not Communist but similar in nature to the Mexican revolution or the Nasser revolution in Egypt?[16]

President Kennedy predicted: "Those who make peaceful revolution impossible will make violent revolution inevitable." Here arises a highly charged question: Can a Christian be a revolutionary? The answer is obvious: in general, not only can he be but he must be one.

Christianity was and is a revolution. It will continue to be a revolution as long as prejudicial conditions of injustice against the rights of the human person continue, as long as there are men who exploit other men, people who subjugate other people.

The dynamic of Christianity comes from a revolutionary force which will always work to destroy whatever structures are instruments of unjust social pressure, which concedes privileges to some and makes others victims. By its essence, authentic Christianity will be on the side of the victims, of the oppressed, of those who have revolutionary ability no matter to what political force they belong.

When the majority is oppressed and a legal government approves of this, then the Christian has the duty to criticize and fight that government. The conservative, conformist attitude rejects the criticism; the dominant groups which hold power do not tolerate it; the tyrants and the dictators proscribe it. Criticism and self-criticism imply a radical non-conformity and this, in its turn, must be crystallized in a revolutionary position.

If Christianity is founded in charity; if charity is the service of men; if the majority of men is seen to be mired in subhuman conditions, the Christian must be a revolutionary. He must face reality. He must face that reality in order to analyze it and to criticize it.

Objective analysis shows him in that reality certain structures, an order, a human totality composed of sectors. These sectors are divided into the exploiters and the exploited: the first constitutes a minority which is typified as a very powerful pressure group, benefiting from all the decisive instruments of power. The exploited sector forms the immense majority without any effective channel of pressure and without any decision-making possibility. Thus, as long as the social reality is a conglomeration of indigent masses and unjust structures, the Christian has the obligation to be on the side of the indigent masses and not at the service of unjust structures.

Man is a subject with fundamental necessities before he is someone with rights and obligations. Necessity precedes rights. As Fernández de Castro shows, before every juridical edict and every legal superstructure the necessities of man regulate his relations and are the force which makes the world advance towards its final organization.[17]

The foregoing serves as a basis for passing judgment on the structures as they are in reality: the perfection or imperfection, the advantage or disadvantage of each social structure, can be judged by the help or hindrance it offers to man to satisfy his fundamental necessities. When the structures do not respond to this command which springs from the very essence of the human person, the Christian must adopt a meaningful position, neither theoretical nor contemplative, but one translated into revolutionary action.

Because as long as indigent substructures and unjust structures exist, there will be a force capable of producing revolutions. The Christian—if he is authentic—will be with the indigent, against structures and political regimes which provoke misery. Neither the conformists nor the complacent will be able to stop it; even if they are Christians and even if they momentarily achieve success in keeping their bourgeois selfishness united with Christian ideals.[18]

The teaching of many representatives of the ecclesiastical hierarchy in this sense is timid, accommodating, calculated, presented in documents full of bland suggestions and nice advice, very paternal and very condescending. They do not want to admit that in that way they check Christianity and arrest the progress of the world.

Men have the obligation to satisfy their fundamental necessities. "But this is not produced automatically; it is necessary to promote it. This is Christianity's great mission. In forcing radical changes, they will eliminate innumerable tragedies."

An objection comes up: Such a procedure leads to the violation of others' rights. Those who speak in that way are the ones who identify rights with privileges. They are the ones who demand of others respect and recognition, silence and abstention from every expression of nonconformity. They demand of the State that it maintain police and soldiers to protect them. They are the beneficiaries of a public system which prevents by bullets the alteration of systems of government which are essentially legalized tyranny.

A tyrant can be a man or a regime. What is disconcerting is that the overthrow of the individual tyrant is easily justified, but not that of the tyrannical regimes disguised as democracy and "established order."

There is yet one last observation: There are Christians who abstain from revolutionary involvement for reasons of conscience. Why?

In the first place, their spiritual direction depends on individuals who are opposed to the change of structures; these individuals receive their orientation from high circles where there are many who defend the established "order" to the death in order not to lose the privileges which it gives them. They forget, as Camilo said, that they must bring about the Incarnation of the Lord; they will do this only if they fulfill their responsibility and involve themselves in the human destiny of their flock.[19]

Secondly, because they have not understood the essence of Christianity. They are still torn between the myth and the scruple; between the superstition and the duty which the present social disorder imposes on them. They have not captured the full meaning of the precept of love for one's neighbor. They continue to give alms without contributing to the eradication of the causes of misery.

What should be the attitude of the Christian regarding revolution? The Catholic magazine *Mensaje,* directed by the Jesuit Fathers, among whom figure the eminent Vekemans, a sociologist, and Zañartas, an economist, as the principal mentors, gives this response:

> The Christian is a child of truth and his activity has to be true. He doesn't have to fight windmills but neither must he hide his head like the ostrich in the fable. Neither ingenuous illusion, nor fearful realism. To be a Christian means to be judged *totally* by the truth without worrying if such a route leads you to the cross . . .
>
> Before a "revolution in motion" it is impossible to remain neutral . . . We do not see how an authentically Christian multitude can be reconciled with a closed antirevolutionary attitude, opposed to the radical and urgent change of structures.
>
> A profound and integral change of structures is required, an urgent change which might give an answer to the breathless and raging anxiety of the masses. And the masses are ready, they are on the move.

Not to be opposed to this movement, and even more, to support it, clearly involves a risk because no one can know exactly where the revolution will end, but life is a risk and Christianity is not a religion of safe ports but of open-hearted folly. The important thing is sincerity, veracity, loyalty.[20]

To be a revolutionary, according to Camilo, is to be conscious that in Colombia it is impossible for the majority to have enough to eat, sufficient clothing and sufficient housing. This is due to the fact that those who have power constitute an economic minority which dominates political, cultural, military, and, disgracefully, even ecclesiastical power. It means fighting against oppressive structures in order to obtain education for the children and access to culture for those economically deprived. To be a revolutionary means for the Christian not to compromise with misery and to recognize in every man whatever right is due him. It means not to protect crime and to defend every citizen from abuse and injustice, without distinction of creed or opinion.

To be a revolutionary means to promote the union of all groups of the substructure and not to allow the exploiters to break that unity. It means rejecting every unjust repression and every tyranny. It means a fight for the integral elevation of man. It implies a profound dedication to justice. It entails substituting effective organizations of the people which are dedicated to the welfare of the community for the present inoperative bodies. The revolutionary must support those fighting honorably for the people and not sell out for money, rewards, promises, positions.

This is how the revolutionary must fulfill his commitment to fight for effective social justice. This will develop an authentic democracy, not dominated by pressure groups, understood as the minority of individuals who have all the influence over the decisions of power. Revolution means fighting against hunger. We are not concerned, he frequently stated, with becoming entangled in discussions of whether the soul is mortal or immortal. The thing that is clear is that hunger is mortal. Camilo, with Josué de Castro, the Brazilian expert, agreed that we live in a juxtaposition of antagonistic worlds: one where people live for seventy years; and the other, where they live for thirty-five years. The earth is principally divided into two large groups: those who do not eat and those who eat but do not sleep because they fear the revolt of the hungry. Each day of each week, ten thousand persons die of hunger—more than in any other period of history. In India alone, in the next ten years, fifty million children will die of hunger. More than one and a half billion human beings live at this moment with hunger in their bellies, hunger in their heart, hunger in their brains. According to the report of the FAO, half of the world's population is hungry or undernourished. The earth is inhabited by three billion persons. Within seventeen years we will be four billion; within thirty-seven years six billion. At each swing of the pendulum of the clock in the Congress of Nutrition, there are three more mouths.[21]

The world production of food must grow at a rate of 30% annually, if it is to keep up with the demographic increase of underdeveloped countries. However, between 1958 and 1965, production increased only two percent and in 1966 the situation actually grew worse.[22] We must remember that in 1965, the world population grew at a rate of 180,000 births a day.

Camilo demanded authenticity as the essential condition of the revolutionary. He was aware of other kinds: the café revolutionary, the office revolutionary, the plaza revolutionary, the opportunist, the egoist and the occasional revolutionary. He knew that some who posed as revolutionaries were exploiters; some spoke revolution with a loud voice; some were revolutionaries of convenience, some for the sake of "snobbism"; some called themselves revolutionaries merely because they played with intellectual theories.

None of these is authentic. All the incendiary and shrieking outcry is nourished by irresponsible and treacherous chatter. This is a characteristic of those who, from the safety of the cafés or from secure positions within the same system they are fighting, never lose anything while inciting the people to revolt.

The people are authentic in their truth, in their affirmation, in their dedication, in their faith, in their heroic life. They are authentic because of the direct contact with the daily tragedy which they sustain. Many will go to the people to propose to them a revolution which, examined deeply, is nothing more than another exploitation, another fraud.

In order to work with the people, especially the worker and peasant, one must be honest and transparent. Such transparency, such clearness, such brightness is the light which illumines the hope of the poor. The theatrical revolutionaries and the tourists, spectators, shouters, clowns, gesticulators, are not authentic. Authentic revolution comes from the indigenous root, Indian and Mestizo, worker and peasant, which nourishes our nationality. Someone said that "all revolutions fit inside the national spirit, but outside it revolution is anarchy." Our tragedy is rooted in the lack of a national spirit, of a national purpose so many times falsely proclaimed by those who defend "evolution" and combat "revolution." It is the problem of not having found ourselves.

As he progressed in the battle, mental and operative manifestations of a growing revolutionary radicalism flourished in Camilo. It was the revolution in action.

On June 15, 1965, at a conference in the Universidad Grancolombiano, he proclaimed: "Not one step back. Down with Yankee imperialism. Long live the revolution. Away with oligarchies. Power for the people to the death." "Long live the Gaitán in the cassock," shouted the students when Camilo appeared. "Rebel Zone . . . Independent Area . . . Keep Out, Gringos" was written in large red letters on the walls along the entire street leading to the building where he was going to speak.

From the podium, he showed that "the revolution must be something constructive. It requires the progressive creation of a movement which organizes all the sectors of the people. This will be obtained by forming a movement which includes intellectuals and university students, united in spite of small groups and parties."

As for our political parties, he said that they did not have platforms or technical plans and that they subsisted only on a sentimental basis.

He held that power in Colombia was exercised through minority pressure groups, composed of twenty-four families, around whom revolve economic, cultural, military, and ecclesiastical power. The National Front was created to defend the interests of those twenty-four families, constituting the first class party to be established in Colombia as a channel for dividing the bureaucratic spoils between liberals and conservatives.[23]

It is fitting to add the following to these previous transcriptions taken from the conference which he dictated in the Universidad Grancolombiano: "The economic, military, ecclesiastical, and political powers will wage war with the people in the face of the revolution which is approaching. Revolution which consists in a change of structures. This change implies violence for those who retain power. But violence is not excluded from the Christian ethic, because if Christianity is concerned with eliminating the serious evils which we suffer and saving us from the continuous violence in which we live without possible solution, the ethic is to be violent once and for all in order to destroy the violence which the economic minorities exercise against the people."[24]

On the 19th of June, during a conference given in Medellín, he stated emphatically: "I am of the middle class, of bourgeois extraction. But I have come to the masses who will make the Colombian revolution and I demand that I be admitted as a revolutionary, promising that from this day I will be completely dedicated as a revolutionary."[25]

On June 20th, he declared: "In Colombia anyone who is opposed to the current economic regime is called a Communist; on the other hand, he can be an atheist and never be called a Communist, so long as he doesn't attack the system."[26]

Concerning the Church, he said: "I believe in the expropriation of the wealth of the Church."[27]

He judged the agrarian reform in these terms: "I find that the great defect of *Incora* is that it has not been sufficiently concerned with the education of the peasants—education not only in a formal sense, for it has created schools and cooperatives, but in the informal sense of creating a consciousness in the peasants so that in the future they might undertake to form a large pressure group, capable of transforming this agrarian pseudo-reform into a true reform for themselves."[28] What Camilo meant was that the peasants should be organized in a group which would develop pressure capable of promoting integral and authentic agrarian reform with all the requirements which modern technology demands.

The increasing radicalism of Camilo became even more evident when he declared: "We young people no longer believe that a minority can direct a country without giving opportunity to the other parties. What we want is—more than anything else—to destroy the National Front and, for my part, I believe that only by a bloody war can we reach that objective."[29]

In his speech of July 3rd, given in the National University, after returning from Lima, he stated: "In the face of repression, we will go to the death for the Colombian revolution."

And he added: "The social revolution, which is the essence of Christianity, makes me a priest. What my brothers are doing in an effective and true way, makes me a priest. We are with the revolutionaries and against the counter-revolutionaries. We have on our side truth, morality, justice. We are the people; we go forward for the Colombian revolution."[30]

On the 5th of August he said in Barranquilla that "if the efficacy of love of neighbor can not be obtained except through a revolution, love of neighbor must consider the revolution as one of its objectives, and if in that revolution they coincide in action and in practice with some Marxist-Leninist methods and objectives, it is not that the Marxists are becoming Christians or the Christians Marxists, but that they are united for the technical solution of the problems of the majority of Colombians and that this solution must not only be permitted for Catholics but obligatory for the priest."

And he added: "We do not serve our neighbor by giving him old shoes, or left-overs from the table of the rich. We serve our neighbor with a fundamental agrarian reform, with free education, with the reasonable distribution of the riches, with equality of opportunity for everyone. And since these are accomplished only by taking power, then, it is necessary to revolt in order to take power."[31]

On August 10th he emphasized in Medellín: "The most appropriate way is, naturally, the peaceful revolution. However, I believe it is not in the hands of the poor, of the destitute, to decide the way of revolution. I believe that we would do better to ask the rulers how they will give power to the majority, through peaceful or violent means.

"I think we should continue to try all the peaceful ways. But always moving forward, for the conquest of power for the people."[32]

In September he said: "The Colombian revolution is now a reality. As far as the seizure of power is concerned, it depends on the rapidity of unification and organization which the various sectors of the people have.[33]

All this reiterates the idea that a Colombian problem exists before which it is necessary to adopt an attitude and now for a solution. Camilo took his position, and with undeniable integrity gave his own solution. He did it with a profound honesty. He was able to see that it would demand of him a total sacrifice. The facts confirmed that he was unalterably faithful to his destiny.

Chapter 6

The Platform of the United Front

Not all dreams are stamped out. Some remain and continue to lift our spirits until they are realized when favorable circumstances present themselves. When did Camilo begin to aspire to the organization of a team and a platform?

Concerning this restlessness of Camilo, I was directed to Dr. Jaime Quijano-Caballero, the university professor who knew Camilo's development very well, since they were intimate friends for ten years. I transcribe here the thoughts of Quijano-Caballero, as an answer to the point I wanted to investigate.

"At the end of 1954, there was founded under the immediate influence of Camilo, through a group of Colombian students at Louvain, a team which then invited all Colombians who wished to place their intellectual preparation at the service of the country.

The first public formulation of the ideals of that group was made at Louvain in the month of June 1956, when they were first known as The Colombian Team for Socio-Economic Research, ECISE. At that time the ideas which were enunciated took the following directions:

"In spite of our party or ideological differences, our union will prescind from the factors which separate us in order to concentrate our attention on that which we have in common.

"They emphasized the fact that Colombian youth did not want to waste their energies and scientific preparation on sectarian battles. Agreement was reached on a proposal that all the members of the team agree to the concept of a prior study of the real situation of the country, for which and through which the group wanted to organize a rigidly objective research team, which would instruct public opinion. These ideas were ratified in a document which was known as Bulletin No. 1 of this team, in the month of June, 1956.

"From that time there were outlined as ideals: the necessity to acquire a technique applicable to the reality of the nation; the necessity of a mystique in the disinterested service of the country through scientific expertise; the necessity to work as a team in order to investigate the realities and propose concrete solutions, and the necessity to form groups of scientists and technicians who would second those proposals.

"Camilo, at my suggestion, sought contact, in many trips made by him and other members of the team, with various groups of Colombian students with a thought to the possible extension of the movement; many persons, now in various leadership positions in the country and students at that time, remember that sections were formed in Rome, Paris, London, and Madrid. Informative meetings were held in Berlin, Bonn, and Geneva. And there was founded in September of 1956 the section of Bogotá.

"Three key postulates of the team were definitively proposed. They were formulated thus: (1) disinterestedness; (2) teamwork; (3) scientific objectivity.

"It was precisely the 18th of September of 1956, when Camilo organized the group. This was after several conversations which put me in contact with him for the first time. Although I never knew why, they chose my place. However, I was always grateful for this. It was there that he organized a meeting in my house from which came that Section of Bogotá.

"In November of 1956 the second Informative Bulletin of the team ECISE was published. In it the four principal events were reviewed: the meetings in Bogotá, Paris, London, and Louvain.

"More than a year had passed since I had founded what was then called the Colombian Institute of Administrative Sciences, INCCA, an autonomous entity, the cradle and origin of the INCCA University. Perhaps this was the determining reason that from there and from that meeting there came an Executive Committee of the ECISE, composed of Fernando Gaviria, economist from Harvard, professor at the Javeriana University and the University of the Andes, head at that time of the Office of Economic Research of the Bank of the Republic; César Garcés Verraza, architect, interim director of the Interamerican Center of Housing, CINVA; Miguel Triana Uribe, priest, Licentiate in Theology from the Gregorian University, spiritual director of the Apostolic School of San Benito; Lucía Holguín Pardo, secretary of the Information Center of the United Nations in Bogotá and wife of the Ambassador to the Organization of American States, Alfredo Vásquez Carrizosa.

"I ended up as chairman of that distinguished committee, and as a result, also of the Colombian Team for Socio-Economic Research in that central committee in Bogotá.

"You could see from the beginning that the idea of prescinding from those factors which separate us and concentrating attention on what we have in common was in the mind of Fr. Camilo Torres. That is to say, uniting around questions we agreed on and avoiding what we didn't agree on. I can say that the most essential part of the ideal of constructing a team based on a platform consisted in this point.

"As for the meeting in Paris, this was held Sunday, September 30, 1956, and an Executive Committee was chosen there also. Among those on the committee were Fausto Rentería and Rafael Rivas, both Doctors in Law; Rita Restrepo, a biologist and wife of

Hernando Agudelo Villa; Ramiro Delgado, doctor in medicine, presently connected with the Universidad del Valle, and an eminent expert in population problems, and Flavio Cruz, also a doctor in Law.

"As for the meeting in London which was held at the end of October of that year, it attracted some students from the London School of Economics among whom was Jaime García Parra.

"Bulletin No. 2 to which I am referring, reference is made to the meeting in Louvain. The text of that informative bulletin was produced and published in Louvain.

"It is worthwhile to select some of the ideas which, according to the Bulletin, were discussed by the members of the Louvain team, which set the pattern, and to which Camilo and Father Gustavo Pérez Ramírez belonged as the principal directors, among others. In the following ideas there is contained a philosophy which shows quite well a tendency which Camilo followed in his actions. Or better, by following it, he marked out a plan for his slowly developing progressive solutions and which objectively show, as I believe, that they are identical with his final publicly known declarations. By a curious coincidence they are also contained in the conference which Father Camilo Torres gave in the INCCA University of Colombia, September 21, 1965. They are also found in the text of an interview given by him, during a visit to the INCCA University on October 6, 1965, for a German magazine, and given to Mr. Armin Hindricks, M. A., as a member of the Federico Ebert Foundation of Bonn; and to Mr. Fernando Foncillas, as a member of the A. Bergstrasser Institute of Freiburg, West Germany. I will make further reference to documents later when concluding my answer to the question which Monsignor Germán Guzmán has asked me.

"In that meeting in Louvain, Bulletin No. 2 says that 'they repeated the desire that the movement should continue its concentration on the investigation and scientific study of the national reality, as an indispensable means to any kind of realistic and objective action, and as a basis for union among differing ideological groups. The problems would be pointed out through these investigations, in order to give their solution a strictly scientific character. The solutions would be discussed in the team with specialists in speculative sciences. Without excluding the possibility of a diversity of ideologies, the existence of certain points cannot be denied, and around these unity could be secured.'

"And the Bulletin continues: 'Without this union of all the constructive national elements, we will not arrive at a lasting solution of our problems. These common points must exist for the sake of what has been already accomplished, and also as we consider the objective scientific solutions according to which every ideology must be justified and suggest its program.'

"And then it adds: 'The orientation of scientific solutions, in those fields in which agreement becomes impossible, would be left to the different currents, without diminution of that which remains in common. The movement as such, would not be responsible except for that on which all agree.'

"Finally, in this second Bulletin, was the information that after finishing their studies, two members of the team, Leonor Martínez, then Mrs. de Rocha, and Leticia Velázquez had arrived in Bogotá from Louvain. And that one of the members of the movement, Dr. Jorge Méndez Munévar, dean at that time of the Economics Faculty of the University of the Andes, together with Hernando Agudelo Villa, one of the members of the so-called team of the Seven Wise Men, of the Alliance for Progress, had promoted, towards the end of 1956, the creation of an Institute for Economic Research which had begun to function in that university.

"It is worthy of note that the objectives described above serve as a thread, in my judgment, for identifying the two greatest preoccupations of Camilo from 1956 to 1965: organization of teams and union around that which was held in common, avoiding anything which could break up the union.

"This team, in its next act, as far as activities accomplished in Europe, made an impression on the 'First Congress of Colombian Students in Europe,' which was announced in December of 1957 in Bulletin No. 3 of the team, and was held in Louvain on October 1, 1958, with delegations of Colombian students from Germany, England, France, Spain, Holland, and Belgium. It was under the presidency of Jaime García Parra. Camilo Torres acted as secretary of the Congress.

"The reports presented there reflect a total orientation. Jaime García dealt with 'the urgency of the movement.' Fausto Rentería presented the 'fundamental ideals,' and Camilo Torres the 'immediate objectives.' In this last report, Camilo analyzed: (1) the necessity of an organization; (2) dangers of an organization; and (3) conditions for an organization.

"In the report of Jaime García there was, among other things, an analysis of the importance and the role which 'human leadership' and 'technology' play in economic development. The necessity of having teams capable of transforming and utilizing the advances made in the world was emphasized. They spoke there 'of how the serious problem of the country is, not its poverty, nor its violence, nor the diverse situations which the moment presents, but the lack of a human leadership, of a class or group of people prepared to look for a solution for the country.' They spoke equally of 'the danger that people who have acquired new ideas may become frustrated because of a lack of cohesion.' And making allusion to the experience of the past, the schema of the report continued in its fourth point, alluding to 'the danger that forces and circumstances provoke the individual isolation of people who think in an intelligent way about the country.'

"As a consequence, there was proposed the 'urgent need for a movement and of an organization which might bring together the different forces of those who have a realistic and technical attitude and mentality concerning the problems of the country.'

"And I continue transcribing the text which forms part of the fifth point of the schema of the report recommended by Jaime García on the urgency of this movement. And which, enlarging on the reason for this urgency, speaks: 'of how a movement of this kind is not only necessary from the technical point of view, owing to the necessity of bringing together the little technology available, but also from a personal point of view, so that the barriers, the ignorance, and the traditional taboos do not dissipate, frustrate, and isolate those individuals who have understood—through different circumstances—that the country needs intelligent direction and that they have had the opportunity to acquire a technical preparation and a fuller vision of what are the destinies of the country' (ECEP, Informative Bulletin, No. 4, January 4, 1959 p. 3).

"No one will be able to deny that there was in the plan a certain prophetic vision in so far as a movement was conceived which would serve, from a personal point of view, as a defense of a new Colombian mentality.

"In the report of Fausto Rentería on fundamental ideals, among those ends there was mentioned: 'to promote in all the territory of the Republic, and in all the groups of students and professionals . . . a movement of coordination, between students and between professionals,' tending to establish between them the commitment to act in a positive way for the country on the basis of disinterest already enunciated, to work in teams and with scientific objectivity.

"And in point No. 5 of the schema of the report in question, it proposes: 'To study the Colombian problems and to present concrete solutions on each one of them to the ruling sectors and to public opinion and to collaborate in the realization of the solutions proposed.'

"For all of which, Camilo Torres sketched 'immediate objectives' in his report, concentrating, as was noted above, on necessity, dangers, and conditions of an organization. And he showed, in the respective schema, which is transcribed in the already cited Informative Bulletin No. 4, that the greatest danger would be the disconnection of individuals from the masses through bureaucratization.

"With a foundation in these previous ideas, it can be said that in the matter of the organization of teams, at this time, there predominated the idea of human leadership which represented a new mentality and which should be careful that barriers, ignorance, and traditional taboos do not dissipate, frustrate, and isolate those individuals thus represented; that this mentality should be sought in an inter-student and inter-professional movement, and that, finally, the studies accomplished by these teams or individuals would present solutions to the ruling sectors and public opinion in the country, offering their collaboration in the realization of the solutions.

"Perhaps for this reason seeing the things from above, we can understand the telegram which the then ambassador of Colombia in Belgium, Dr. Juan Uribe Cualla, dispatched to the Minister of Foreign Affairs on the first Congress, telling him on October 5, 1958, among other things, the following: 'From the 1st to the 3rd of this month a Louvain Congress of Colombian students residing in Europe was convened with delegations coming from Belgium, France, Germany, Spain, England, Holland. They determined to organize a Colombian team for study and progress under the sign "ECEP." It will have a permanent Louvain secretariat with different responsible directors from the university centers of Europe. They have adopted magnificent conclusions.'

"And then: '24 delegates participated. Last night I offered the participants at the Congress a reception at the Embassy. The Congress of Colombian university students was a great success. The young intellectuals of our country are disposed to effectively contribute their technical studies to the serious national problems. Colombian Ambassador Juan Uribe Cualla.'

"Summing up, they selected as ideals proposed in the Congress, the cooperation between students and professionals, scientific investigation and the formation of teams. Concretely, the formation of scientific and technical teams facilitating and increasing access to specialization in the Colombian situation would bring together the minimum necessary requisites. And among other things, ECEP, as one of its immediate objectives, proposed to facilitate, even economically, the formation in Europe of Colombian university students and the specialized training of the greatest possible number of young people and workers.

"But adverting to the fact that in reference to Europe, where there already existed bases ready to fulfill their commitment, ECEP began to adapt itself to form teams in the United States. Camilo Torres was commissioned by the Congress for that task. At this stage Camilo's desire to work with a team and a definite platform appears clearly. From Bulletin No. 4 of January 1959, published by the General Secretariat in Europe, I have taken the previous references. The General Secretariat of ECEP at that time, with headquarters in Bogotá, was under the direction of Father Gustavo Pérez Ramírez, a colleague of Camilo. The General Secretariat for Europe, with headquarters in Louvain, was placed under the direction of Luis Patiño, an alumnus of the Modern Gymnasium of Bogotá, as were Camilo and many of those who were involved. Very many of the connections which Camilo enjoyed at this time had been born of youthful relations formed in that school.

"Four more European sections were organized in Belgium, France, Germany and England. Besides Jaime García and Fausto Rentería, Jorge Plata in Belgium and Germán Duque in Germany were involved.

"In the meanwhile Camilo had established a General Secretariat for the United States, and he was informed of sections established in Minneapolis, Chicago, and New York, each with three members.

"This was the situation as far as the team is concerned. And as for the Platform, a text of Gustavo Pérez, one of the first promoters of the Team, was transcribed in which a synthesis of the common ideology was made. It insisted that there be a minimal ideological content. Considering it of special interest for understanding the tendency Camilo followed in his actions, I wish to transcribe part of this synthesis:

" 'The problem of a social organization is to make sure that one arrives at a minimal ideological content which is enough to accomplish the necessary integration and cohesion of the society without demanding that each member commit himself to a complete world vision.

" 'It seems that such content is contained in the idea of the acknowledgment of man by man, a humanism which is based on a common denominator. This philosophy can be the object of a universal consensus. The Christian can adhere to it even though for him, humanism has otherworldly dimensions.

" 'This historical experience,' continues Father Gustavo Pérez, 'is present today in the case of Colombia. There must be an ideological minimum on which agreement can be reached by Colombians in view of the common good. Here we find the total significance of the Colombian team. Humanism would be the common denominator which would polarize all the living forces of the country.'

"And then he added, insisting on the same constant, that 'in order to obtain the unity and the solution' of the Colombian problem, 'it is necessary to leave to one side all that would cause dissension.' Thus, through mutual respect of political and religious ideology, it was thought that, at least in part, a community of interests for the good of all would be obtained.

"The foregoing, in my own opinion, now presents a type of platform of a kind of United Front, united according to what was believed possible.

"I must confess that my persistent doubts about the efficacy of these ideas in terms of action and in the face of reality slowly drew me away from ECEP.

"In November of 1958, I had taken office as Administrative Secretary of the National University. In 1959, there began, in my judgment, a new, important stage in the developing activities of Camilo Torres. He also, associated with the National University, began to produce, especially towards the end of the year, some very significant work. Together with Gustavo Pérez, Orlando Fals Borda, Leonor Martínez de Rocha, mentioned above, César Garcés, Gerardo Tamayo, three other persons and Camilo Torres, we were called by our friend and colleague, Nemesio Camacho Rodríguez, Secretary General of the Ministry of National Education, at the initiative of Dr. Abel Naranjo Villegas, Minister of Education, to constitute what was called the Committee for the Promotion of Common Action, the first organization of this kind on the national level in Colombia.

"Between us, Orlando Fals, Camilo Torres, Gustavo Pérez and I drew up, at the request of the Minister Naranjo, a document called 'Platform for Common Action,' which was then circulated, without mention of the authors, as an official document of that Ministry in the national press, in order to inaugurate a vast campaign of common action in the country. I remember that the national campaign was begun with the presentation on national television of the whole group, presided over by the Minister of Education. This occurred as a development of the celebrated decree 1761 in 1959 which introduced the movement of community action in Colombia. I recall only one key phrase from that platform: 'the most humble citizen is a potential resource and not a liability.'

"At this time or stage in the action, in respect to the activities of Camilo Torres, he tried to initiate the University and Professional Movement for the Organization of the Community (MUNIPROC).

"Basically, they were concerned with fulfilling, as the name itself says, the ideals which were outlined by the Congress of Students in Louvain, which he had inspired. Once again, it was an inter-student and inter-professional movement, but this time not only to present solutions to the ruling sectors and public opinion in the country. Here, I believe, there was introduced a new development which slowly grew in importance: the action was oriented towards several sectors of society—the suburban communities, for example, and certain peasant groups.

"One of the last activities which I fulfilled during my stay in the National University was to organize the First Inter-university Seminar on Community Development, in September of 1960. I had proposed it since the beginning of the year as a new task which would commit the Colombian University to new responsibilities. Orlando Fals, Camilo Torres, Andrew Pearse, a visiting professor from UNESCO, and I were involved in the organization of the Seminar. In this Seminar, we now saw the results of a very considerable concern, in comparison with those propositions which had risen from the experiences and anxieties articulated by Camilo in the Louvain stage, six years before.

"MUNIPROC, among many other organizations and movements, felt the same desire to organize people and unite them under the same ideals by leaving to one side all that could cause dissension.

"Even the objectives proposed for a platform continued to be fundamentally the same, but the means for accomplishing the union, that is to say, the character of the teams, had changed.

"This process, in my judgment, continued. Along with the identical objectives, the persons to whom the call for action was given changed. And they continued to change until Camilo found himself with the principal adherents following him.

"The identity of the intentions is verified, I feel, by the words which Camilo had spoken in beginning his conference on September 21, 1965, in the large hall of the University INCCA. I had invited him there so that in a free dialogue, he could express his ideas. In the same way I had been permitted to invite Dr. Carlos Lleras Restrepo to give his views. One of the first disappointments which Camilo suffered in the National University was when they prevented this dialogue from taking place.

"Then Father Camilo Torres, alluding to my introductory words, said: 'As Jaime Quijano has said, it is profoundly significant for me also that after meeting for ten years in his small apartment, the cradle of the INCCA University, today I see that small apartment converted into a great university. It was there that for the first time we began to discuss with Marxists, Christians and persons of many different ideologies the need to work out, in unity of action and prescinding from whatever might divide us, scientific and technical solutions designed to fit the concrete situation of our country.'

"This indicates the consistency of Camilo's thinking in terms of his objectives as he gradually formulated a platform. Once again, as I said in citing the interview he gave on October 6, 1965, in the University, this shows in my judgment how right he was to progressively and gradually develop the means he needed to accomplish his goals.

"When his interviewers asked him, 'Do you approve of the influence of the non-oligarchical middle class?', Camilo answered: 'Unfortunately, in Colombia there are very few elements of the middle class who are not also part of the oligarchy. In Columbia there is a very small middle class. From the economic point of view, the majority of Colombian capitalists are associated with foreign capitalists. They have a tendency to be foreign-oriented. For our middle class it is a sign of pride to be educated in foreign countries; not to use national products; to use foreign speech; to have a foreign culture; to look down on what is native. Therefore, there is not really a nationalist middle class here. Secondly, almost the entire middle class is allied to the oligarchy which holds the real power. Some sectors of the small middle class come from the upper classes as in the case of families which have lost their wealth. Among these people there may be some good influences, in my opinion; after all, I myself come from the middle class.'

"And when he was asked in this same interview: 'How is your movement organized . . .?' he answered: 'This movement came out of the University like so many movements in Latin America. Nevertheless, for the past six years, as a result of the programs of community development and the trade union courses, I have had many contacts with the peasants and the workers. The movement is principally oriented towards them. It attempts to organize them from below upwards. Because of this, I believe that it has a broad base among the peasants and workers . . . a broad popular base.'

"Finally, he replied to the question, 'How can you reconcile your priestly state and your revolutionary position in which, without doubt, many Marxist-Leninist elements are present?'

" 'I come from a family who were not practicing Catholics; they were even free-thinkers. I discovered Christianity as a way of living one's life for his neighbor as love among equals. When I realized what importance this had, I resolved to dedicate myself completely to the love of neighbor, and therefore I became a priest. When I saw that if love was to be sincere and true it was necessary that it be effective, then I saw that it was necessary to unite it to science. Therefore, I became a sociologist. But in studying sociology, I realized that in order to give enough to eat to the majority, in order to give them houses and education, paternalism was not sufficient. It was necessary to organize society in a different way. I thought that lay Catholics would do this. I thought that they would accomplish a structural transformation in Columbia that would benefit our brothers. Nevertheless, I saw that either they did not wish to do it or they couldn't do it. Having tried it through many means, and having gone to the politicians of the opposition, I resolved to present my plan to the people directly.'

"Camilo had been anxious ever since Louvain, and perhaps even before that, to organize a team with a platform for action which would have contact with technically prepared groups. Regarding this important point of the organization of technical groups, it is important to transcribe what was surely his ultimate public stand, when during this interview he answered the following question of Messrs. Hindrichs and Foncillas: 'Does your movement have technically prepared groups, should you occupy power through a revolution?' And Camilo responded:

"I believe that Colombia does not have technically prepared teams. Much less does the movement; but since this is a vicious circle, we must break out of it on some side. I believe that there are not sufficient technically prepared groups, because neither education nor society has been organized so that those groups might exist. On the other hand, one of the great obstacles to organizing education and society is the lack of technically prepared groups. Since it is necessary to break out of this vicious circle on some side, I think that we are going to break out of it with what there is. And after, as it is commonly said in Colombia, we will fix things on the way. We will do this with few technicians, trying to prepare them practically with people who have practical experience. Even though they will not have high academic levels, I believe that it is possible to reconstruct a country, naturally with great emphasis on education at all levels.'

"Thus Camilo passed through various slow and successive adjustments from the heights to the level of the people. ECEP had stayed behind. Nevertheless he continued to be faithful to its objectives, in the form and condition in which he conceived them."

Up to here I have transcribed the judgment of Dr. Jaime Quijano Caballero in answer to my questioning.

Since ECEP (Colombian Team for Study and Progress) works at the level of the ruling classes, it receives only praise and encouraging messages; but when Camilo worked at the level of the lower classes, this brought him insults and curses. The fact was that in the initial activities, the structures of society weren't touched.

From the foregoing we can see that the principles and program of the Platform and the United Front had antecedents in the experiment at Louvain. What, then, led to the program for a movement of popular unity, which Camilo presented in 1965?

Let us begin in the final months of 1964. In the face of the national confusion of that time and of the urgent need for a coherent politics, people on many fronts were asking why the Left remained silent, why it did not act. Someone asked Camilo who composed the Colombian Left, who its leaders were, what sort of revolution they were seeking. People asked him whether it would be worthwhile to meet the leaders of various Leftist groups and listen to them. It was suggested that he promote a meeting for the progressive groups.

Camilo jotted down the various names, called numbers of people on the telephone, suggested a meeting at a specific time and place. The response was very encouraging. When the day of the meeting arrived, reporters from *The New Press* asked Camilo for an interview beforehand. In the apartment of the publisher of this magazine, they spoke of objectives, results, positions, and political momentum, in order to make it clear that the five present were in agreement with Camilo fundamentally but were not participating in the general meeting for personal reasons.

At night, the finest leading politicians of the various progressive tendencies came to Camilo's house; and they established a completely open dialogue with regard to the doctrinal position of each group and of the minimal basis of understanding for later joint actions of a revolutionary type to be accomplished through legal channels. They concluded that what was indicated was to work from this basic premise: To emphasize the cohesive forces and not insist on factors of disunion. They found three points on which all were in agreement: anti-imperialism, commercial international relations with all the countries of the world, and the necessity of a pronouncement in the face of the Cuban situation. Afterwards, Camilo traveled to Europe, having been invited to the International Congress of the Pro Mundi Vita movement.

At the beginning of 1965 new contacts and other methods were sought to bring everyone together. They had another meeting with a large number of important participants from the various progressive groups.

Camilo insisted that, in order to proceed with revolutionary spirit, they ought to abandon negative positions and sharpen those criteria which would exclude anything derived from the self-interest of the group.

Starting with an analysis of the Colombian situation, he then spoke of the advantage of arriving at a consensus on the basis of the following themes, which were introduced to the participants and discussed along general lines: neutralism and self-determination; international relations; attitude toward Cuba; nationalization; industrialization; agrarian reform; business and tax reform as well as general monetary reform and redistribution of the national budget; private investment policies, economic planning; cooperatives; control of the cost of living; unemployment; the trade unions; social security; violence; the outstanding social problems; public health; the political parties and the general condition of domestic politics; the armed forces; educational policy and the university particularly; freedom of the press and of religion; the emancipation of women.

Immediately committees were created to study each theme and to develop a report in no more than ten pages. Each study was to be exchanged with the studies of all the other committees for criticism and revision before a final draft. It was agreed to publish a book containing all the reports and ending with a manifesto or platform, written to be representative of the various groups and viewpoints. Camilo was commissioned to draft this platform, and he began to work on it a few days later.

In March, he went to Medellín, at the invitation of the Independent Young Conservatives.

During a meeting when he showed some friends the projected Platform, they snatched it from him and made him read it. It fell like a bomb, and immediately the Platform was converted into a banner for the progressive groups and, on the part of the others, was a declaration of war against Camilo Torres. Two forces faced one another again: the advanced and traditional.

Upon the return to Bogotá, this dialogue developed:

Camilo: The bomb has exploded. The Platform has been discovered in Medellín. It produced a brutal impact. They took it and are now distributing it. What do you think?

Speaker: That it is an error. What you did was precipitate and tactically foolish. Moreover, it was only a rough copy, something too sketchy.

Camilo: How do you say it? Putting my foot in my mouth?

Speaker: Yes. The plan is cancelled.

Camilo: It was a blunder which had to be committed some day. There are only two committees that have developed their projects. In any case it is done now and no one can undo it.

Speaker: On what day did that happen?

Camilo: The 12th. . . .

On March 17, 1965, the *Platform for a Movement for the Unity of the People* became public. Only on May 22nd did Camilo publicly present the text which can be called the original, during a student gathering in his honor in the University City in Bogotá. He read:

PLATFORM OF THE UNITED FRONT OF THE PEOPLE

In order to unify in concrete objectives the various sectors of the Colombian people, we present the following platform to all Colombians, to the popular associations, to the teams formed for common action, to the trade unions, the cooperatives, the Peasant Leagues, the Native Worker Communities and Organizations, to all nonconformists, and to all those not aligned with traditional political parties.

MOTIVES

1. So that Colombian politics might be directed to the welfare of the majority and not the minority, the necessary decisions will have to be taken away from those who have power now.
2. Those who actually possess real power constitute an economic minority which makes all the fundamental decisions of the national politics.
3. This minority will never make necessary decisions which might affect their own interests or the foreign interests to which they are tied.
4. The decisions required for a socio-economic development of the country to benefit the majority and for national independence will necessarily affect the interests of the economic minority.
5. Those circumstances make indispensable a change of the struc-

ture of political power so that the majorities might produce the decisions.

6. At the present time the majority rejects the political parties and the prevailing system, but does not have a political apparatus capable of taking power.

7. The political apparatus which is organized must look for the greatest support from the masses, must have technical planning, and must be built on principles of action rather than on a leader, so that the danger of influential coteries, demagoguery, and personality cult might be avoided.

OBJECTIVES

I. Agrarian Reform

The land will belong to those directly working it.

The government will designate agrarian inspectors who will present titles to the peasants who fulfill certain conditions, but it will see to it that the cultivation is through cooperative and community systems, in accord with a national agrarian plan, with credit and technical assistance.

The land will not be purchased from anyone. If it is considered necessary for the common good, it will be appropriated without indemnification.

Those indigenous groups will enter into real possession on the lands which belong to them. The development and strengthening of the indigenous communities will be promoted.

II. Urban Reform

a. All those living in houses in the cities or towns will be owners of the houses where they live. Persons who have only the rent as their source of subsistence will be able to keep it, even though they don't live in the same building, if they prove this situation.

b. Every building not sufficiently used in the judgment of the government will entail a fine for the owner, which will be invested by the State in its plans for housing.

III. Planning

There will be an obligatory plan for substituting for imports, increasing exports, and industrializing the country.

Every public or private investment will have to be submitted to the national plan for investments. Dealing in foreign currencies will be done exclusively by the State.

IV. Politics of Paying Taxes

There will be a progressive tax for those who receive more income than is necessary for a Colombian family to live decently (e.g. 5,000 pesos in 1965). Excessive income which is not invested in the sectors designated by the official plan for investments will go completely to the State. No institution will be exempt from paying taxes. Salaries, up to a certain limit (e.g. 5,000 pesos monthly in 1965) will not be affected.

V. Nationalizations

1. The banks, insurance companies, hospitals, clinics, pharmaceutical plants, public transportation, radio and television and the exploitation of natural resources will belong to the State.

2. The State will give free education to all Colombians, respecting the ideology of the parents until the secondary education is completed and of the student after that.

Education will be compulsory until the end of secondary or technical school. There will be penalties for parents who do not comply with the obligation to have their children educated. The financing will be seen to in the official plan of investments through an increase in taxation.

3. The ownership of the subsoil will belong to the State and the exploitation of petroleum will be done on all accounts for the purpose of serving the national economy.

Petroleum concessions will not be given to foreign companies unless the following conditions are present:

a. the State's share is not less than 70%.

b. The refining, distribution, and production of the fuel are public utilities under their control.

c. The salaries of the Colombian workers and employees will be at least equal to those of foreigners of the same category.

VI. International Relations

Colombia will have relations with all the countries of the world and interchanges of commerce and culture in conditions of equality and mutual benefit.

VII. SOCIAL SECURITY AND PUBLIC HEALTH

The State will enforce a complete and progressive plan for social security which freely guarantees the people the right to health and medical attention (without prejudice to the private exercise of the medical profession) and considers all the aspects of unemployment, of sickness, old age, and death. All the personnel in the health professions will be functionaries of the government and will be paid in accord with the number of families (up to a limit which the law will fix) under their care.

VIII. FAMILY POLITICS

There will be sanctions for the parents of abandoned children. The protection of the woman and the children will be assured by a law with effective sanctions.

IX. ARMED FORCES

The budget of the armed forces will be adequate for its mission without affecting the necessities of health and education of Colombians. The defense of the national sovereignty will be the responsibility of the entire Colombian people. Women will have the obligation of civic service after they are eighteen years old.

X. RIGHTS OF WOMEN

Women will participate on an equal footing with men, in the economic, political, and social activities of the country.[1]

As is seen, Camilo only touched on ten of the thirty points which were in the study.

The university and worker groups sympathizing with the ideas of Camilo distributed the platform by thousands.

The reaction of the various sectors can be synthesized thus:

Ruling Sector: Negative Reaction, Placed on guard.

Oligarchical Sector: Total hostility.

Clerical Sector: Condemnatory reaction in the hierarchical structure and on the part of the clergy. Of sympathy, among young and rural clergy.

Official Sector: Adverse Reaction shown in assignments of espionage and attitudes of obstruction.

Military Sector: In the higher circles, rejection of the plan because the platform had Communist theses. In the lower grades of officers a more open position.

Minority Sector With Decisive Power: Reaction of absolute rejection and head-on opposition.

Progressive Sector: Reactions of endorsement and decision to fight.

Sector not Politically Aligned: Decision of commitment in some; of waiting in others.

Student Sector: Reaction of absolute acceptance by the majority.

Worker Sector: Total reception both independently and in political groups.

Peasant Sector: Sympathy and expectation.

Sector of the Common People: Support by the masses.

Sector of the Press: Condemnation of Camilo and repudiation of his thesis through campaigns carefully planned.

The platform is presented to Colombians so that they might study it, discuss it, add to it, correct it. However, immediately they give it the category of absolute force and it is converted into maxims or into an unquestionable theme by some, into an untouchable thesis by others, and into a battle cry for the leaders of reaction.

The thinking of Camilo was absolutely explicit regarding these things.

"It is a working document," he said, "which must be discussed by scientists and perfected. Shamefully until now, outside of really progressive circles, in the sectors which feel themselves affected, the platform has produced a sentimental reaction, at times a little emotional, but it has not produced a reaction of serious criticism around the technical points which can suffer from defects. A plan which has brought forth such reactions must contain something respectable."[2]

In the present moment in Colombia any platform which contradicts the faults of the system, touches the interests of North American domination, or those of bureaucratic capitalism is anathematized and condemned by the regressive sectors.

The platform of Camilo produced a formidable impact. It represented the protest of the people, the discontent and the anxiety for justice hidden in the urgency of a necessary change. Therefore at the initiative of the workers and peasants and with its limited means, it was reproduced in an impressive way throughout the entire country.

This fact was the first widespread support, on a national scale, for the thesis of Camilo. Moreover, it was strengthened by the captivating personality of Camilo and by his priestly status. He was the hoped for leader, all the nobler since he was a priest with the practical courage to defy the oligarchy and the system. Camilo rose as a great scandal and the people followed him because they felt themselves to be understood by him.

Without millions spent on propaganda, without having the walls of every city and village papered with his picture, without technical opinion polls introduced by foreign specialists, Camilo had mobilized the masses in these last days. For a very simple reason: Between his political honesty and the honesty of the people there was a precise correlation.

One day, after returning from Cali, a friend asked him: "How did it go in Cali?"

"Better than I expected. They didn't leave me alone for one minute in three days. The largest concentration of people I have seen until now was that of Cali."

"And what did you say, Camilo?"

"The same talk I always give because I don't have another right now," he responded, smiling. "There are things one has to keep on saying. The people feel that I am not tricking them. I am convinced that the people will march forward some day."

Camilo was not a politician who lived by inventing tricks through demagogical speculations in order to fool the masses.

He planted not for transitory, immediate objectives but for the effective and complete construction of an inevitable future.

The platform acquired the significance of a standard. The immense growing wave of adhesion to the programs of Camilo made those unlawfully holding all power tremble.

The pharisees, who preach love for the people without really caring about them, also trembled; also those who say they work for the people but actually exploit them and those who pity their misery but do nothing to eradicate it.

All because they feared that the people might say: "That is enough!"; that they might break their chains; that they might intervene, act, and decide; that they might wake up. It was the fear of inhuman leaders at the prospect of losing their privilege as bosses. Camilo wanted every man of the people to learn this: He who tells you not to get involved in the fight for justice—that man is a boss. He who forces you to keep quiet about your rebellion—that man is a boss. He who is pledged to obstruct your freedom—that man is a boss. He who suggests to you that you hate those who fight for you—that man is a boss.

He who induces you to persecute your brothers for differences in political opinion or religion—that man is a boss and a criminal. He who gives you sermons and false teaching opposed to the achievement of justice for yourselves—that man is a boss. He who says that any progressive attitude you have is an attempt against the Church—that man is a boss. He who tells you that to be a Christian you must not travel the precarious way of justice—that man is a boss. Tear off their disguises! Trample on their disguises!

The battle is not against your faith but in support of your faith. It is not against Christ but for implanting the teaching of Christ in justice and effective love. Your battle is not against the truth but for the truth, which is Christ, the Son of God, Truth Essential. The tragedy of the Colombian substructure comes from the absence of solidarity and unity. Thus in the long run it becomes a very large, very weak, very abandoned, and very exploited mixture. The people have not yet understood this fact: Unity Is Liberty.

Every person possesses dignity and inalienable rights. It is wrong that a human being be in misery, die of hunger or malnutrition, not have access to culture or be exploited. Every creature of God has the right to the means of production in order to live, to the shelter of a roof, and to the earth to work. We are not concerned with reducing property to the limited use of goods. We are concerned that property fulfill its social end by serving the common good. We must arrive at freedom from a position of slavery. One has the right to seek liberation from misery. We must pass from the exploitation of the human person to the free exercise of all the powers of man; and pass from conformity to constructive nonconformity. We will achieve these things through justice and charity: Justice because every man has the right to what is recognized as belonging to him. Charity because the dignity of man as a human person and as a Son of God, within a Christian context, is safeguarded. Both constitute the foundations of the common good. But what is the common good?

The answer must start with this postulate of John XXIII: "In every human community which is well organized and productive, it is necessary to hold as fundamental the principle that every human being is a person, that is to say, naturally endowed with intelligence and free will, and that rights and duties are directly born of that same natural endowment, and these are absolutely inalienable.[3] The same good John defines the common good in *Mater et Magistra* thus: "It is connected with social conditions which permit and favor the complete development of the person."

Among other elements which the common good demands are first, favorable external social conditions. The human being needs appropriate conditions to secure his well-being and development in all aspects: material, physical, technical, cultural, moral, and religious. The Popes point out three indispensable conditions: social peace, security, and liberty. If the social situations benefit only a few or a group, there is no common good in a society. Even when the privileged groups prosper, their progress will be only apparent and partial. What is demanded is a just distribution of all goods, material, intellectual, cultural and spiritual.

It is not enough that a minority possesses, enjoys, and profits from those goods. An equitable distribution of them among all the members of society is necessary if the common good is to be satisfied.[4]

What was the social content of the points which Camilo made in his platform? How far did they go beyond the present Colombian situation? There is a significant fact. The response of the people showed a clearer grasp of their situation. Through their growing influence they will be mobilized less each day on political levels, and more through formulas and goals of social content.

The Platform had for its specific purpose to establish the basis for a United Front of the People.

But, how did Camilo view the Platform itself and the United Front?

"The United Front of the People," he said, "is the result of several years of experiences and reflection. The intent to unify the opposing political groups and the other discontented Colombians had to face two principal problems:

"The first, the lack of sufficient openness; and the second, the lack of a clear definition. The openness would have been easily limited by religious motives, by traditional politics, by the feeling of a group, or by the reactions of bossism. It was necessary to set up a union around concrete objectives which should unify all Colombians without distinction of religious beliefs, political group, or individual affiliation. The platform of the United Front of the People cannot be accomplished until after they seize power. Its only novelty consists in the fact that it looks for common points of revolutionary character, without entering into religious or party differences. It can be accepted by Catholics and non-Catholics, by poor liberals and poor conservatives, by the revolutionary elements of the M.R.L., the Communist Party, the ANAPO, Christian Democrats, etc., and especially by the revolutionary elements not aligned in these groups. However, it is necessary to state that this platform leads to the establishment of a socialist state, with the condition that we understand "socialism" in a unique mixture with other ideological elements. It is a practical and not a theoretical socialism.

"When speaking of a revolutionary platform many are very adept. However, when stating precisely that the revolution consists of a fundamental reorganization of the State with the application of technology and science in order to obtain reforms favorable to the majority, many excuse themselves.

"For those of us who follow the platform, when establishing for ourselves the seizure of power as the indispensable condition for applying it, we must necessarily come to a tactical decision:

"That of going to the ultimate consequences and that of using any way left open by the oligarchy for this seizure of power.

"This attitude does not have great ideological consequences because the Church itself has established the conditions of a just war. However, the fact is, many 'revolutionaries' do not want to go to the ultimate consequences.

"A platform which attempts a type of socialist state and the liberation of Colombia from North American imperialism cannot be indifferent to the movements which lead to socialism and which plan the liberation from imperialism. Even though these movements might have differing ideological elements, they are the closest to ours in the scientific, positive, and practical aspect. This solidarity in practice estranges many timorous 'revolutionaries' who insist more on the ideology than on the revolution.

"It is quite evident in the movement of the United Front that the movement of the masses has been formed in a short time. Therefore many are recently arrived. The reasons for their arrival differ. Some came into it in order to acquire positions, and they left defrauded. Others thought this was a new party, and they left in the same way they came: very rapidly. While the revolutionary life of the United Front continues to be formed each day more definitely and sharply, those 'companions' of the revolution will continue to straddle the fence in order to return to their place of origin or to wait until the revolution succeeds so that they might join it.

"The important thing is that the Colombian people continue to advance without one step backwards, in spite of the defections, the false rumors, and the betrayals. The decision of the poor that they do not want their children to accuse them in the future of having betrayed their historical and revolutionary vocation will be what determines the situation. They can know that I will go to the ultimate consequences, and that if there remains with me only a handful of committed men, I will continue the fight with them.

"Even though this will be a prolonged fight, what is important is that everyone who has decided to become involved in it has decided also to continue to the end."[5]

Never in the history of Colombia has a political platform taken root so swiftly and so strongly nor its translation into a movement been organized so feebly. The United Front justly surprised both followers and adversaries. Camilo did not understand the need of the military organization, since his work room was converted into general headquarters where he worked day and night receiving and answering correspondence, planning meetings, interviews, dialogues, encounters, visits to the principal cities of the country, which acclaimed him with thousands of red flags, with the sign of Unity! Unity!

These exhausting journeys strengthened the forces of the people, revitalized the hopes of social redemption but at the same time alerted the enemy.

The political movement of the United Front of the People, as the priest leader had predicted, reached a climax and took over the plazas. All the advanced political sectors together saw their own desires and momentarily put aside their long internal differences. It was necessary to organize the movement through committees in order to form teams capable of continuing the agitation, consolidating the organization and educating the people. It is here the first obstacles rise: lack of basic leaders and of a clear concept about who should be the orienting force capable of bringing things happily to a conclusion. Various phenomena are produced: The organization does not advance but the adversary does; the political acts in Bogotá and other cities in the country are violently put down; the leader is continuously besieged and struck down; the dispersed multitude are at the mercy of rifle butts and tear gas bombs.

It is evident that the unity of the progressive sectors was not made of steel: within themselves the petty group positions continued to cause havoc. Their differences smarted in the pleasant shade of the new leader who was pledged to unite the left with the non-aligned sector which, with the national majority, had to be incorporated into the great revolutionary torrent which was begun with the masses. The workers, conscious of the basic forces in the large cities, gave him all and, at the side of the students, were always determined to continue the fight which the leader announced would be long, very long.

Then came the desertions: That of the Christian Democratic party, barely in formation; the frontal attack of the armed forces under ex-General Rojas Pinilla; the discreet isolation of the leaders of the Revolutionary Liberal Movement (M.R.L.).

Camilo began to understand the political wavering better and to suffer the diatribes of his own companions in fraternal dialogue.

This divisive procedure constituted a great mistake, a lamentable error. Those who committed it, forgot—as Stefan Zweig writes—that, in history, lamenting what has succeeded does not make time stand still, and a thousand years are not enough to recover what is lost in only one hour.[6]

The revolution of the progressive left which Camilo favored was pushed back decades.

Chapter 7

Confronting the Establishment

It must be very clearly established that Camilo did not deny any dogma of the Catholic religion. There is no foundation for holding that he belonged to the group which says: "Christ, yes; the Church, no." Neither was he a renegade. "With the grace of God," he said, "I want to continue in my faith and in the love which I have for my priesthood and for the Church."[1] He was concerned with judging only the external structure and limited his criticisms to the Latin American Church and the Colombian case.[2] But here we find ourselves face to face at once with a taboo, affecting both clergy and laity.

It is a sacred norm that the Church's defects and failures must not be aired in public. Such an attitude proceeds from the feudalistic interpretation which the hierarchy gives to the concept of authority, according to which we have princes with absolute rights and servants obliged to obey. As regards priests, the loyalty demanded is greater because on the day of ordination they make a solemn vow of obedience to their bishop.

On the other hand the bourgeois hierarchy and clergy constitute a monolithic clan. They make an especially strenuous effort for cohesion, and consequently they will do absolutely nothing without the consent of the bishop. Unity, rather than being understood in the evangelical sense, is interpreted as common defense or attack, or as a common front in temporal affairs, e.g. to support a political party, to organize elections, to persecute Communists or Protestants, to show respect for the State . . . when this favors their caste interests.

The Church has enjoyed a privileged position in Colombia derived from the public and economic powers and from the oligarchy. The political parties at all times avail themselves of every means to keep it propitiated and favorable. It is an understatement to say that, in defense of those privileges, the Church has been extremely jealous. For that reason, it appeals to the Concordat and to the sustaining of the elite in power. This makes it appear an institution which has more need of the rich than of the poor. To assure the support of the rich and the submission of the poor, its decision-making power becomes consolidated and autocratic.

"It is now an accepted reality that the Church is in a crisis. When it is faced with a crisis, no matter from what camp, it has three alternatives: the first consists in ignoring the problem and saying 'nothing is happening here' and, in accord with this thinking, following its usual line of behavior. The second tends to destroy everything in the conviction that nothing is working and it is necessary to begin anew. The third, which is a reflective reaction, consists in holding on to what it has and introducing necessary transformations, without thereby destroying what is basic."[3]

Which of the three courses did Camilo choose? He called for an immense effort of thought, but it was his conviction that the Colombian Catholic Church in its temporal structure could be analyzed with the techniques of the social sciences, just like any institution where you have bureaucratic organization and an authoritarian regime. The Church is a social institution, with the characteristic elements of any other institution at the sociological level: status and roles, personnel, material possessions, norms and values in greater or less degree of internationalization. The Dominican Sociologist Alain Byrou, close collaborator of Lebret, in *Sociology and Religion* teaches: ". . . It was incarnated in the world. It was visibly constituted, committed in time and with earthly life, it has a history and *is a society*."[4]

The Roman Catholic Church, holds Monsignor Ivan Illich, is the largest non-governmental bureaucratic organization in the world. It employs 1,800,000 workers full time—priests, brothers, religious, laity. These employees work within a corporate structure which has been considered by an American consulting agency as one of the best-directed organizations in the world. The institutional Church functions on the same level as General Motors or Esso. This well-known fact is accepted at times with pride by some persons. But for others, this very effective functioning of the machinery is considered a source of discredit. Men suspect that the institutional Church has lost its meaning in the face of the gospel and the world. Vacillation, doubt, and confusion reign among its directors, functionaries, and employees. The giant begins to totter before it collapses.[5]

In observing the many facets of the phenomenon, we can deduce that the Church is too much compromised with temporal power and that it will be tenaciously opposed to any attempt at a change in the structures. Excluding the rural clergy, without homes or possessions, and those who work in the city slums, the mentality of the ecclesiastical personnel is bourgeois and regressive. In such a sense, it remains very distant from the people. This places the clergy at a high level of society. Lebret, a Dominican priest, holds that "Colombian society seen as a whole seems more like a society of castes than of classes." The people slowly become more anticlerical even when they continue to believe. How long will they be forced to remain devoted and submissive to the priest? Perhaps until they are convinced that the fear of Communism has been used to exploit their faith, in defense of a structure which is not basically committed to radical social change.

As they had promised, the bishops in 1967 placed at the disposition of the Colombian Institute of Agrarian Reform the lands of the Church to be parceled out. Even though they do not amount to much, it looks like a gesture in the right direction. But they have not taken any effective steps to discontinue the schools, which are the most lucrative business of many religious communities.

They appeal to the works of social action which the Church develops in order to demonstrate their effective love for and interest in the poor. If an analysis in depth is made, we discover an excess of verbiage: "Does a mother need to continue repeating that she loves them, to prove to her children that she really loves them?" By not favoring radical changes, by establishing more local works which are undertaken without planning, (with the result that many of them are ephemeral), by too many speeches bordering on paternalistic sentimentalism, by more donations received from foreigners, the Church will continue a reformism which in the long run leads to failure and frustration.

It is easy to predict that not a few priests who feel compelled to respond to the people's needs in terms of something more genuine than "angelism" will be thwarted by the closed attitude of the hierarchical structure and its obstinacy in rejecting revolutionary changes. They will search for more effective and less restrictive ways to give testimony as Christians among the poor. They do not do it in order to escape the Church but with a very honest and highly respectable sincerity. The cases, more frequent each day, support this forecast.

Before the realistic panorama which the external structure of the Church presents, what are the theses of Camilo?

In what pertains to the area of Indo-America, he thought that "at the time it gained independence from Spain, Latin America had been evangelized widely but not deeply. There were many baptized but few with a Christian conscience. Moreover, the scarcity of clergy, caused by the emigration of the Spanish priests, aggravated the situation. The Latin American Church continued to be a Church of external rite and not of Christian faith. Even today when one asks the workers in the cities: "Who is the most Holy Trinity?" they almost always firmly respond, "The Mother of Our

Lord Jesus Christ." Nevertheless, the Latin Americans love one another. Not always in a rational or constructive way; but in spite of everything, we find in our people love, cooperation, hospitality, and a spirit of service. It is different within the upper class. At the risk of gratuitously generalizing, it can be said that those who boast more of their faith and their clericalism are those who love their neighbors less; and those who serve their brothers more are, many times, those who do not practice the external cult of religion. This, of course, is not always true. Identification as a Christian is made in relation to the practice of love. When speaking of things Catholic, the people refer to external practice. The Church seems to consist of a majority of persons who practice but do not know their Faith and a minority who know their Faith but do not solely practice it externally. Can it be said that the majority is Christian?"[6]

He held, moreover, that "the primordial criterion of promotion in the present structure of the Latin American Church is conformity. For example, in some countries, the bishops are not chosen without the acceptance of the candidate by the entire national episcopacy, all of which encourages candidates who are basically conformists. Thus there is created—in underdeveloped countries—a social material mobility but not a socio-cultural one. Only those become bishop, archbishop, or Cardinal who are in conformity with the values of the dominant minority."[7] This criterion is applicable to Colombia: The Church is linked to the temporal superstructures.

"But the heaviest burden of the Colombian Church," Camilo roundly asserted, without fear of stirring up a hornet's nest," is in the possession of wealth and political power. This forces the Church to follow in its decisions the wisdom of men rather than the wisdom of God, as St. Paul said. The wealth and political power of which I speak are the result of an attitude of those leaders who have surrounded the Church with economic and legal guaranties. Because of that, the Church is an economic and a political power. As Christ says, it is very difficult to serve two masters, God and mammon. The Colombian clergy is more backward than any other in the world, even more than in Spain. It is evident that the only progressive Churches are the poor ones. . . ."[8]

The conservative periodical *El Siglo* points out what those goods are: "Without excluding churches and rectories, ecclesiastical wealth in Colombia totals $5,000,000,000* in real estate evaluation according to official statistics. Such a figure was arrived at through reports which periodically were developed in the Agustín Codazzí Geographic Institute, the Office of Taxation of Bogotá and its branches in the city of Mendellín and the Department of Antioquía. If the theories of the priest Camilo Torres were accepted, such wealth would be liable to expropriation or could be distributed, in great part, among needy people, as the Chilean bishops are doing.

"The ecclesiastical wealth located in the jurisdiction of the Special District of Bogotá has a tax value of $176,250,330.00 distributed thus: wealth in the adjacent municipalities $60,936,-350.00; wealth in Bogotá $109,313,980.00 In the adjacent districts there are six churches valued at $614,500.00, and 25 convents and high schools, valued for their real estate at $16,502,-530.00. In the metropolitan area there are 118 churches with a value of $66,321,850.00 and 137 convents at $92,811,450. These figures do not include the lots which different ecclesiastical entities hold nor the personal properties of priests and religious."[9] Everyone knows that the tax value is much less than the commercial value, which would quadruple the tax estimates.

The Church will achieve authenticity "when Christians live fundamentally for love and so that others might love; when Faith is inspired by life, especially by the life of Christ; when the external rite is a true expression of love within the Christian community. Then we will be able to say that the Church is strong, without economic and political power, but with charity."[10] "It is not the representative of a philosophy, much less of a political or economic system. It is a life, which takes different forms in accord with technology, with the historical moment, with the society in which we live.[11]

* Not, of course, American dollars. See above, Chapter 3, note 7.

In the eyes of public opinion, "the Colombian clergy appear as a group with a feudal mentality and, at least some of them, with an unadulterated capitalistic mentality. This is obvious in the higher hierarchical circles, and is especially true in the cities where the desire for wealth becomes more patent."[12] And he adds: "I am a supporter of the expropriation of the Church's wealth, even if there is no revolution."

As regards our Concordat, he thought that it was "unique in the world, the most anachronistic, the only one which has not been reformed, among other reasons, because it has become a political issue. The Concordat is a taboo; it is impossible to speak of it because they fear that it may produce a schism. It has become an issue between the traditional parties."[13]

Camilo was right: the Conservatives defend the untouchableness of the treaty in order to assure the support of the clergy with a view to using it for political purposes; the Liberals demand its revision in order to gain sympathy with public opinion; the hierarchy fights to maintain a tool which assures it exceptional advantages. The truth is that the general consensus is inclined to a revision of this outdated pact signed in 1897 between the Holy See and the Colombian Government.

In education, Camilo proposed that the monopoly of Church schools be abandoned and that pluralism be accepted. As a consequence we should permit academic freedom in order to eliminate the social and psychological factors which prevent a conscious and personal commitment to the Church on the part of those who want to love and give of themselves for others. Among such factors he lists the economic and political power of the Church and clericalism, the meddling of the clergy and hierarchy, with a spirit of ownership, in the temporal world.[14]

In the fifth point of the Platform No. 2 further precise points appear. It is evident that the ideology, plans, and activities of Camilo contradict multiple stereotypes of our culture. He thought with Einstein that "it is easier to split the atom than it is to dismantle prejudices ingrained in the human conscience for centuries." Camilo was an absolute enemy of prejudice.

He did not refuse debate on his ideas. He looked for a response to his theses with daring—it could almost be said, with a challenging romanticism. I heard him say one day: "Let them fight me with valid arguments and not with preconceptions; nor with ambiguous accusations; nor with interpretations accommodated to individual caprice; nor with emotional interpretations."

But real dialogue was avoided, in the hope that he would fall into irreverent iconoclasm against the old enduring idols which could then offer the last word in absolution or condemnation. The totemic untouchability of reactionism was not willing to support a daring Camilo, a shouting Camilo, a challenging Camilo, an upright Camilo, who said things without permission which were of such unfortunate implication for the continuance of one of the ruling superstructures. Would it not have been right to give explanations when he honestly asked a reason, even a microscopic reason?

He resented the arrogance of those who stubbornly conserve, by any means whatsoever, submissive genuflections and the offering of silent insincere submission. In order to save the principle of authority, should they not have dialogued with Camilo? No! In this way he could be condemned without a hearing.

Basically his anxiety coincided with that expressed in the document which an unknown number of anonymous bishops distributed in the Second Vatican Council on December 7, 1965, and which introduced three emendations to Schema XIV. This is the text, taken from a reliable source:

We, bishops, meeting in the Second Vatican Council, having carefully considered the failure in our lives of poverty according to the Gospel; strengthening one another in a movement in which each of us would desire to avoid singularity and presumption; united with all our brothers in the Episcopacy; counting, above all else, on the strength and the grace of Our Lord Jesus Christ, on the prayer of the faithful and on the priests of our respective dioceses; placing ourselves through thought and prayer before the Trinity, before the Church of Christ, before the priests and the faithful of our dioceses, in humility and conscious of our weakness, yet strengthened by the firmness of our resolve, for which may God give us grace, commit ourselves to the following:

(1) We will try to live according to the ordinary standards of our people as regards housing, food, means of transportation and all else. (See Mt. 5:3; Mt. 6:33,34; Mt. 8:20.)

(2) We renounce for ever the appearance and the reality of riches, particularly in dress, and in the insignia of precious materials (these signs should rather be evangelical). (See Mk. 6:9; Mt. 10:9,10; Acts 3:6.)

(3) We will possess neither moveable nor unmoveable possessions nor bank accounts, etc., in our own name; if it is necessary to possess anything we will place it in the name of the diocese, or of social or charitable works. (See Mt. 6:19,21; Lk. 12:33,34.)

(4) We will confide, as far as it is possible, the financial and material negotiations in our dioceses to a committee of competent laymen conscious of their apostolic role, with a view to being less administrators and more pastors and apostles. (See Mt. 19:8; Acts 6:1, 7.)

(5) We refuse to be called orally or in writing by names or titles which signify grandeur and power (Eminence, Excellency, Monsignor). We prefer to be called by the evangelical name of Fathers.

(6) We will avoid in our behavior and in our social relations whatever seems to concede privileges, priorities, or even some preference to the rich or to the powerful (e.g. banquets offered or accepted, social classes in religious services). (See Lk. 13:12,14; I Cor. 9:14, 19.)

(7) We will avoid, at the same time, encouraging or flattering the vanity of anyone who might want it as a recompense for soliciting gifts, or for any other reason. We will invite our faithful to consider their gifts as a normal participation in religion, in the apostolate and in social action. (See Mt. 6:2,4; Lk. 15:9,13; II Cor. 12-14.)

(8) We will give all that is necessary of our time, thought, heart, actions, etc., to the apostolic and pastoral service of workers who are economically weak and underdeveloped, without neglecting the other persons in the diocese. We will support those laymen, religious, deacons, or priests whom the Lord calls to evangelize the poor, participating in their life and their work. (See Lk. 4:18,19; Mk. 6:4; Mt. 11:45; Acts 18:3,4; Acts 20:33,35; I Cor. 4:12 and 9:1,27.)

(9) Conscious of the demands of justice and charity and of their mutual relationship, we will try to transform the works of mercy into social works based on charity and justice, which take into consideration everyone and all needs, as a humble service of the competent public organizations. (See Mt. 25:31,46; Lk. 13:14 and 33,34.)

(10) We will do everything possible so that those responsible for our government and for our public services might decide and apply the laws, the structures, and the social institutions necessary for justice, equality, and the harmonious and total development of each man among all men, and we will labor for the coming of a distinct and new social order, worthy of the sons of man and the sons of God. (See Acts 2:44,45, Acts 4:32,33,35, Acts 5:4; II Cor. 8 and 9 complete; I Tim. 5:16.)

(11) The College of Bishops, finding their most evangelical work in becoming aware of their responsibility for the human masses in a state of physical, cultural and moral misery—two-thirds of humanity—we promise: to participate, according to our means, in the urgent needs of the episcopates of the poor nations: to work together, on the level of international organizations, giving testimony of the Gospel like Pope Paul VI in the U.N., for the introduction of economic and cultural structures which will not construct proletarian nations in a world more and more rich each day, but which will permit the poor masses to leave their misery.

(12) We promise to share in pastoral charity our life with our brothers in Christ, priests, religious, and laity, so that our ministry might be a true service, thus:

We will be strengthened in "revision of our life" with them;

We will vigorously promote our companions so that they may be more on fire, according to the Spirit, as more effective leaders, according to the world;

We will try to be more humanly present, to be more understanding;

We will show ourselves open to all, no matter what their religion might be. (See Mk. 6,8:34, 35; Acts 6:1,7; I Tim. 3:8,10.)

(13) Upon returning to our respective dioceses, we will let everyone know our resolution, asking them to help us through their understanding, their collaboration, and their prayers.

May God help us to be faithful.[15]

Camilo retained hope for a return to the humility which might permit them to say with complete honesty: In Columbia, we have sometimes been mistaken. Didn't the Pope publicly ask pardon of his brothers for faults committed? He hoped to fight for a Church not mortgaged to temporal pressures of the oligarchical or political coteries. What image of the hierarchical structure do many Christians and many priests strongly desire, along with Camilo? Let us look at "The Open Letter to the Argentinian Episcopacy" (Buenos Aires, November 1965):

We want poor bishops—authentically and really poor—without official honors, extraordinary privileges, dangerous compromises with the wealthy classes, with the military, with the businessmen, with the sources of power. An episcopacy which serves and is not served. An episcopacy which renounces now the prerogatives of cult and all subsidies and financial stipends. An episcopacy which, perhaps, cannot travel in such luxurious cars, or live in the best houses, or build magnificent churches, universities, and high schools, but bishops of whom all can be proud because they are a testimony of the Church of the Poor.

We want a free Episcopacy—authentic and really free—without any kind of institutional links with the State, without submission to any force other than the Truth "which makes us free," without the permanent play of political attitudes.

We want a courageous Episcopacy—authentic and really courageous—armed with the necessary courage for preaching the Gospel fully, especially when the Gospel condemns the god of riches, when it singles out those who exploit and treat unjustly their brothers, when it denounces those who pretend to be Christians and persecutes the poor, salving their consciences with a charity which gives enormous temples, which helps their bishop and priest friends, but which at the same time denies their workers and peons a salary which might allow them to really live as sons of God. An Episcopate which does not fear to confront the powerful of the earth because it maintains an independence which permits it to defend the defenseless in all circumstances; an Episcopate which does not offer such clear suspicions of accommodation with every kind of "pressure" when it should be giving testimony of the Truth and of Justice. We also need the courage and the daring of the bishops so that instead of being paralyzed, frightened, and reacting against the changes and the tensions which the Council provokes and awakens, they might be disposed to take this new reality of the Church as the point of departure for a permanent renovation and conversion. Without this courage the changes will cost many difficulties and oppositions, and the internal tensions of the Church will be finally resolved with the sad experience—which many priests and laymen are already suffering—namely that which forces a choice between fidelity to the Gospel and to the Council and obedience to a hierarchy which is not disposed and ready to accomplish among us all the necessary changes.

We want a faithful Episcopate—authentic and really faithful to all the demands of the Vatican Council. We know that this faithfulness will bear fruit in a real commitment to the People of God, especially with the personal and concrete history of those who are hungry, of those who do not have homes, of those who are unjustly dismissed from their jobs, of those who suffer persecution for wanting to exercise their sacred rights, of those who are submerged in present subhuman and pre-Christian situations.

We want an evangelical Episcopacy—authentic and really evangelical which understands that the new vision of "evangelizing" in our country and in Latin America is to contribute first and fundamentally to free all men of exploitation, misery, ignorance, sickness, and all those serious sins which in the name of "western Christianity" mean the death of thousands of babies and a life of hell for millions who survive.

We have bishops who do not teach, because their pastoral concerns are dictated by a magisterium which is not that of the Church of the Second Vatican Council; because their silences and omissions separate them from the historical reality in which we as Christians must commit ourselves; because their personal and/or collective attitudes are contrary to the spirit of poverty, service, and humility which are the strongest reasons for every teaching; because pastoral reflection is so disconnected fom the concrete problems of men and of the world in which we live, that it is received with indifference and frustration by those to whom it is directed.

We have bishops who do not govern, because their closed minds do not agree with the first function of governing which is that of being Fathers; because in their treatment of priests and laity they do not consider dialogue valuable and rather insist on a principle of authority corresponding to the best traditions of feudalism; because in not having obtained true union around their own person they must resort to the use of sanctions in order to resolve the permanent tensions in the clergy because living as they do in their small world of curias and sacristies they cannot see the reality of a sheepfold from which the ninety-nine sheep are lost or separated and the one which remains chokes the pastor with preoccupations which are not those of the Christian people.

We have bishops who are not channels of sanctity in its richness and fullness, because unless the episcopal ministry of teaching and ruling is exercised in the spirit of the Council, the preaching of Christ's gospel and the celebration of the Mystery of the Lord's Supper become, in the last resort, a mere rite of cult and of sacraments; because the poor, sacrament of the Lord and privileged with His love, neither participate nor can participate—because of the way the Church offers it to them —in the life of grace and of salvation.

The new conditions of the Church in the world clearly demand that in our country the bishops truly teach, govern, and sanctify. They demand that the Argentinian bishops drop their appearance as "functionaries" of the State or of the Church and assume the new conciliar attitude of service and testimony. They demand even that bishops renounce legitimate rights in order to manifest the sincerity of their function and in order to blot out forever the image of an Episcopate which does not dialogue, does not listen, and does not understand the needs of the poor.

They distribute the sorrow and the anxiety to the poor of our country who will, once again, be the victims of "order" and "national recovery" announced as liberation and actualized in acts such as a new step of economic plunder, of political dictatorship, and social tensions.

Our Church pains us, pains us in knowing that it is financially identified with the rich, socially with the powerful, and politically with the oppressors. It pains us because we feel it in the flesh and blood of all the poor, the defenseless, the oppressed which—inspite of the sorrow and the scandal which the hierarchy causes—still persist with hope in the liberation announced by the Gospel and join themselves decisively with the revolution—in which they wanted to see their Church committed also—in order to obtain in this world the happiness of those who are hungry and of those who thirst for justice.[16]

Could we ask for better testimony?

During a meeting someone, referring to Camilo, said: "When the history of the Colombian Church of this period is written in the future, they will not be able to condemn everything. You, as a member of that Church, had the courage to say in public what you believed should be corrected." Camilo responded: "I am a Christian. I believe, I am a priest. I love the Church. My criticisms are directed against accidental aspects. That being so, I have committed the sin of being honest. . . ."

Chapter 8

Camilo—Against The Church?

In order to clarify this question, it is necessary to make a synthesis of the facts before entering into the documentation:

Immediately after some of the positions in the Platform became known to Medellín (March 17, 1965), there began a series of pressures on the Curia of Bogotá and on the National Government to dismiss Camilo from the School of Public Administration.

The argument adduced was simple: Camilo's salary was paid with official money as he was a public employee. The law forbids State employees to intervene actively in politics. Camilo contravened that regulation and therefore should be dismissed as Dean of the Institute of Social Administration (IAS).

For some time those spokesmen of reaction were engaged in a quiet and cruel campaign against Camilo and some of his immediate collaborators. They went to such unheard-of extremes as searching for supposedly compromising documents in the desks of certain employees of the IAS, alleging that Camilo had converted the Institute into a center of conspiracy against the legitimately constituted powers.

Complete credence was given to the treachery of these dishonest informers who, eager to receive adulation, were engaged as secret agents, pretending at the same time to be friends of Camilo. They proposed to him that he go to Europe to finish his doctorate in sociology at Louvain or that he enter the Office of Pastoral Affairs of the Archdiocese. Because of the rumor of his possible leaving, the National Federation of University Students (FUN) promoted a public celebration in his honor for May 22nd to see him off. In the invitations it was stated that Camilo's trip was due to the maneuvers of the oligarchy and the peremptory orders of his hierarchical superior.[1]

The development of the events follows this sequence:

Camilo is dismissed from the ESAP through pressures of the Governing Board and the decision of the Cardinal.[2]

He agrees to the celebration of the students honoring him, since he wants the Platform to be known.

He decides to leave for six months.

The press makes public the Declaration of the Cardinal, May 26th.

Camilo cancels his trip and throws himself into the revolutionary fight.

DOCUMENTATION

1. *An unpublished letter:*

The situation which is created for him in ESAP and the attitude of his superior, who yields to outside influences, move Camilo to write a first document, which he doesn't send, because some of his intimate friends ask him not to send it. I remember very well that he said, "It will be better to destroy it." Then he observed: "It is better not to send it. Nevertheless, keep it in case anything happens." It is published now because of his courageous testimony.

"Bogotá, March 20, 1965

Your Eminence:

Permit me to ask of your Eminence that you proceed with the necessary canonical steps for my reduction to the lay state.

I make this petition after mature reflection having concluded to the necessity of considering this solution as that which I must follow in conscience.

When I chose the clerical state I did it thinking principally that in that way I would better serve both the Church and all Columbians. After more than ten years of priestly ministry I realize that, in the particular historical circumstances of the Church, of Colombia and myself, I can obtain these objectives more effectively as a layman. I believe that the circumstances to which I refer oblige me to take positions in the temporal world which I cannot refuse without damaging my fidelity to Christ, to the Church, and to Columbia.

I am disposed to give all the explanations which your Eminence considers proper and necessary, so that your Eminence might be able to assist in what I do in accordance with my conscience.

With the grace of God I want to continue in my Faith and the love which I have for my priesthood and for my Church. I am acting only through love for His Church and for the people whom he redeemed.

Respectfully in Christ,

Padre Camilo Torres Restrepo"[3]

2. *The following Statement of the Cardinal precipitates a series of decisions and events:*

"May 25, 1965

The Cardinal Archbishop of Bogotá declares:

1. It is absolutely inexact that the trip of Father Camilo Torres is due to the dispositions of the ecclesiastical authorities or to pressures which he has suffered in such a sense.

Several months ago Father Torres spontaneously asked the Archbishop of Bogotá for permission to leave the Archdiocese so that he might present his doctoral thesis at the University of

Louvain; this permission was given and, afterwards, repeated by the Coadjutor Bishop before a new petition of Father Torres.

2. In the platform for political-social action presented or supported by Father Torres, there are points which are irreconcilable with the doctrine of the Church.

L. Cardinal Concha
Archbishop of Bogotá"[4]

3. *Letter of Father Camilo Torres to the Cardinal:*

"Bogotá, May 28, 1965

His Eminence
Luis Concha Córdoba
Cardinal Archbishop of Bogotá, E.S.D.
Your Eminence:

Bishop Rubén Isaza was kind enough to communicate to me the desire of your Eminence that I leave immediately the School of Public Administration and assume some duties in the Office of Pastoral Research of the Curia.

He showed me also that the remuneration would be relatively small, a fact which would necessarily affect the physical and mental health of my mother, as Bishop Ernesto Solano can testify. The classes which I taught in the National University had made it easier for me to face the family problem created by my leaving the School of Public Administration; nevertheless, Bishop Isaza told me that your Eminence did not agree with this solution.

In view of all this, in order to alleviate a little the problem to which I have referred, I ask of your Eminence permission to leave the country for six months, under the auspices of ESAP, in order to finish my doctoral thesis in sociology, according to conversations which we have already had and to finish a project which I have not yet been able to finish because of my important work in the School.

In hopes that my petition is kindly received by your Eminence, I remain,

Respectfully in Christ,

Camilo Torres Restrepo"[5]

4. *Concerning the possibility of going to the Office of Pastoral Research of the Curia, Camilo establishes his terms in a document addressed to the Coadjutor Bishop:*

"Your Excellency:

This traditional form in which I address your Excellency does not mean that it is not sent in a spirit of fraternal love to an older brother whom God, in His Providence, has placed over me as His representative.

When your Excellency proposed that I should leave my present work in order to conduct a study of all that is necessary for an Archdiocesan Pastoral Plan, I asked for the terms before acceding to your request.

The reasons I gave were based on motives of charity for the many persons who depended on my work and whose situation would be precarious if I were to leave my work immediately. I believe these reasons were valid and that your Excellency agreed.

Without taking anything away from its validity I have thought much about the personal reaction which your proposal produced in me: I felt a profound repugnance at the thought of working with the clerical structure of our Church.

I have attempted during my spiritual retreats to delve a little into this reaction, which in a priest seems, if not absurd, at least improper. My work as a priest has developed during these ten years under the authority of the bishop but a little outside the clerical structure. This situation has caused many difficulties for my priestly spirit, but it can also lead to advantages for the life of the Church.

One of those advantages can be that of having acquired a more objective vision of the structure to which I belong but in which I have participated less than the others, who due to the limitations of their positions, could have less possibility of analysis, because they are more involved in the phenomenon which I try to describe.

When I thought about the possibility of working in the Curia, doing research, I sensed the security of a separation from the world and from the poor in order to be included in a closed group, an organization pertaining to the powerful on the earth.

When I considered how I should direct the studies, I encountered theoretical problems, the solution of which I believe will be, for my part, different or opposed to the sense the Hierarchy might give to what would be validated by the data I would study.

I believe that it is vital for the success of a study that the solution of the problems will depend on the orientation of the study; and since it is impossible to study everything, it is necessary that the one doing the studies and those who have the responsibility for accomplishing a Pastoral Plan for the Archdiocese have a common program.

As regards my own plan I wish to write to your Excellency so that you might judge if I am the right person for this proposed study.

I. By Pastoral, I understand a number of activities which must be exercised in order to implant or increase the Kingdom of God in a definite society and historical epoch. In order to arrive at a consensus on the essence of the Pastoral, it is necessary to agree on what is the Kingdom of God. And in order to direct a study, it is necessary to agree on a series of hypotheses regarding Colombian society at this present time:

A. The Kingdom of God is supernatural life, the justification of mankind. To extend the Kingdom of God or establish it is a problem of life. The activities which must be exercised in order to implant the Kingdom are those which lead more securely and effectively to life. Among these, there are some priorities. In my thinking, the emphasis which one must place on the means for establishing the Kingdom must follow this order:

1. Bring the people to live, a total love (agape).
2. Preach the Gospel.
3. Cult, Eucharist, and Sacraments (Sacramentals, Parliturgies).

B. Colombian society is mainly a Catholic society in so far as cult is concerned (Baptism, Confession, Communion, Matrimony, Burial, Mass, Extreme Unction, Processions, Novenas, Scapulars, First Fridays). Colombian society, in the greatest part, does not recognize Christian Doctrine, even though it knows some catechism answers by heart. Within Colombian society, there are many who love others with a committed love, but who deny they are

Catholics or at least deny that they belong to the Church, understanding by Church, this present clerical structure.

II. If pastoral efforts are concentrated on preserving the present situation, it is possible that the establishment or the increase of the Kingdom of God will not be obtained. If the priority of love over everything else is accepted and also preaching is given preference to cultic activity, the Hierarchy will be seen to advocate a pastoral program of mission.

III. Mission supposes:

A. Emphasis on quality and not on quantity. It will insist more on personal convictions than on family and social pressures. It will abandon private education and will accept pluralistic education. It will permit academic freedom. It will emphasize biblical catechesis both for children and for adults.

B. Emphasis on bringing the people to love rather than to faith and religious practice.

C. More emphasis on preaching than on cult.

D. Elimination of those social and psychological factors which prevent a conscious and personal allegiance to the Church, on the part of those who want to love and to give themselves to others. Among these factors we find: the economic power of the Church; the political power of the Church, both formal by means of laws and concordats and informal (clerical domination in the temporal order); cultural, sociological, and psychological separation between the clergy and faithful; lack of solidarity with the poor; and lack of a scientific spirit in the Church.

If the pastoral plan which is proposed is a pastoral plan of conservation, it will be very difficult for me to be able to cooperate in an effective way, especially since I would do it for obedience but against all my rational convictions.

Therefore, I have thought it to be basic honesty to explain these points of view to your Excellency.

Joined to this letter is a study which I was permitted to make on the primacy of charity.

As regards my positions, I believe that either I can supprt them theologically or they constitute working hypotheses which must be proved with empirical investigations.

Nevertheless, I am ready to retract as soon as I have been convinced I am in error, and I will submit if there is anything which goes against dogma or good customs.

Fraternally with your Excellency,
P. Camilo Torres Restrepo"[6]

5. *A New Letter of Camilo to the Cardinal:*

"Bogotá, May 28, 1965

His Eminence
Luis Concha Córdoba
Cardinal Archbishop of Bogotá
E.S.D.

Your Eminence:

In the press on May 26th of this year I was surprised to find a statement of your Eminence regarding my next trip and some ideas which I had presented or to which I had subscribed.

I immediately went to the Curia to speak personally with Bishop Rubén Isaza, coadjutor bishop of Bogotá. I thought it was much more proper to clarify a situation with my Prelate personally and not through the press, since I feel that relations among Christians, and especially between priests and their bishop, should be family relations of mutual confidence.

Easter Tuesday I had a long conversation with Bishop Isaza in this same atmosphere of familiarity and confidence. In that conversation I told his Excellency, in a completely spontaneous way, of the difficulties which I have encountered for having read a socio-economic platform in the development of which I had participated and which contained strictly technical points of order which many Catholics consider indispensable for the common good.

I am concerned over the statement which your Eminence made through the press and which Bishop Isaza confirmed as the correct opinion of your Eminence. For my own tranquility and that of all Colombians who are engaged in a change of temporal structures so that there might be a more just society in Colombia, in Latin

America, and in all the so-called underdeveloped countries, I am writing to you. I am concerned for all those who consider the doctrine of the Church a beacon of progress and feel that they would exist only on the margin of history, if they cannot participate in the fundamental socio-economic changes which humanity needs in order to accomplish, even in part, the supreme precept of charity. For the tranquility of all those persons, your Eminence, it is necessary for me that you clarify at least two essential questions:

1. To which socio-political platform does your Eminence refer in the statement of May 26th?

2. What points which I have subscribed to or defended does your Eminence consider as 'incompatible with the doctrine of the Church'?

In full confidence that the paternal benevolence of your Eminence will graciously receive this petition, in which I believe the temporal action of so many Christians and so many men is committed, and assuring you of my total submission to the judgment of the Church, I remain, your Eminence,

Faithfully in Christ,
Camilo Torres Restrepo"[7]

6. *The Cardinal's reply:*

"Bogotá, June 9, 1965

Father Camilo Torres Restrepo:

In your letter of the 28th of May last year you ask me what are the points in the programs profusely divulged by you which are in opposition to the doctrine of the Catholic Church.

I do not understand—or better, I don't want to understand—the motives which have induced you to ask such a question.

You know perfectly well the teachings of the Catholic Church concerning the points which you have treated in your programs and which have been knowingly removed from those teachings. It is better to say things clearly and without beating around the bush.

I wish to add that from the beginning of my priesthood I have been absolutely convinced that the pontifical directives forbid the priest to intervene in political activities and in purely technical and practical questions in the matter of social action properly speaking. In virtue of that conviction during my already long episcopate I have forced myself to keep the clergy subject to my jurisdiction separated from intervention in the matters which I have mentioned.

This letter puts an end to the business it treats. Nevertheless, any time you wish to speak with me you can be sure that my doors will be open.

Sincerely in the Lord,
L. Concha Córdoba
Archbishop of Bogotá"[8]

7. *In the meanwhile, Camilo preached his revolutionary doctrine before very different audiences: workers, students, proletariat. He gave interviews to periodicals and publications of every tendency. From the farthest corners came messages of support. The attitude of the hierarchy of the Colombian Church stirred up the reaction of the masses and of many of the faithful who found in the theses of Camilo an answer to their anxiety. The tension increased with a new statement from the Cardinal:*

"Bogotá, June 18, 1965

The Cardinal Archbishop of Bogotá believes he has an obligation in conscience to say to Catholics that Father Camilo Torres has consciously separated himself from the doctrines and directives of the Church.

It is enough to open the Encyclicals of the Supreme Pontiffs to realize this lamentable reality, a reality all the more lamentable insofar as Father Torres proclaims a violent revolution with seizure of power at the very moment that the country is involved in a crisis caused in no small part by the violence which he is making great efforts to promote.

The activities of Father Camilo Torres are incompatible with his priestly character and with the very ecclesiastical habit he wears. It can happen that these two circumstances induce some Catholics to follow the erroneous and pernicious doctrines which Father Torres proposes in his programs.

L. Cardinal Concha
Archbishop of Bogotá"[9]

8. Camilo decided to solve the impasse definitively; between the external exercise of his priesthood and the practice of charity as a total commitment to the people, he opted for serving men without renouncing his Christian witness. He chose between the exploiters and the people, between a pseudo-order and the search for authentic order, between selling out to a minority and the rights of the majority. The ecclesiastical structure failed to convince him it was free of connections with political power to which it had been tied for years.

At this time he sent this petition to the Cardinal:

"Bogotá, June 24, 1965

His Eminence, Luis Concha Córdoba
Cardinal Archbishop of Bogotá
Your Eminence:

Agreeing with what we have discussed it seems to me necessary, as a testimony of fidelity to the Church and to what I consider essential in Christianity, to ask your Eminence for reduction to the lay state and for exoneration from obligations inherent in the clerical state.

Hoping that your Eminence will kindly accede to this petition, permit me to sign myself,

Faithfully in Christ,

Camilo Torres Restrepo"[10]

With this request, he left the formal juridical structure to go in search of the masses of the hungry, the naked, and the oppressed, which none of the judges who condemned him had dared to do.

9. *Camilo dispelled any doubts about the rectitude of what he was*

doing and affirmed his resolve to accept all the risks which would result from his decision:

CAMILO'S STATEMENT

June 24, 1965. When circumstances exist which prevent men from giving themselves completely to Christ, the priest has as his proper function the obligation of combatting those circumstances, even at the sacrifice of his ability to celebrate the Eucharist—which is itself unintelligible without the commitment of Christians. In the present structure of the Church it has been made impossible for me to continue the exercise of my priesthood in matters of external cult. The Mass, which is the final objective of the sacerdotal action, is fundamentally a community action. But the Christian community cannot authentically offer the sacrifice if it has not first authentically fulfilled the precept of love of neighbor.

I chose Christianity because I thought it contained the purest way to serve my neighbor. I was chosen by Christ to be a priest forever, motivated by the desire to commit myself totally to the love of my fellow man. As a sociologist, I had wished that that love might become effective through technology and science. In analyzing Colombian society I have realized that a revolution is necessary in order to give food to the hungry and drink to the thirsty, to clothe the naked and to obtain the welfare of the majority of our people. I think the revolutionary fight is a Christian and priestly fight. Only through it, in the concrete circumstances of our country, can we accomplish the love which men must have for their neighbors.

Since I began exercising my priestly ministry, I have used every means possible so that the laity, Catholic or non-Catholic, might dedicate themselves to the revolutionary fight. In the absence of a massive answer of the people to the action of the laity I have resolved to offer myself, thus fulfilling part of my work of bringing men through mutual love to the love of God. I consider this activity essential for my Christian and priestly life, as a Colombian. With all that, it is a labor which actually is at odds with the present discipline of the Church. I do not want to go against that discipline nor do I want to betray my conscience.

Because of that I have asked His Eminence the Cardinal to free me from my clerical obligations in order to serve the people in the temporal world. I sacrifice one of the rights which I love very deeply, the power to celebrate the external cult of the Church as a priest, in order to create the conditions which might make that cult more authentic.

I believe that my commitment to effectively fulfill the precept of love of neighbor demands this sacrifice of me. The supreme measure of human decisions must be charity, supernatural love. I will run all the risks which this measure demands of me.[11]

10. Communication of the Cardinal to Father Camilo Torres:

"We, Luis Concha, Cardinal Priest of the Holy Roman Church of the Title of S. Maria Nuova,

By the grace of God and the holy apostolic See, Archbishop of Bogotá and Primate of Colombia

In conformity with Ecclesiastical Legislation, at the petition of the priest Camilo Torres, we decree his reduction to the lay state within the terms of the solicited pontifical rescript.

Given in Bogotá, June 26, 1965.

L. Cardinal Concha
Archbishop of Bogotá"[12]

11. The Episcopate speaks:

On July 7, 1965, the press in the country learned about the document in which the Colombian hierarchy, meeting in episcopal conference, determined the position of the Church as regards some theses of Camilo. They didn't expressly name him, but the doctrinal statements allude to the Platform and to his political conduct.

We transcribe the pertinent sections:

The Colombian Episcopate, meeting in its regular annual assembly, in order to study and coordinate various pastoral activities, cannot ignore or underestimate the difficult and painful situation present in the moral, political, economic, and social order of the country.

In the face of the anxiety which is seen in all and the hope which many have in the light of Christ, the Episcopal Conference addresses itself to all the Colombian people to offer orientations of thought and social action.

I. Function of Priests and of Seculars

. . . The noble function of the priest in the social field is precisely to sacrifice every personal political interest so that, guided by the Magisterium, he may faithfully interpret the demands of the Word of God in social life. . . .

III. The Right of Property and Its Social Function

. . . The responsibility of the rich is not satisfied through almsgiving, although this is demanded in numerous emergency cases.

Wealth must reinvest capital for the common good, not for private interest, but for the production of new wealth and the creation of new sources of employment which will benefit society.

It would be a serious error to confuse the right of property with its use, holding that the goods possessed are destined exclusively for the benefit of the property owner. Its use cannot be determined without having in mind the needs of others.

IV. Errors Regarding the Right of Property

It would destroy the true responsibility included in the right of property to reduce it to mere right to use its fruits. Practically, this is the error of those who attribute by law the ownership of the land to those peasants who cultivate it solely because of their cultivating it, the ownership of the benefits of capital to the employees of a business, and the ownership of houses to the inhabitants. Within that system ownership would be reduced to a right which would end when the necessity to use it disappeared in the judgment of the State.

Such an ordinance is not the authentic right of ownership. It does not confer a true power to dispose of it, nor does it permit man to satisfy many necessities which the State neither can nor should take over. It is also not sufficient to guarantee the liberty of the citizen from the State. Much more would go wrong with a fiscal system which would absorb all income which is more than enough for individual or family necessities.

According to those false principles, the State would have complete economic responsibility and the individual person would be deprived of it. In this system, only the State would have the power to give ownership of the land, of the profits from capital, of homes, and also the right to determine the incomes themselves.

Without sufficient reflection, the transfer of the temporal goods of the Church to the State is suggested at times as a solution to the social problems.

The Church is the People of God. As a visible society it needs material goods to fulfill its duties among men. But religious authority is careful that those goods are of service to the Christian community within the spirit of evangelical poverty and the supernatural ends of the Church. We do not condemn criticism in those cases in which the properties or their investment do not comply with the ends of service which justify them, no matter who are their direct owners or administrators. . . .

VI. Violent Revolution Is Not the Solution

Violent revolution, because of the immense material and moral damage it causes, with the destruction of goods and of lives, with the mutual hatred it instigates in souls, is not the proper solution. There is no greater danger in the present situation of the country than that of Christians betraying their responsibility and accepting violent revolution instead of creating by their intelligent and dynamic action the possibilities for a rapid and peaceful solution.

We can still hear the voice of His Holiness John XXIII who in *Pacem in Terris* says: "here is no lack of men of great courage who, faced with situations in which the demands of justice either are not fulfilled or are fulfilled in a deficient way, moved by a desire to change everything, do not allow themselves to be carried by an impulse so violent that they seem to recur to something similar to a revolution.

"We would like to remind these men that all things require time to grow in successive steps and thus, in virtue of that law, we do not arrive at improvement in human institutions unless we work from within, step by step.

"Our predecessor of happy memory, Pius XII, recalled this when he said: 'It is not in revolution but in well-planned evolution that justice and salvation are found.'

"Violence has never done anything but destroy; it does not build; it ignites passions; it does not appease them.

"Accumulating hatreds and destruction, not only has it not succeeded in reconciling the combatants, but it has brought men and parties to the hard necessity of slowly, with much labor, rebuilding on rubbish piled up through discord, the old work having been destroyed."[13]

12. *Pastoral Letter of His Eminence the Cardinal read in all the churches of the Archdiocese of Bogotá, August 15, 1965:*

"The ancients considered the two-edged sword one of the most deadly weapons. In these days we could compare certain words to the two-edged sword, because of the variety of meanings to which they lend themselves. One of those words is the word Revolution. The Spanish Dictionary defines it: 'Violent change of the nation's political institutions.' And this is the sense which spontaneously comes to mind when one hears or reads the word Revolution. Sometimes in pronouncing or writing it we intend to give it another meaning, omitting anything which might explain that we do not want to speak of 'violent change,' which causes confusion in the spirit of our hearers or readers. Other times we add another explanatory word saying, for example, *peaceful revolution* or something similar. But would it not be better to prescind from the word *revolution* when we want to understand an evolution, a change which is justifiable, peaceful, and lawful.

On June 11, 1943, Pope Pius XII said: 'Not in a revolution but in a well-planned evolution do we find salvation and justice. Violence has never done anything but destroy; it does not build; it ignites passions; it does not appease them. Accumulating hatreds and ruins, not only has it not succeeded in reconciling the combatants, but it has brought men and parties to the hard necessity of slowly, with immense labor, rebuilding on rubbish piled up through discord, the old work having been destroyed.'

Very wise words which seem to be especially written for us today when revolution is preached as the only remedy for the critical situation in which we certainly live. Isn't the havoc produced through many years of violence enough to force Colombians into a position of prudence? What would be accomplished with the sacrifice of more lives and with the accumulation of more wreckage? Will it be necessary to destroy what our fathers constructed with extraordinary efforts and sacrifices in order to build afterwards on the ruins? Would not this be a program of madmen? No one denies that there is much to do, that there are many things to correct and many injustices to repair; but the remedy is certainly not to destroy everything that exists and to create chaos in order to begin anew and to arrive at who knows where. We hear the teachings of the Pope and we will not be seduced from what Christ teaches by false prophets who come to us with sheep's clothing but inwardly are wolves.

The advocates of revolution proclaim the fall of the existing government and, since they start out from the inadmissible basis of revolution, they do so logically. So certain is this that those among us who promote revolution judge that it is necessary to begin with 'the seizure of power.' But to make an attempt against a legitimate government is condemned by natural law, and if the mandate of the natural law would seem doubtful to some, that of the Sacred Scripture promulgated by the Church would show, as the Supreme Pontiffs have constantly taught, that it is illicit when it means disobedience, rebellion, or the overthrow of civil power legally constituted.

St. Paul, with words which leave no room for doubt, wrote in his Epistle to the Romans: 'You must all obey the governing authorities. Since all government comes from God, the civil authorities were appointed by God, and so anyone who resists authority is rebelling against God's decision, and such an act is bound to be punished.' (Rom. 13: 1-2) And it is interesting to advert to the fact that St. Paul wrote when the tyranny of the pagan emperors was manifest and presaged days of tremendous trial for the Christians. Nine years after the writing of the Epistle to the Romans the head of St. Paul fell under the sword of the executioner.

The teachings of St. Peter in respect to the duties to legitimate authority do not differ from those of St. Paul and, if you wish, are even more strict than those of the Apostle to the Gentiles.

But what is of extraordinary significance in this matter is that during all this time in which the Roman emperors governed the Roman Empire, the Christians who were the victims of atrocities and bloody persecutions never attempted rebellion against the tyrannical imperial authority. On the contrary they always obeyed it and respected it in everything which was not against the Law of God. St. Cyprian declared in the presence of the judge who had the power to condemn him to death that 'the Christians prayed for the welfare of the Emperors.'

It is undeniable that every nation must have changes in its institutions, in accord with the circumstances of the times. But it is equally undeniable that, under pain of falling into chaos and anarchy, these changes must be verified in a regular and legal way and never in a violent way. Certainly there are many evils which must be cured among us, as happens everywhere, and it is undeniable that every effort must be made to remedy them. The use of violence for this reason would only bring greater evils and would not correct the existing ones.

Those who proclaim revolutions seduce the multitudes with illusory promises. They promise them an ideal world in which they will be free of all those evils which weigh on them, a true paradise on earth. The final result is infinitely far from what was promised. In changing a legal regime which can be diseased with deficiencies, like every human system, and yet within which they could make their voice heard, they finally come under the domination of an absolute master or a tyrannical oligarchy which suffocates their more just requests and their now useless laments.

L. Cardinal Concha
Archbishop of Bogotá"[14]

13. Last communication from the Cardinal:

"Bogotá, September 20, 1965

The Cardinal Archbishop of Bogotá has not judged it opportune or convenient to make a statement about the situation of Camilo Torres as regards the Catholic Church nor about his situation as regards Canon Law. He had not thought that such a statement was necessary because he believed that Catholics had sufficient evidence to form for themselves an exact concept on one or the other point.

Nevertheless, the Cardinal Archibishop of Bogotá has arrived at the conclusion that there is a Catholic group, not very large, which is still uncertain as to what to think about the situation of Camilo Torres before the laws of the Catholic Church.

For this reason the Cardinal Archbishop of Bogotá has decided to make the following statements:

1. Camilo Torres spontaneously sought reduction to the lay state. In virtue of reduction to the lay state, Camilo Torres was dispensed from the obligations of the priestly state, except for the obligation of celibacy.

2. Reduction to the lay state, which certainly does not blot out the sacerdotal character which is indelible, implies that Camilo Torres will never be able to return to the exercise of his priestly ministry. Reduction to the lay state, spontaneously requested by Camilo Torres, and given to him, is not a simple temporary permission given by ecclesiastical authority, which permits him to dedicate himself to activities foreign to his sacerdotal character with the supposition that afterwards he will be able to return to the exercise of his priestly functions.

3. The Cardinal Archbishop of Bogotá believes he must call the attention of Catholics to the activities, notoriously at odds with the teachings of the Catholic Church, in which Camilo Torres is found to be engaged: inciting to the subversion of public order which can even mean the use of violence; seizure of power (in an illegal way, of course) peacefully if possible, by force if it becomes necessary. Anyone can see the unfortunate consequences which will follow if such activities of Camilo Torres are accomplished according to his plans.

4. The ecclesiastical authority fulfills its responsibility and does it so that Catholics might know that it categorically disapproves of the procedures of Camilo Torres, because they are opposed to the doctrine of the Catholic Church.

Finally, the Cardinal Archibishop of Bogotá makes a public manifestation of the profound and paternal sorrow which the actions of Camilo Torres have caused and do cause him, for he is failing in his obligations to the priesthood of Christ.

L. Cardinal Concha"[15]

14. Last Clarification of Camilo:

The Cardinal reduced me to the lay state by a decree in which he says that this reduction will be in accord with a rescript which comes from Rome, but that rescript has not arrived. In Rome they asked him to speak to me before imposing the sanction on me and he did not heed that order.

Disgracefully, the Cardinal gives the appearance of continuing in the same key: without explaining or proving that I am against the Catholic

Church. It seems that he acted under the pressure of the groups who have control of the country.

The public statements of his Eminence the Cardinal are contrary to his private statements. When I spoke personally with him, we saw that the only way to save his conscience and mine was for me to ask for reduction to the lay state. He told me that it was a sad decision for him but that he hoped that in the moment I would consider convenient, I could return to the exercise of my priesthood and he would receive me with open arms.[16]

As final commentaries to this chapter, which was intentionally presented in an oversimplified way so as not to detract from the objectivity of the documents, those of Canon Houtart and the magazine *Mensaje* are worthwhile:

The first says:

Camilo arrived at an open conflict with his bishop, and for a priest this implies, certainly, a very bitter reality. All this must be seen in its context. On the one hand, the way authority was understood was not proper. The ignorance of the social realities was such, that perhaps the conflict was inevitable. On the other hand, the use of polemical speech on both sides must be deeply lamented.

This should help us to reflect on the ideas we have concerning the exercise of authority in the Church on the one side and on obedience and submission to the hierarchical Church on the other. I believe I can say that on both sides they committed serious mistakes, explicable, without doubt, because of the existing climate but which, in all honesty, it is necessary to admit.[17]

The text says:

Could Camilo Torres choose another way without infidelity to his vocation and personal orientation? Did not the very circumstances of Colombian politics and the chosen attitude of the Catholic hierarchy force it?

The attitude of the Prelate (the Cardinal) was authoritarian. In observing it from Chile it seems to us that it was in excess. A bishop who consents to enter into public argument with one of his priests is not disposed to listen, but only to proclaim and condemn without appeal. Perhaps events would have taken another direction if the Cardinal had responded privately to the first letter received from Camilo Torres. And even once Camilo made it public, as bishop he had other means to address himself to his priest.

On the other hand, in the heat of the argument the bishop used phrases which are unacceptable from the doctrinal point of view such as admitting, in effect, that the Church has nothing to do with social problems.

Nevertheless, those planks of Camilo Torres in his Platform and in his other writings contained many doctrinal errors and suffered, moreover, from a simplification in solutions bordering on childishness. The Cardinal could have made him see that with full reason.

. . . It will not be difficult to see that the Cardinal was right when he found more than one point against the social doctrine of the Church. Little or nothing remains, in fact, of the right of property and of the subsidiary role of the State, to indicate just two important points. Would it not have been desirable if the ecclesiastical authority had not refused dialogue with its people, and especially with its priests. . . . even though it might have reasons for not believing very much in its efficacy?[18]

Chapter 9

And His Brothers Judged Him

The "Camilo Torres case" could not remain merely a conflict between the revolutionary priest and the Cardinal. The preaching of each had an audience in the entire nation. The warnings, teachings, and condemnations of the Primate logically aroused support in the clerical structure and approbation, doubts, or rejection in the various other sectors of public opinion.

As useful material for *post factum* analysis, it is fitting to cite the more detached manifestations of ecclesiastical opinion.

AMONG THE BISHOPS:

Bishop José Ignacio López Umaña, Archbishop of Cartagena, speaking before the Union Radio Newscast, said: "As Father Torres has his superior, who is Cardinal Concha, I am unable to give my opinion as to what the sanction can be, but by all means I think it should be imposed on him. I cannot interfere in that authority. In any case, I completely support any decision which His Eminence Cardinal Concha Córdoba takes."[1]

Bishop Norberto Forero, Bishop of Santa Marta, when interviewed on the same newscast, said: "I have not read the statements of Father Camilo Torres, but if it is true that he is meddling in politics, it seems to me that he should be sanctioned by the Cardinal. It is a problem when priests speak about politics. Clearly we have the rights of a citizen, but we must exercise them without the necessity of giving our opinion or of immersing ourselves in problems which only touch the civil world."[2]

The same prelate responded for the Monserrate newscast: "It certainly seems to me that Cardinal Concha Córdoba must impose a sanction because I consider it very serious when a priest proclaims political theses no matter how important they might be. By all means, I think Cardinal Concha Córdoba must impose a sanction on him."

To this question: "Does your Excellency feel that the theses of Camilo Torres are really unchristian?", he responded: "I think that Father Camilo Torres has expressed some theses, which even though they are bitter, merit study. He may hold various erroneous concepts, but by all means, they should be studied."

"Your Excellency: What do you think of the statement of Father Torres that the Colombian clergy are backward?"

"It seems to me that it is an erroneous concept, especially since it is a generalization. There are many very important persons in the Colombian clergy and it seems to me that the accusations of Father Camilo Torres are an offense against the Colombian clergy."[3]

Most Reverend Bishop Rubén Isaza, Coadjutor Bishop of the Archdiocese of Bogotá, said: "A sanction has not been imposed on Father Camilo Torres. I think that if the situation does not change, things will remain as they are today, that is to say, that there will not be further consequences. But if the problem should become more serious, the resulting difficulties would also be more serious."[4]

Most Reverend Bishop Arturo Duque Villegas, Archbishop of

Manizales, said: "It is possible that the Holy See might begin to study the feasibility of sanctioning the priest who, two days ago, predicted a revolution within five years for the country, after foretelling the future of four political leaders as presidential candidates."[5]

Bishop Tulio Botero Salazar, Archbishop of Medellín, declared: "Only Cardinal Luis Concha Córdoba can handle this problem."[6]

The Archbishop of Cali, Doctor Uribe Urdaneta, made the following comment: "I am sincerely convinced that the Catholic Church must take a more direct role in the social changes which modern life is demanding with greater urgency every day. But we must act with a Catholic outlook. The Church has a hierarchy and a laity. It is the duty of the first to teach and of the laity to labor responsibly in accord with doctrine. Political problems, economy, and technology do not pertain to the priest."[7]

The Bishops of the Ecclesiastical Province of Medellín made this communication public:

"The Archbishop and the Bishops of the Ecclesiastical Province of Medellín inform all Catholics of Antioquía that

1. Camilo Torres, having renounced the exercise of the priesthood, has lost the category and the rights of the clergy and both the authorities and the faithful must consider and treat him as a simple citizen.

2. In such condition the ex-cleric Torres does not represent nor is he the voice of the Church in the programs and ideas which he divulges publicly or privately. Also, in the exercise of these activities, he is subject to the norms which the laws of the Republic impose for any citizen.

3. Mr. Torres is not now Father Camilo Torres. He is a layman now and the people should not listen to the erroneous propaganda which invites them to hear 'Father Camilo.'

4. Finally we advert to the fact that the programs and the social, econmic, and political theses which Mr. Torres proposes, lead to erroneous applications, harmful consequences, dangerous evasions, and to actions contrary to the teaching and methods of the Catholic Church.

The present statement must be read in all the churches and

chapels of the Diocese of Antioquía, at all the Masses next Sunday.

Medellín, August 2, 1965.

Tulio Botero Salazar, Archbishop of Medellín; Miguel Angel Builes, Bishop of Santa Rosa de Osos; Guillermo Escobar Vélez, Bishop of Antioquía; Alfredo Rubio Díaz, Bishop of Sonsón; Augusto Trujillo Arango, Bishop of Jericó."[8]

AMONG THE PRIESTS:

Monsignor Víctor Viedemann, Vicar General of the Archdiocese of Medellín, said: "It is forbidden for us priests to write for the public without the consent of the Most Reverend Archbishop. I am sure that Father Torres has not obtained it. The fact is that he is knowingly disobeying ecclesiastical regulations.

"We cannot think that the organization of the State is perfect and does not require renewal. The Church, for her part, certainly needs it. But for all, there are procedures, whether in the civil or the ecclesiastical order, for the innovations which need to be made. The recognition of the hierarchy is indispensable. It is the duty of the clergy in public life to act as directors in the religious field, but this authority cannot be used for political proselytism."[9]

The Priest, Doctor Mario Revollo, Director of *El Catholicismo,* said: "The statements of Father Torres have two aspects: a profound one which deserves study, but not independently as he is doing it, and another unacceptable for taking public positions at odds with the regular conduct established by the Church. No Christian, and even less a priest, can speak of their mother, the Church, in that way. Father Camilo Torres is acting outside the Church as an agitator."[10]

The old conservative politician and ex-minister of Government, Doctor Luis Ignacio Andrade, today Father Anselmo, made the following comments: "I don't know Father Torres nor have I had any relationship with him. As a priest, I prefer to make my mistakes in union with the hierarchy rather than set myself up against them. I am with the Cardinal. I am with my bishop and my hierarchical superior."[11]

A very vocal ecclesiastical declared: "Let us suppose that the doctrine of Camilo Torres was orthodox and had not been separated in any point from the teachings of the Church. Even so, the sole fact of disobeying the Cardinal is wrong."[12]

Father César Jaramillo Velásquez, S.J., Dean of the Faculty of Medicine of the Pontifical University Javeriana, said: "Father Camilo Torres, in some things, may be right from the viewpoint of the Church. In others he may be giving his own personal opinion. He should not propose such concepts except under the guidance of the Church. If the Cardinal has said that he does not agree with these opinions, Father Camilo Torres should not disobey the hierarchy."[13]

The Jesuit Father Félix Restrepo, President of the Colombian Academy of Languages, asserted: "Father Camilo Torres must subject himself to the opinion and authority of the Church before teaching such ideas."[14]

From the open letter which Father Hernando Borrientos addressed to Camilo: ". . . There is a priest who likes to jump from one podium to another preaching revolution and there are many adolescents who are confusing him with the Messiah and many heedless people who believe that he is really a good priest.

"It would be better for him to take off the soutane and conduct the war against the hierarchy from outside, reduced to the lay state, and not hiding behind the soutane. . . . A war behind a mask is not noble. Thus, as a layman, one would be able to analyze his ideas without having the distasteful impression of playing Judas.

"If you, Mr. Scholar, are called to the revolution of the forces of the left, do you think that we who are not Communists are going to stand by with our arms folded? Don't be naive, Mr. Scholar Torres.

"It is not fear of the revolution which discourages us. It is seeing that you, Scholar Torres, have been given the task of organizing apostasy among the students and the uninformed."[15]

The Claretian priest, Father Efrán Gaitán Orjuela, Director of the magazine *El Voto Nacional,* responded for the Union Radio

Newcast: "Father Camilo Torres finds himself down a dead-end street, for if he turns back, the students and his fanatical followers lynch him, and if he persists he falls into the hands of ecclesiastical justice. All of which means that his sacrifice is useless, for they will eliminate him before he has begun the revolution of the people.

"I am ninety-five per cent identified with Father Camilo Torres. The remaining five per cent with which I do not agree would be in his confrontation with the hierarchy. I know that there are not a few priests who have adhered to the theses of Father Torres, but all have done it privately. It seems to me that presently there is no priest in Colombia who wishes to attack the supreme hierarchy of the Colombian Church. This would be to work against unity which is one of the foundations of the Catholic Church. I think that if Father Camilo continues in that attitude and is not reconciled with the Cardinal, the priests partial to him, who sympathize with him, will leave him alone in the conflict.

"It is evident that Father Torres has separated himself from the teachings of the Church. In social matters, perhaps the same thing could not be said. Many of the things which Father Torres affirms are as old as Christianity and the Encyclicals. However, sociology is a science in formation, and therefore the social and economic platform which Father Torres in company with other technologists has proposed has not been presented as a dogma of the faith, but as matter for discussion.

"A moderate anti-clericalism within the clergy can be healthy, since it helps to correct the defects in the priestly class. I favor a revision of the Concordat and a tax placed on those ecclesiastical goods which are not directly at the service of the welfare of the community. Father Camilo must humbly settle the quarrel with the Cardinal; he must declare publicly that he is not leaving as an outcast and is taking a trip to Europe, but without compromising his ideas, which are very good."[16]

The Superior of the Claretians in Colombia, Father Mariano Izquierdo Gallo, emphatically rejected the statements of Father Gaitán Orjuela and asserted of Camilo: "Father Camilo Torres is insane, a maniac. He has taken a position of mental paroxysm. He lacks spiritual serenity. The expropriation of ecclesiastical goods is a theory which must not be listened to. There are laws and ecclesiastical authorities which regulate the possessions of the Church, and Father Torres cannot proceed against them nor does he have the right to do so. The Church does not possess superfluous goods and the income produced by the faithful is hardly sufficient to maintain the churches, sustain the religious services, and support works of the apostolate and charity."[17]

Father José Antonio Sánchez blames Camilo thus:

"1. Marxism is an antiquated doctrine and, amusingly, opposed to violent revolution almost by definition, since if the evolution of human society inevitably leads to a communist organization, to look for an acceleration by means of violence is either premature or useless.

"2. Since Communism is essentially international as a political party, how does Father Torres accuse us moderates of receiving our orders from the United States? Why does he forget that his orders come from Moscow or Peking?

"3. Where does Father Camilo get his money for continuous airplane flights, for his hotels, and for all the other expenses of conferences?"[18]

Father Fernando Gómez Mejía, in an article titled "Neither Apostle Nor Liberator," said the following: "The whole country is following with curiosity the episodes provoked by Father Camilo Torres, who is now calling himself the revolutionary priest. The forces of the left and the naive have saluted him as a liberator and authentic apostle of Christ.

"In order to avoid errors and open the way to a correct understanding of the problem let us establish some facts. It has been said that Father Torres is persecuted because he has taken up the defense of the poor. Nothing is further from the truth. We find fault with his errors and his methods. His supporters say that he is concerned with sociological matters. We have attentively listened to his discourses and have found the affirmation of theses and statistical data which are continuously proposed by those who treat of such themes. Every person of moderate culture knows these theories and hearing them in the words of Father Torres does not produce any new enlightenment.

"The originality of Father Torres lies in having taken the path of rebellion against his legitimate superior and of having rashly abandoned the direct field of priestly action in order to enter into the political life of the country against the very clear norms of ecclesiastical discipline and law. The rejection of this erroneous behavior does not imply a denial of an acute Colombian social problem, nor the acceptance of injustice, nor ignorance of the causes which created it and maintain it today. Neither does it mean malicious obstruction of solutions or gratuitous persecution of those who, with prudence and courage, are engaged in the correction of the system and the renovation of the unjust structures. The fact that he uses Gospel texts, Catholic social doctrine, and pontifical documents, for his political activity does not legitimize his errors.

"Some have wanted to argue for a complex of fear and inferiority on the part of the Cardinal before the Challenge of Father Torres. Such a challenge is disrespect on the part of an inferior, who has wished to compromise the Cardinal in a polemical periodical unworthy of the Primate of the Colombian Church. With a great feeling for prudence and dignity the Cardinal did not bite at the bait. Since he did not accept the challenge, they malign the dignity of the Cardinal as fear or ignorance. The theories of Father Camilo are guilty of an essential lack of focus in that he approaches the solution of the problem from a merely economic angle. Consequently, his theses are exclusively concerned with economics. Therefore, he touches only the materialistic side of the problem which is far from a satisfactory solution. If Father Camilo retains, as I believe he does, priestly sensibility, he must be deeply worried because he has lost the basis for peace of conscience, having set out on the path of disobedience. There are few seeds which bear fruit as immediately as those of Father Camilo. His revolutionary speeches have not obtained a single act of love of God or the repentance of a single sinner. But they have sown, in less than one month, more hatred for the Church and for the Colombian clergy than have unbelievers and perpetrators of malicious campaigns after many years. It is evident that in these times he does not act as an authentic apostle, even though the indelible character of his priesthood remains, because he now places himself outside of obedience to his Bishop and the disciplinary norms of the Church.

"Neither is he a liberator. The revolution which Father Camilo wants will not lead to the solution of our problems. In his speeches he speaks a lot about objectivity, but this is precisely what is lacking in his political campaigns. As a sociologist he knows that an authentic revolution does not happen overnight. It needs to go through the process of sowing, growth, and maturation. It is necessary to form leaders and electrify the atmosphere, to create a mystique and move the masses behind those leaders towards the realization of a national ideal which not only counts on enthusiasm but on the doctrinal, technical, and administrative capability which the recovery of the country requires. This is not the path taken by our revolutionary priest. He has expressly said that he accepts the collaboration of all the nonconformist groups without any kind of discrimination in order to make the revolution successful. Therefore he is engaged in the impossible task of reconstructing a tower of Babel rather than the country. He has been converted into an agitator for change in this convulsed country where we have more than enough demagogues and not enough leaders.

"You may know, Father Camilo, that the patience with which the Cardinal has treated you and the gentlemanly behavior of the clergy do not mean, in any way, a fear which rumor says that we have of you or of the leftists. We fight Communism because it is essentially the enemy of God and of the liberty and peace of the people. We are fulfilling a duty of conscience, not the counsel of fear. If you make a show of strength in order to betray the Church and the country, the other priests of the country are equally firm in shutting out renegades and traitors."[19]

Father Juan Cuervo, S.D.S., sets down his position: "Our opinion, in all due respect, is that both the Cardinal and Father Torres are partially right. We young priests are nonconformists and cannot accept the social, economical, and political situation in our country. If revolution means to change the present structures for others more dynamic and effective, then we are revolutionaries. It is not important that these other changes are given the name of evolution, a word which makes less of an impression on the leading Colombian classes.

"Let us not counsel our brother in the priesthood to return to Rome. In the best of cases, this is the answer which would arrive: 'The Holy See has not found anything in your socio-economic and political ideas contrary to the teachings of the Gospel and of the Church. The opportuneness, or the way you express such ideas, must be judged by your own hierarchy. Submit, therefore, humbly to the decisions of the Ordinary.'

"Concretely, the situation of Father Torres from the viewpoint of Rome is that the Cardinal must save face and Camilo must lose."[20]

Some observations of Father Tomás Calvis, S.J.: "We are sure of the uselessness of Father Torres' resolution to abandon the ecclesiastical state. The influence which he had yesterday over the youthful masses depended, more than anything else, on his priestly character. Voluntarily deprived of it, it will be difficult for him to be able to replace it with purely human talents. How true is the phrase of the French thinker. 'The youth, who at fifteen years old is not a communist, has no heart; the young man, who at thirty years old is a communist, has no head.' We regret that a priest of such excellent social talents as Father Torres has taken a step which, far from contributing to the welfare of the proletarian class, will create, without benefit to anyone and with harm for many, great confusion and social unrest."[21]

A priest writes to Camilo from El Poblado (Antioquía):

"What is the change of structures which you propose? When it becomes necessary to change the columns which support a building to substitute others, these must be ready and proven to be better; otherwise everything, including the good which one wanted to save, will founder. This has been the lot of every violent revolution which destroys without being able to replace.

"Will there be a change of government? If it is done in accord with the Constitution, as we see happen sometimes, then that is where political machinery is to be mobilized and where the Church must not be committed unless the hierarchy judges that a definite system of government is a threat to its human-divine structure.

Otherwise, it should operate very much above political parties so that it is not contaminated with sectarianism.

"Or, if it is this structure which Christ left to his Church that you want to change, remember there have already been those who have dedicated themselves to do it. Then you are doing nothing else than spreading the ideas of Luther, Calvin, etc., although I don't think that you can measure up to the standards of those revolutionary geniuses in order to try something different.

"Will it be, then, a change of the Constitution that you offer for Colombia? You must, if you are not to work irresponsibly, have the principles ready, the substantial foundations of which have been shown to be better. Why haven't you shown them to us? Write, at least, a thick solid book which will withstand the critics, and don't dedicate yourself any longer to exploiting the credibility of the masses. Or if you want a copy of the atheistic and materialistic principles of Marx, say so clearly, define yourself, don't try to deceive. Don't play games with Colombian communism, don't serve it, as they say today, as the 'useful idiot.' "[22]

Father Edgar Alfredo Casas, of Popayán, stated for the press: "This situation of misery and of social injustice needs a change. We have been talking about it for some time now. The Archbishop must give us the direction."[23]

The moral assessor of the UTC, Father Vicente Andrade Valderrama, S.J., refers to the theses of Camilo in the following terms: "To say that every activity of the Church in the social field has been paternalistic is pitiful ignorance; and if someone says this who has had by his office the right and the opportunity to know the truth, then it is reasonable to assert that his attitude casts doubt on his good faith.

"It is, therefore, clear that Father Camilo Torres, both in his affirmations which sully the work of the Church, and in the role which he wants to assume in the politics of the country, is not acting in agreement with his duties as a priest, nor with the loyalty a Christian owes his Mother the Church.

"The Platform of United Action not even once mentions the trade unions and the other associations as instruments of social reform. The State must do everything and everything must be under its control. In these circumstances, every guarantee of the individual before the State would disappear and we would fall into Nazi or Communist totalitarianism."[24]

Another Jesuit, Father Manuel Foyaca de la Concha, Director of the Latin American Secretariat of the Social Apostolate of the Society of Jesus, commented on the Platform of Camilo noting, along general lines, that he gives exaggerated importance to the intervention of the State and that "in some points it is tinged with a certain communist inspiration."[25]

Father Miguel Betancur writes: "Demagogues preach only their own and almost always exaggerated and fallacious rights. They never speak to their party or social class of the duties which their followers necessarily must have.

"I would prefer to see Father Camilo Torres supporting the League of Alcoholics Anonymous or working on our farms, in schools and sports programs to preserve our young men from vice rather than stimulating the animal instincts of men. . . . Which profitable position they (the Communists) have ultimately adopted in order to discredit the social work of the Church which hurts them because they haven't done anything.

"I prefer a thousand times vertical, beneficent, creative, active paternalism, full of charity, to horizontal, non-workable, disorganized, violent, and lazy fraternalism."[26]

Monsignor Gustave E. Vivas wrote:

"The Platform of Unity of Action, the ambitious project of my friend Father Torres, whom I met in the University of Louvain, has raised a cloud of dust which impedes clear vision. It is a socio-economic agenda which must not be thrown out. He has good points and the best intentions for our suffering people; he also has a good foundation in pontifical social doctrine, even though there are serious errors and difficulties in his application of authentic Catholic sociology. The most serious effect of these theses of Father Torres is the confusion which he has caused in the conscience of many convinced Catholics."[27]

Father Nicolás Nicholaes, in a long article for *La Patria* of Manizales, said among other things: ". . . It seems to me that Torres does not know the Colombian clergy very well. He speaks as though our clergy were living in the midst of great material wealth. I know priests who have worked years and years without receiving the slightest remuneration, barely living from alms or with the aid of their parents or religious communities. The apostolic zeal of our priests is an example not only for Colombia but for the entire world. I don't know if Father Torres has worked in mountain parishes, alone, without resources, completely cut off from other priests, administering the sacraments day and night and in situations which are very hard, miserable, and eminently precarious. We must study much more deeply the social thought of the Church and leave to the laity the technical application of that doctrine."[28]

Father Gómez Mejía wrote again: "The more Camilo speaks, the more deeply is he committed to Communism. . . . Camilo said: 'If a materialistic, unbelieving atheist speaks of his positions in this matter, nothing happens nor does anyone say anything. But if someone who believes in God, who has faith in Jesus Christ, and loves the Church, attacks the interests of the oligarchy, they immediately brand him a communist, not to signify that he belongs to a party, but so that he may be repudiated by those whom he has been teaching . . .' Camilo must bear in mind that he is not being attacked for fighting for social justice nor for condemning the abuses of the oligarchy. He is being attacked for having embarked on a revolutionary adventure with Communism at the helm. Communism is essentially atheistic, the enemy of Jesus Christ, and an implacable persecutor of the Church. Here is its sin. It is a contradiction to say that you believe in God and love Jesus Christ and his Church and then place yourself in the front lines of a party which is essentially its enemy.

"Communist hands pull the strings of the puppet. The people do not believe that Mr. Torres is acting alone and purely on his own initiative. Nor was this situation produced suddenly. This has been coming for many years. They were waiting for the right moment and they couldn't have picked a better one because of the misery, the political confusion, parliamentary irresponsibility, and the desperation of the people. They were only waiting to seize the psychological moment. This is the reason for the eruption of Camilo

Torres in the political life of the country. The antireligious MOEC, aggressive and energetic, has proclaimed its leader: his name is Camilo Torres."[29]

Father Luis Enrique Sendoya said: "I attended the celebration which some friends had given for Camilo Torres when he visited Cali. The problem is that some theses and theories of Camilo Torres are not in agreement with Catholic doctrine according to the Colombian ecclesiastical hierachy. This places him in a dangerous position. But at the same time it demands that we treat him honestly and with the kindness which anyone deserves who commits errors, whether they be large or small.

"To make this distinction is not to compromise the truth but to approach a delicate situation with a heart free of hate and without any kind of prejudice. John XXIII hastened to distinguish with intelligent charity—these are his own words—'between him who errs and the error, even though you are treating of men who know the truth or only know it partially whether in the religious order or in the order of moral practice, since he who errs does not thereby lose his humanity nor has he lost his dignity as a person and he will always deserve the consideration which comes from this fact.'

"Such noble words, essentially Christian, since they are those of a Pope, are incompatible with the way the writers and adversaries of Camilo are treating him publicly, without the decency which a citizen deserves, denying him even the rights which our laws set down as applicable to every citizen. 'Following the truth' and following the truth 'in charity' of which St. Paul speaks, are authentic expressions of a true Christian, and rather than be destroyed, they will simultaneously complement and perfect one another.

"Personally, I don't agree with Camilo's attacks on the ecclesiastical hierarchy and the Catholic priesthood. They seem to me unjust and beneath someone who was distinguished many times by the same hierarchy. . . . Neither are our bishops some kind of public relations directors for plutocratic capitalism. Nor have the priests enriched themselves with that 'depraved activity' which Veblen attributed to the bourgeoisie in a famous book on the idle rich."

What can be added? Jesus Christ taught: "By this love you have for one another, everyone will know that you are my disciples" (Jn. 13:35). As far as words, polemics, apologias and defenses are concerned, there were more than enough. But as regards real effort at contact or action to bring brothers together in personal dialogue, we did not do what we could and should have done.

We are left with our good intentions and with the record of our statements to the press. Was this the only way? Or, did we lack real charity? The problem was not political success but love. Did we go into the streets, into the city or even into the hills to save him and "his insane adventure"? Or, did we give him up as lost once and for all.

I honestly believe, the case of Camilo will mean for many of us only one thing—remorse.

Chapter 10

The Newspaper *Frente Unido*

Adherence to the theses of Camilo increased as he came into contact with the people. Owing to the fact that his theories seemed very radical and unheard-of, the majority of people reacted favorably when they saw in the new leader a man of indisputable honesty, capable of sacrificing everything in order to serve the poor.

Camilo sounded out opinion and proposed a crusade to abstain from voting in order to remove all pretense of justification from the obligarchy in power. This was contrary to the opinion of some groups who sympathized with the United Front. While Camilo called for abstention from voting as a weapon in the struggle, others of his friends judged this tactic counterproductive because they thought they could more advantageously carry on the opposition from Parliament.

If the suggestions of the revolutionary priest were followed, a massive failure of the electoral machinery would result. Camilo perceived that the National Front rapidly detected the urgent necessity of a change of course and modified its entire program to condition it to immediate tactics more in accord with electoral considerations and more accessible to the masses. In this way we see the Front for National Transformation rise and support Doctor Carlos Lleras Restrepo for President of the Republic. They immediately included within the plans for future development the necessity of socio-economic change as an answer to the general anxiety of the people. They felt it was necessary to accommodate themselves to the moment, to speak a new language in order to win popularity.

In face of the determination of his friends to go to the people in the ballot boxes, Camilo decided to give his reasons for not participating in the elections: "The Platform of the United Front of the Colombian People," he wrote, "does not have a set revolutionary tactic as regards the electoral fight. In order to accomplish the unity of the revolutionaries we must insist on everything which unites us and prescind from everything which separates us. If the electoral problem is an obstacle to this union, it is better to avoid it, especially when we are still not sure the elections will take place.

"As for my participation in the elections, the most logical thing would be to offer a slate and to present myself personally as a candidate. In my thinking this would be to form a new group which would divide the opposition even more. This attitude would hinder the work I have imposed on myself: to unify the Colombian people.

"I do not consider myself a representative of the Colombian popular class, nor the head of the United Front, nor the leader of the Colombian revolution, because I have not been chosen by the people. I hope to be accepted by them as a *servant of the revolution.*

"As long as the United Front does not choose its leaders, I am not the leader of the United Front, except in those cases where the members want it. Since I am not going to participate in the elections, I have to explain to the people the reasons for this decision.

In addition to the reason just given, I have the following reasons:

"1. In the present voting system, the Colombian popular class must be divided into liberal and conservative; anything which divides the people is against their interests.

"2. The electoral apparatus is in the hands of the oligarchy and therefore 'the one counting the votes does the electing.' The elections take place more in the offices of the oligarchical government than at the voting tables.

"3. Since it is impossible to beat those who control the electoral machinery and all the power, the opposition groups who get to Parliament will never be able to bring about revolutionary transformations. On the contrary, their presence in Parliament makes it easy for the oligarchy to say that there is a democracy in Colombia because there is an opposition.

"4. It does not seem to me to be good revolutionary education to tell the people in words not to trust the obligarchy and to tell them in deeds to give the system something as precious as their political opinion.

"5. I believe that the time and the money which will be used in gathering lists, discussing expenses, substitutes, and leaders, can be used to organize and unify the common people with a solid foundation.

"6. In the case that the miracle would work and the oligarchy should err in counting the votes and the majority gets in, we know that, as in Argentina with the triumph of Peronism, the oligarchy can annul the elections and bring about a coup d'etat. An oligarchy which has not hesitated to kill revolutionary leaders, to turn over the country to violence and to support military governments, will not turn over power because the opposition may win a majority in the voting, a majority which, as we have already shown, it is morally impossible to obtain.

"Personally I favor electoral abstention—not a passive abstention, but an active, belligerent, and revolutionary abstention. Active: because it will be a rejection of the entire system including the elections; for that it will have to be politically motivated. Belligerent: because the revolutionary commandos will receive precise instructions on how to act before the electoral process. Revolutionary: because it will be employed to unify and organize the lower class for the final assault on power."[1]

Camilo had had just a few months of political experience. During that time he learned that the directing role of the leader—with a continuous multiplication of duties—can only be accomplished with the help of an organ of publicity which keeps the call to action alive; which coordinates on a national scale the tasks of the movement; which denounces intrigues; which makes possible the formulation of programs and disseminates messages and assignments, at the same time enhancing the political capacity of the affiliates. The periodical would have to be the agitator, the organizer, and the mover of the United Front. Consequently, they search out first contacts with intellectuals and newspaper people in order to lay the foundation for the organ of the movement, with the suggested name of *Frente Unido,* registered in the Offices of Intellectual Affairs and the Press of the Ministry of Government; they obtain a temporary license for it, the director being Camilo Torres.

A great propaganda campaign throughout the entire country precedes the first issue of *Frente Unido,* a weekly of eight pages at a price of one peso an issue; that is to say, twice the price of any other national paper. The first edition appeared on August 26, 1965, and 50,000 copies were sold, which is unheard of in the history of Colombian journalism, since not even the periodical of Jorge Eliécer Gaitán, *Jornada,* achieved such a figure in its first editions. It is enough to note that with the university students, 7,000 copies were sold at the National University in the first few hours of the morning. At noon *Frente Unido* was sold out. It was moving to see old people, women, children, students, workers, and intellectuals talking about the new weekly in the streets, theaters, cafés, universities, factories, and workers' neighborhoods, house by house. It seemed that everyone now felt the revolution moving because of their conquest of the streets, convinced that the enemy was incapable of making a frontal attack in the field of freedom of expression.

The clamor of the people filled the streets like an explosion. "There goes the mother of Camilo," the people on Carrera Séptima, the principal street in Bogotá, would say. There, Doña Isabel

Restrepo, widow of the eminent Doctor Calixto Torres Umaña, accompanied by a group of students, very dignified and noble, would be offering the pedestrians her son's weekly. "Buy *Frente Unido,* the newspaper of the people." What contrasts life has! Doña Isabel, accustomed to the company of the highest aristocracy, now mixed with the people, defying the anger of her former friends.

What was the progress of the periodical *Frente Unido* after the surprising success obtained in the first edition? When the texts are examined we must conclude that the objectives of Camilo were not perfectly fulfilled. In the first place, a publication of that kind needs unity of political thought which *Frente Unido* did not have. It fully achieved its objective of agitation, but, owing to the lack of political unity on the part of its editors, it failed to obtain the support of the masses.

Camilo's aim of attracting the "unaligned" to the revolution was itself an important cause of the split in the movement. Two trends arose among the leaders of the United Front: that of Camilo, who felt it was necessary to win over to the fight the millions of Colombians who wanted to produce a movement of the masses; and that of some of his companions, who wished to create a new political party along with the non-militant groups. This corrupted the thought of Camilo, detracted essentially from the ends of the United Front as a movement and discredited it in the eyes of the other revolutionary forces.

"Between the 70 per cent of the abstentionist Colombians and the militant sector of the non-aligned included within this number, there can be neither drawing apart nor coming together. Both see themselves as a large popular and revolutionary unity which, through the United Front, will carry out the indispensable tasks to establish this movement as *the true party of the Colombian revolution.*"[2]

This text caused a violent reaction among the members of the movement bent on integration. These addressed themselves to Camilo in the following terms: "The Coordinating Committee of the United Front of Valle del Cauca, in session May 22 of this year and with the assistance of the representatives of the Communist Party, the MRL, the Popular Nationalist Vanguard, the Federation of Workers of Valle, the Independent Trade Union Block, the Association of Women Democrats, the National Office for Housing, the non-aligned movement and some students, unanimously approved the following considerations:

"First, in number four of the periodical which you direct, it is stated that the United Front is a new party and that this new party will gather together the large masses who abstained from voting and who theoretically belong among the non-aligned.

"This point of view is expressed in a vague manner in your 'Message to the Non-Aligned,' and in an open and direct way in the articles of Julio César Cortés and Ricardo Valencia; for example, this last statement that the United Front will be 'the true party of the Colombian revolution' and that those non-aligned will be 'Its one fundamental support.'

"This new focus implies an essential change of the 'United Front' with many political consequences. In this conception, the United Front is not a unifying movement which seeks to glue together all the revolutionary forces on the basis of a minimal program; i.e., an alliance of parties and other organizations, without a new party being formed by the non-aligned.

"In accepting this conception, the first and most serious consequence would be that all of us in the revolution who are aligned in definite political parties would be left facing this dilemma: either to renege on our parties in order to enter that of the non-aligned, or to continue faithful to our organizations and not belong to the United Front.

"It will not escape you that this conception of the United Front, as the party of the Non-Aligned, is divisive and sectarian, and therefore contrary to the spirit of the examples you initially gave and which won the support of the masses.

"Since then, we have not lost that same point of view, and we are disposed to continue in the fight for a United Front without exclusiveness or hierarchies, ready to step away from every divisive factor. It is clear that neither are we opposed to the fact that the persons who are non-aligned might form a revolutionary party. On the contrary, we think this would be another step forward in the Colombian revolution. But it would not be right that this party be formed in opposition to the other revolutionary organizations nor that it should be identified with the United Front.

"Second, the articles of Julio César Cortés and Ricardo Valencia contain calumnious and irresponsible expressions about various parties which presently participate in the unifying movement of which you are a part. Thus, Mr. Cortés speaks of 'small revolutionary groups' or simply 'those in opposition' in order to refer to the organizations which make up the United Front as distinct from the sector of the Non-Aligned. Mr. Ricardo Valencia is more bold in his Olympian disdain, when he says that such 'groups' have won the rejection of the people because of their incapacity to move the Colombian revolution forward.

"We are unaware of the vast masses which follow these columnists, just as we don't know anything about their effective revolutionary labor, but we think that even though there are many who follow them and you multiply the revolutionary merits which they have, this does not give them the right to express themselves in the terms indicated.

"We reject, moreover, this and other calumnious expressions which abound in these articles, and we think that they represent a real danger for popular unity, and therefore it becomes necessary to raise the revolutionary vigilance in the ranks of the United Front.

"We ask that these considerations be published in our periodical *Frente Unido*."[3]

To what could these internal fights lead except to negative results? As for the periodical, it seems that the order was given to the youth organizations not to distribute it. I don't know of any document which would prove my hypothesis, but the packages could be seen piled up in the sites, and even on occasion they would not reclaim them in the Post Office.

In reality, Camilo never planned to start a new political party; his object was to unite with the revolutionary forces the immense majority of the people who had abstained from voting. Unfortunately, his absences, due to continuous trips through the interior of the country, were used by anti-Communist elements who, disguised in revolutionary clothes, injected venom into the controversy on the role of the non-aligned with the simplistic argument that in case the several movements in the United Front withdrew their support, it would be necessary to construct a political apparatus capable of pursuing the tasks of the revolution. On the other hand, the extremist elements were encouraged in the thesis of electoral abstention which Camilo proclaimed, in order to mark as opportunist the movements which considered participation in the elections a proper means of denunciation and elevation of the popular conscience. The extremists and the anti-Communists operated under the negotiating table, using the absence of Camilo, who found on his return a chaotic situation which he tried to correct with a new editorial, placing the facts clearly.

All this is the reason why he had not obtained political unity in the direction of the periodical *Frente Unido.*

Thus, from the first editions, the controversy grew in the very pages of the weekly, and this division passed on to the commandos in the provinces. The reactions against this divisive attitude reached the seat of the movement, creating an atmosphere of tension, taking away strength from the popular offensive in the streets and plazas and using up precious energies to consolidate the organization. All of which, added to the pressures not to publish the weekly, its high costs, the lack of funds, the refusal to distribute it, led to an end of the paper. They succeeded in publishing No. 13, dated the 9th of December, 1965; that is to say, thirteen editions in the course of five months.

In general, the entire progress of the periodical *Frente Unido* was a matter of improvisation. And in the field of cultural activity, you cannot improvise—much less permit trends in two directions. Courageous denunciations continued in their pages; important documents were published; it had a good initial presentation; but it failed in its mission to unite the people. These are sad experiences which must be borne in mind for the future. Because a political periodical without unity of command and without discipline is a boat without a rudder.

Chapter 11

Camilo and Some "Advanced" Groups

In the eyes of the progressive movements, Camilo rose both as a cohesive force and a factor for polarization, largely because of a dialogue directed towards operative activities based on a common agreement. Since the human being needs liberty, peace, justice, solidarity, he reasoned that he must not give himself to any advanced group whose philosophy, implicitly or explicitly, excluded such necessities.

But since undeniable divisionary tendencies appeared within the particular answers to the human problems, Camilo detected their real possibilities and dedicated himself to hastening the psychological thaw of the walls separating the progressive groups. At least, he arrived at the conclusion that it was possible to speak with all of them, not in terms of conversion, recrimination, or polemics, but of coordinated action. It was a first blow at the inertia of our sedentary revolutionaries. Camilo was looking not for the neutralizing of the particular activities of each group but for a transcending of self-interest, an acquisition of new attitudes.

He set down pluralism as the basis for coming together. In society and in man new values have risen in the face of which it is not reasonable to adopt a Manichean position. Therefore, it is necessary to look for new expressions and new language in a common effort for drawing closer.

Pluralism, he wrote, has been recognized as characteristic of present society-ideological and institutional pluralism. The opposing religious, philosophical, and political systems have had to come realistically to terms with coexistence. Coexistence cannot succeed, in any case, unless it has a basis in common agreement. An important joining of common points offers programs for action. Action on behalf of men, executed by men, is never totally good nor totally bad. When it is produced, when it passes from projects to realizations, it is presented as a challenge to the conscience of all those who are searching for the welfare of the community. The challenge of the action is difficult enough. To accept a program of action implies that you assume the inevitable defects which it has; to reject it means to discard the advantages which it must also undeniably have.

Nevertheless, action is something concrete. The variables which condition it can be controlled, in the main part, by objective observation, since facts do not lend themselves to interminable discussion. In addition, action for the service of others, among the values of today's world, has come to occupy one of the highest places. In our pluralist world, unity in action on behalf of men is unity with an essentially Christian foundation. Within this context Pope John XXIII wrote the encyclical *Pacem in Terris* and discussed contacts with opposed ideologies on the level of action.

On the plane of dialogue, Camilo sought contact with the various groups of the Left. But what was his opinion of the Left?

"The predominant criteria in the underdeveloped countries," he said, "have conditioned the orientation of those who have been called Colombian groups of the Left. Our progressive leaders, on many occasions, place themselves in such groups through an altruistic sentiment which we can identify with that of the utopian socialists, without scientific foundations and without reasonably established tactics.

"Traditionalism works in them not directly but by reaction. That which is traditional, even though it appears scientifically advisable, is often rejected through resentment. The normative and speculative spirit of these same leaders brings them to give more emphasis to theoretical planning than to the practical solutions of our socio-economic problems. This orientation is narrowly tied to the ideological colonialism of our Left. Slogans and clichés are used in a special revolutionary jargon. They apply solutions prefabricated outside the country to Colombian problems. They make public manifestations of solidarity with the oppressed people of other lands and forget the situation of our own oppressed. Sentimentalism frequently leads to demagoguery and consequent frustration.

"While the small but all-powerful ruling class is united to defend its interests, the leaders of the Left attack one another, produce confusion among the people and resemble very closely the traditional, sentimental, speculative criteria of ideological colonialism."[1]

At the beginning, the initiative of Camilo had the desired effect, but after a short time there was a return to insularity and many progressives scurried away when it was rumored that Camilo had gone over to the Communists.

"He holds Communist theses, associates with Communists, and uses Communist methods," they said. Weren't these good reasons for abandoning him? And they left him alone—instead of deeply committing themselves to re-enforcing things within the initial program. They could not stop being what they had been until then—an archipelago: islands surrounded with prejudices, calculations and suspicions; islands of pseudo-orthodoxy and sectarianism; islands tallking to themselves.

The Christian Social Democratic Party at first responded to Camilo's call with enthusiasm. July 20, 1965, it made public this communication:

The Christian Social Democratic Party in its Fifth National Council:

Reaffirms its commitment to the Colombian Revolution and its decision to accomplish it with an organized and prepared people, within a vigorous democratic spirit and a definite Christian inspiration.

Considers it its duty to identify itself with the objectives sought by Father Camilo Torres in his Platform and recent campaigns. They coincide essentially with the Christian Democrat plans.

Assumes the responsibility which belongs to it in the national revolutionary process within an independent, dynamic, and loyal unity, as it belongs to a force which constitutes, without doubt, the great hope of the Colombian people.

Invites the different popular groups to exercise a powerful social pressure for a plebiscite which might serve to reflect the will of the people as regards the large institutional changes demanded for justice.

Alvaro Rivera, President of the Council[2]

Another statement said:

The Social Christian Democratic Party of Manizales, considering:

1. That the socio-economic theses expressed by Father Camilo Torres have wakened an unusual reaction of alarm within the oligarchy represented in the companies, the press, and the high ecclesiastical hierarchy.

2. That these theses are a faithful interpretation of the Christian thought expressed in the Encyclicals.

3. That the myth of Communism has stopped being an effective weapon of the oligarchy for combating those nonconformists who are simply claiming justice.

4. That the vindication of the people demands the integration of all groups and all progressive and revolutionary persons in only one front, declares:

1. That the Social Christian Democratic party of Manizales identifies itself with the socio-economic Platform of this illustrious priest; and at the same time that it offers its spiritual and material endorsement, it condemns the ill-intentioned reaction of those who retain power and exploit the Colombian people in an inhuman and anti-Christian way.

2. That the attitude of certain people who call themselves Christians

and deliberately refuse to recognize everything from the works of mercy to the pontifical documents is irresponsible.

3. That the people no longer fear the oligarchy nor the epithet of Communist, and they have decided to fight for their rights, call them what you wish.

4. Lastly, the Christian Social Democratic Party of Manizales feels itself obliged to issue a call to all the peasant worker organizations and to all conscientious men, so that, forgettting differences, we might constitute one front in the fight for a system which guarantees the dignity of the human person and the social, economic, cultural, and political progress of the country.[3]

A leader of this party had already written: "The Platform for action presented by Father Camilo Torres can be rejected or not, in accord with its viability and utility, but it is very difficult to classify it as irreconcilable with Catholic Social Doctrine; because, among other things, this doctrine, in its technical application, is in perpetual development, according to what circumstances might require. As, for example, if in one era the right of private property obviously extended to all the social classes was defensible, presently the practical impossibility of applying this system, at least in so far as it refers to the means of production and large investments, can bring us to defend a type of collective private property perfectly compatible with human dignity. In the same way, social security can serve to guarantee the liberty of the man and his family.

"On the other hand, it is an invitation to the laity to assume fully the responsibility which directly relates to us in these temporal matters, exonerating the priests of that responsibility.

"The leading classes of the Colombian economy would tolerate neither Lombardi nor Lebret."[4]

The Youth set down their position in the following document:

As for the Christians, there were some who openly supported Father Camilo Torres and had decided to accompany him to the end. These Christians came from different social strata, but when they became deeply involved in the battle they noticed more and more the Marxist influence in the strategy, the politics, and even in some of the ideological planning of the movement which Father Camilo Torres directed. When they saw that they were helpless to prevent the take-over by organized Marxist forces, they were struck little by little with the sense that they were frustrated once more in seriously beginning the fight for the liberation of our country.

Disgracefully, the desertion of many of these Christians and the lack of participation of the majority, was due fundamentally to the absence of a fighting spirit, to the non-existence of a global vision, to the formation of an escapist Christianity, to flight from sacrifice and from the demands of a commitment which is too great for them.

How much responsibility can they have, since the sincerity, honesty, and courage of Father Camilo Torres have been laughed at and betrayed and his person used by the Communist Party and Marxist pro-China forces? How much responsibility can all these Christians have, who in a given moment supported him without understanding the magnitude of the responsibility and the effort which was demanded of them? We qualify and denounce as mediocre the activity of the Christian Social Democratic Party, since if it possesses a revolutionary ideology with national political ambitions, it has the obligation of breaking the circle which the Soviet Communist Party and the other Marxist forces have placed around Father Camilo Torres.

As for the Social Christian Student Movement, it supported Father Camilo Torres as the leader of the Colombian Revolution until the moment he resolved within his revolutionary strategy to opt for armed guerilla warfare to seize power. For we believe that the guerilla warfare, in the actual context of the international and specifically Latin American situation is not a revolutionary solution. On this occasion we must show that, contrary to the opinion of the students and of the country in general, our movement did not withdraw its support from Father Camilo Torres on the occasion of the Congress of Worker-Student-Peasant Solidarity, celebrated in Medellín last September, as many have made him believe, even though our relations became worse owing to a certain ideological confusion—but not to a doctrinal confusion, either on his part or ours.[5]

A demonstration of what disorder was produced when Camilo was accused of playing games with Communism is the following statement:

The Executive Committee of the Regional Christian Social Democratic Party of the Department of Santander,

1. In face of the partiality of Camilo Torres in favor of the Marxists in the Worker-Student-Peasant Congress of Medellín, in not recognizing Heliodoro Agudelo Rivera, the Christian leader of CLASC, to whom his United Front owed more and with whom he should be identified as a Christian, which it is said that he is:

2. In face of the Marxist-Leninist orientation of his weekly, badly named *Frente Unido,* and the ignoring of Christian Social Democracy in all the acts realized in the name of this Front;

Thinking, moreover, that we have more advanced Platforms than the Platform of Unity of Action, Declares:

1. That it withdraw from Camilo Torres' movement and, since we are Christians, we cannot play games with Marxism, whose electoral strength we don't know.

2. That it denounces to the people of Santander and Colombia how they are being tricked by a movement directed by such Marxist-Leninists as Julio César Cortés and Jaime Arenas but which is made to appear Christian through using Camilo Torres.

3. That it affirms that the Christian Social Democratic Party of Colombia does not need anyone's permission to be revolutionary, and that the revolution in freedom which we preach, with the same ardor as always, is the only salvation for Colombia, to free it from every type of imperialism which wants to exploit it through its capitalist or Communist lackeys.

4. That it forbids Christian Social Democrats of Santander to take part in the committees of the United Front, either in their own name or in the name of the party and orders them to inform the citizenry in general that Christian Social Democrats continue to form one popular force, which is capable of winning the revolution in liberty which we preach.[6]

The falling-out between Camilo and the Christian Democrats, it seems according to the foregoing document, came about on the occasion of the Worker-Student "Encounter" (Sept. 17 to 19, 1965); it came up in the discussion of these four points: armed warfare; position regarding Cuba; pronouncement against imperialism, and electoral abstention.

The thinking of Camilo regarding the Cuban fact did not admit of any ambiguities: "The United Front, as a factor for cohesion does not care to sow discord through its international politics. Its position against colonialism and neo-colonialism comes from its anxiety that Colombia possess a genuine economic, political, diplomatic, and cultural sovereignty. It defends every movement which, in its own way, operates in this sense, throughout Latin America and the Third World. Even though it may not be identified with it, it considers as positive any objective activity against all politics of expansion and of war. Hence, we have manifested, without theoretical commitment in other aspects our sympathy for Frei in Chile. We have also shown support for Goulart in Brazil, and we considered certain acts of the Mexican government worthy of applause.

"Equally, as regards the Cuban revolution we believe that any attempt against its self-determination is a problem not only for the country of Martí, but one that is of interest to all of Latin America. We do not agree with those who give it no value. As a complex phenomenon, Cuba is today the first experiment of Socialism in the Western Hemisphere and was the symptom of the despair of the Indian, Negro, and Mestizo masses of our poor and underdeveloped continent. We also strongly repudiate the North American intervention in the Dominican Republic.

"The case of Egypt is important as a nationalist example, even when all of the aspects of its foreign policy cannot be equally evaluated. The conduct followed by the Socialists as regards the developing countries is not only positive but decisive. It is impossible in today's world to turn your back on facts such as this.

"Our neutralism, moreover, insists on friendship with all nations and it is active in its solidarity with the Third World and its fight for de-colonization."[7]

The delegates of the Christian Democratic Party rejected some of the four points proposed by Camilo and accused several of his friends of having formulated openly Communistic programs, by which the spirit of the United Front was broken and directions coming from one group were imposed. Camilo, by supporting his companions, lost the support of the worker sector of CLASC. It was a tactical mistake. He fell into that intransigence of the reactionaries of the Left. They all persisted in quarreling, but they failed to win a battle.

According to Camilo, two negative elements were evident in the "Encounter": 1. insistence on fixed positions in an attempt to convince others and the use of reasons which are divisive; 2. irrational reactions to opinions which they could object to or reject by reasonable means.[8]

Camilo sought a revolution purified of every oligarchical or imperialistic taste. He did not want to continue operating with a foundation in the middle-class criterion of the liberty-pretext which consists in the sophistry of using liberty to exploit the people, to oppress them economically, to enrich the few, to justify the attitude of the few and the poverty of the many who get poorer each day while the others get richer. The Colombian bishops themselves had declared on July 6, 1965: "The misery of the small farms and the slums, the contrast between the wasteful spending of the few and the necessities of the many, the inertia of so many as regards the urgency of developing the economy of the country, are an offense to the human conscience and the principles of the Gospel."[9]

The head of the Revolutionary Liberal Movement (MRL), Doctor Alfonso López Michelsen, once said to Camilo: "We agree with you. We have no difficulty in signing the Platform, even though there are some observations we could make about it." That is, there was no break at that moment, but everything awaited the debate of March 1966 regarding the parliamentary elections. López counted, above all else, on the electoral mechanics. Camilo proposed abstention, but the MRL would go to the polls. As a group, there is no official document showing that they had been deeply committed to Camilo's movement.

The FUAR, the National Revolutionary Vanguard, and the Marxist-Leninist Party (pro-China) supported Camilo in the beginning, but they withdrew from the United Front after the "encounter at Medellín" and ended by debating each other endlessly.

The MOEC (Worker-Student-Peasant Movement) on the 7th of January "emerges as the result of an historical necessity of the Colombian people and as a popular answer to the opportunism of the revisionist of the poorly named Communist Party of Colombia."[10] We can clearly see in this the inter-group antagonism which characterizes, among other things, this sector, which also faced serious internal crises. In criticizing some negative experiences in the campaign of the United Front under the direction of Camilo, they emphasize that "an authentic United Front must be supported in the militant alliance of the workers, both poor and middle-class. It is not enough to interest some leaders of the opposition from the Left, or simply to agitate the masses, without making that agitation concrete through a respectable organic apparatus. Camilo Torres had the idea of the United Front, he agitated the crowds of the dispossessed, but he did no more than barely outline the necessity of organizing them. A United Front cannot be constructed with nebulous alliances between discredited chiefs of little factions with revolutionary aspirations, nor through the merely emotional agitation of the masses, nor by using the workers and poor peasants as the central attraction for the other sectors because of their seriousness and organic and numerical importance. To conciliate unions of leaders and not seriously organize the alliance of exploited classes—which is what the United Front is doing—will only contribute to stimulating the desire for a better life and produce a parallel to many of the present opportunistic and unscrupulous leaders of the factions of the Left.

"It was demonstrated that there was an absence of a Leninist organization of the vanguard which would serve as the channel for uniting the masses who would make up the United Front. Various groups furiously disputed the direction of the United Front by means of subtle strategies, a direction which was not very good, in part because of an excess of liberalism stimulated by Father Torres, who was determined that the union would be more generous than prudent in that it should not discriminate against anyone. The result was the interference of the revisionists and every kind of opportunists and even such elements as those of the National Vanguard, clearly known as agents of the enemy."[11]

The United Front slowly disbanded, owing to the increasingly radical attitudes of Camilo and his contact with the Marxists, to group suspicions and temporary political agreements. Camilo thought that it was a phenomenon of purification, of simple consolidation, and he had the illusion that the "non-aligned" were the supreme authentic and definitive force.

He started out from two premises: The first was that the people had decided to become unified and organized. This was an optimistic evaluation, because even if the people might manifest such a need, full awareness of the means of bringing it about was lacking. Moreover, they lacked the means of communication with the masses to channel and precipitate the proposed change.

When Camilo saw that it was necessary to consider the time factor in order to prepare adequate staffs who would work at every level, and especially at the level of the peasant, with revolutionary programs, he said, "Yes, it is necessary but we are running out of time." He held, moreover, that the people in the cities, heartened by the theses of a revolutionary priest, would create a climate of insurgency in the peasantry, based on the recognized need for justice and for a change. This did not in fact occur.

The second premise was this: "The people have the irrevocable determination to seize power." This presupposed a polarization of forces, an historical crossroads determined by absolutely intolerable circumstances and a conviction which was generally shared. Camilo finds the masses in the cities and towns. Was he at home in such an encounter? Wasn't he the brilliant professor? Perhaps he suffered from alienation, from a confusion with regard to the real desires which made him believe in a groundswell shaking Colombia. The crowd does not deliberate; it is emotional; when the reason for its coming together disappears, it breaks down without any scruple on the part of the indivdual.

Hope in the non-aligned sector obsessed him. Were the 70% of the Colombians who did not go to the polls for the election of Guillermo León Valencia in 1962 abstentionists in opposition to the National Front? Camilo thought that, in general, they did it as a protest, and that, by the same token, there were people with revolutionary sympathies who did not subscribe to political groups. Those were the "non-aligned," and he concluded: "The principal activity of the United Front must be the organization of the non-aligned. With the organization of this sector we will have taken one of the most important steps forward in the revolutionary movement towards the conquest of power. When this is obtained, there will have appeared in Colombia the great movement of the masses which is indispensable for realizing the revolutionary change frustrated by the assassination of Gaitán, by the political violence, and by the dialectically real impotence of the other political movements. When this fact appears and is realized, the condition and the historical base which have made possible, and even developed, the long domination of the oligarchy over the Colombian people will have been suppressed."[12]

"Organization from below upward, with their own leaders and with an iron authority, but one stripped of bossism. It is necessary for the non-aligned to realize the gravity of the moment and their historical responsibility. Each minute we lose is a minute of advantage we are giving to the oligarchy."[13]

Camilo believed and totally trusted in the non-aligned, in their noncomformity, in their capacity for reaction, in their number, in their possibilities. He thought that they were a growing force disenchanted with the rigid and stultifying system, which should be liberated as the first and principal factor of change. He thought they were uncontaminated by political sordidness. They were the pure, those whose support could not be bought. He did not advert to their lack of a sense of politics, their rigid petty-bourgeois conformity, their aversion to commitment, their reluctance to act, their stubborn determination to stay in the background, not to protest, their complacent self-satisfaction. They were a frigid, rocky lump, and Camilo shattered himself against it without ever becoming aware of their quality.

He presumed that the electoral abstentionists were aligned in his ranks. He dreamed that their abstention was a mute protest, a sign of nonconformity with the ruling oligarchy. Trying to get them to take a step forward in order to initiate the historical gesture consumed too much energy. Only a few recruits came forward. He spoke with them, promoted "encounters," round tables, conferences. He explained with ardent fervor the idea which was guiding him. At the end of the dialogue, these famous "non-aligned" would sneak away into the shadows of their cowardly irresolution.

In that moment I was convinced that Camilo was a solitary figure within the grandeur of his dreams. Actually, in the "Message to the Non-Aligned," he predicted his destiny: "We are competing with the oligarchy. It is possible that it may assassinate me before I have succeeded in creating a solid organization among the non-aligned. I think it would be very stupid for them to put me in jail or to wage war with me solely by words. Therefore, I believe that I will be assassinated. The important thing is that the Colombian people have precise assignments if this happens." And it did happen!

If the present state of the Left and the progressive Colombian groups is analyzed, now that Camilo is dead, it seems possible that their anarchy may be opening the way to fascist groups which are daily becoming more prominent and more violent in their actions. The purity of Camilo's intentions survives him, and the influence of his sacrifice. But no leadership has been established on an objective basis for any corporate action.

Chapter 12

Camilo and Communism

Camilo's relations with Communism and its adherents forms one of the most complex and controverted aspects of his career. To understand it we must analyze the various reasons why Marxist ideas exercise such an influence in today's world.

Following the analysis of Jorge M. Cottier, O.P.,[1] we can account for the widespread resonance of these ideas by the fact that in many ways they express the authentic aspirations of our time.

In the first place, Communism proclaims that our epoch marks the historical moment of the lower classes. The people are not only a new people, but an authentic protagonist of history who for a long time had been burdened and scoffed at. Treated in the past as passive historical matter, which paid with its silent sacrifice for the excesses of the rich, the people finally find their meaning in history. Today they have taken over their own interests and dignity. This means that in the future, control of their destiny will be in their own hands.

In these modern times man fully realizes the power of his own reason when he applies it to a systematic study of the world and of the individual as a social being. In this way reason becomes a means for conquest. The expression "scientific socialism" owes its prestige to the fact that it puts into action the role of sovereign reason, as the mistress of destiny and the creator of happiness. We must add that the principal object of the activity of reason is society—i.e. man himself, because in Marxism man is essentially social and derives all his meaning from his relations with the community.

The word *plan* in Marxism has a great attraction. This is due to the fact that it is the entrance into action of "consultative reason." At the same time both myth and idea, the *plan* is opposed to an irrational society in which the exploitation of man by man dominates.

The Marxist vision also takes in the past. This represents the alienation, the privation, of man, while the Communist action is oriented towards the "reappropriation," the finding again, the recovery, the return of man who was lost to himself. The implacable reproach of the past and the status quo increases the ardor of the battle. Christianity and "Christian Civilization" (no distinction is made between them) constitute an immediate blank. Christianity has not only hindered, but it has also sidetracked humanity towards illusory solutions: this is one of the meanings of the "alienation."

As a consequence of all this, the rupture between generations is radical. This, undoubtedly, also has an undeniable force of attraction. The young are the new heirs, and they find no valid reasons for taking charge of a legacy which has continued without aims. The new generations are constantly tempted to liquidate the past in the name of the "revolution." To apply this to the underdeveloped Catholic regions, what is in evidence is one sociological aspect of Catholicism, by which it is inextricably confused with a particular state condemned to disappear: feudal mentality, alliance with the great landowners, conservative spirit, absence of any effort for fighting against ignorance and misery, lack of human culture in the clergy, parasitic character of some inactive religious communities, whose "mendicant" status is anachronistic, etc.

Another factor of the attraction of Marxism is its revolutionary passion. It could be defined as an awakening of noble and generous sentiments. Behind this awakening there is a radical pessimism regarding the motives of human action, in so far as this is exercised within the structures of the present society. If man is master of the structures, he has previously been determined by them. He owes them his goodness or his evil in such a way that pessimism regarding the power of the individual person is matched by an almost unlimited confidence in the value of institutions.

Within this model Christians are reproached for being lukewarm, with feeble wills and useless scruples. Their intention to help the poor is immediately held back by the desire to respect established privileges and to attract the support of the powerful. The question of property proves it. It is certain that in the doctrine of the Church, property is conceived as the economic prerogative of the person and of the exercise of his responsibility. But, has there rightfully been a reaction against the uses, and even falsifications, which are made of this doctrine in order to keep the domination of the rich? Before what appears as a dishonest compromise, Communism presents itself as the movement which has the courage for radical solutions and which is the first to dare to confront the true problem; the rigor of this radicalism has, evidently, great repercussions.

I think that within this context, what has been called "Camilo's closeness to Communism" can be studied.

It surprised and amazed the Colombian Communists to see a priest rise up whose advanced theses broke the traditional roles, whose priestly voice defiantly demanded with urgency a change of structures, one who preached "power for the people" and predicted a revolution and held that it would be bloody if the ruling structures stubbornly held on to power when the hour arrived and sheltered themselves behind a powerful and highly competent military apparatus.

Within the designs of the economic, social, cultural, and political order, touching on a practical dimension—never in the field of philosophical ideas—Camilo agreed with the Communists on the necessity of stimulating the masses—i.e., a movement with roots in the people, by the people, with the people and for the people was what he demanded. This was the highest moment in his political career.

The Marxists realize that Camilo worked with undeniable honesty. From seeing him at first as a clumsy revolutionary, they came to recognise him as a phenomenon without precedent in the historical politics of the country, because of his priestly character, his ability, and his enormous power for bringing together the forces of the people. They applauded his attitude and supported his program without, naturally, sharing all his points of view.[2]

"Father Camilo Torres," writes Gilberto Vieira, "entered the revolutionary battle with complete sincerity and unlimited self-denial."[3]

The image which has been created for Communism in Colombia is that of something diabolical. In an atmosphere such as ours, the contact of Camilo with Communism was converted into a pretext for abandoning him.

I enumerate the "reasons" which were used at that moment: (1) The comrades employed Camilo to take a huge leap forward, using him craftily as long as necessary. They would get rid of him in their own time. (2) They would exploit him to obtain the cohesion of the proletarian masses which they had been unable to accomplish after thirty-five years. (3) They would endeavor to show that the great pro-Camilo movements were made up mostly by members of the party or sympathizers. (4) Camilo was moved more and more by theses of Communist inspiration. The surrender of Camilo to Communism was inevitable. (5) Therefore, the Communist did not abandon him. They had detached elements, with special assignments, to inform the party on each step of Camilo, where he went, with whom he spoke, where he stayed, what activity he displayed. (6) This circle often prevented Camilo's friends from having easy access to him, and he entered the tactical planning of the moment. (7) The comrades attempted to take over the periodical *Frente Unido*. An internal fight was unleashed in it between the non-aligned and the Communists.

The application of these "criteria" gave free rein to a double game: The base from which Camilo operated was the union of the separatist progressive groups, with a goal and a common revolutionary action, for the benefit of the people. Nevertheless, they brought pressure to convince him that he had the right to attract all the groups except the Communists and could work with everyone except the comrades.

Camilo did not submit to such directions and he continued to follow the norm as outlined. How is his conduct explained?

Starting out from the teaching of John XXIII in *Mater et Magistra* and in *Pacem in Terris,* Camilo looks for dialogue with the Communists, gives a conference in the headquarters of that party, allows them to accompany him on his trips, to speak to the crowds because, according to him, they also had the right to express their theses; he establishes contact with the Communist trade leaders and makes it easy for writers in that movement to collaborate in the periodical *Frente Unido*.

But, he makes his position very clear regarding the Communists in the Message he directs to them:

> I believe it is necessary to make very clear for the Colombian people my relations with the Communist Party and their position within the United Front. I have said that I am a revolutionary as a Colombian, as a sociologist, as a Christian, and as a priest. I think that the Communist Party has authentic revolutionary elements, and for that reason, I cannot be an anti-Communist as a Colombian, as a sociologist, as a Christian, or as a priest.
>
> I am not an anti-Communist as a Colombian, because anti-Communism is oriented towards persecuting nonconformist patriots, Communists or not, the majority of whom are poor. I am not an anti-Communist as a sociologist, because in the Communist plans for fighting poverty, hunger, illiteracy, the lack of housing, the lack of services for the people, we find effective and scientific solutions.
>
> I am not an anti-Communist as a Christian because I believe that anti-Communism condemns everything the Communists defend; and, among those things they defend, there are both just and unjust things. In condemning them all together, we expose ourselves to condemn equally the just and the unjust, and this is anti-Christian. I am not anti-Communist as a priest, because even though the Communists themselves may not know it, you have many among them who are authentic Christians. If they are in good faith, they have sanctifying grace; and if they have sanctifying grace and love their neighbor, they will be saved. My role as a priest, even though it is not in the exercise of external

cult, is to see to it that men find God; and for that, the most effective way is to help men serve their neighbor in accord with their conscience.

I don't think I have proselytized my brothers the Communists, trying to get them to accept the dogma and practice the worship of the Church. I do try to get all men to work in accord with their conscience, to sincerely search for the truth and love their neighbor in an effective way.

The Communists must know very well that I will not enter their ranks, that I am not, nor will I be, a Communist, as a Colombian, as a sociologist, as a Christian, nor as a priest. Nevertheless, I am disposed to fight with them for common objectives: against the oligarchy and the domination of the United States, for the seizure of power by the people.

I don't want public opinion to identify me with the Communists; and for that reason, I have always wanted to appear not only in the company of the Communists but also with all the independent revolutionaries and all the other movements.

It is not important that the press persists in presenting me as a Communist. I prefer to follow my own conscience, to not give in to the pressure of the oligarchy. I prefer to follow the norms of the Pontiffs of the Church rather than the pontiffs of our own ruling class. John XIII authorized me to cooperate with the Communists in his encyclical *Pacem in Terris*. . . .

When the popular class seizes power, thanks to the collaboration of all the revolutionaries, our people will discuss their religious orientation.

The example of Poland shows us that it is possible to construct a socialism without destroying the essentials of Christianity. As the Polish priest said: "We Christians have the obligation to contribute to the construction of the socialist state always when we are permitted to adore God as we wish."[4]

"Camilo was never a Marxist, and when he said he wasn't a Marxist, he spoke the truth; but his Christian humanism brought him to an understanding that the Incarnation, carried to its ultimate consequences, demands harmony between humanity in so far as it belongs to the world of nature and the new humanity brought into being by Christ."[5]

"Camilo works for an honest opening. He doesn't wait for

orders, permissions, or consent, or soundings for advantage in order to launch the dialogue; simply, he dialogues. He passes from the Syllabus of Pius IX—the impossibility of communication—to John XXIII—a drawing near to man and to the world. He thinks, with Mario Gozzini, that just a few years ago the atmosphere in the Church was still counter-reform: a Church Fortress, at the service of men, certainly, but from the high battlement of its superior certitudes."[6]

Camilo makes two points: that the Church, today, does not reject dialogue and that Communism looks for dialogue. "not having any possibility of philosophical reconciliation between historical materialism and transcendental faith, it could appear that the Marxist and the religious man have nothing useful to say to one another and that, simply, each one can only try to convert the other to his own conception of the world.

"John XXIII has been a sign of division and not of unity, for those who proclaim themselves Christians but who live a life diametrically opposed to Christianity. He has been a stumbling block for those who have been accustomed to consider the priest as a petty policeman and the Pope (it has been said) as the chaplain of the Atlantic Pact. He has been the cause of continual scandal for the pharisees and the merchants of the temple. He has been the Pope loved by the people, the Pope with a heart, for those who live Christianity as a means for freeing themselves from self-interests and privileges. The scandalous Pontificate of John XXIII has permitted the ardent heat of this Christianity to break the conservative crust of a discipline which was supported but never accepted."[7]

Luciano Gruppi, a Communist, notes that the development by communism in Italy, as a definite principle, in theory as well as in practice, of the autonomy of the Italian Communist Party with respect to the international communist movement even in the sphere of the international solidarity of the worker movement, brings it about that on the plane of the political concept, the concept of democracy and of the socialist revolution, obstacles of principle are not in opposition to an undersanding and a collaboration between Communists and Catholics.[8] Alberto Cecchi, Ignacio de Logu, Salvatore Di Marco, and other leading Italian Communists think the same.

Advanced Catholics think that in order to make the dialogue easier, the Communists must strip themselves of a certain style and custom of treating every question in a political way, which makes it difficult for them to adopt the necessary openness for dialogue. Cecchi notes that the insistence on the part of the Marxists on defining religion as alienation (the famous opium of the people) raises in Christians and in all believers the resented suspicions of one who does not understand why he is made to feel relegated to a species of intellectual inferiority that, evidently, can be neither accepted nor admitted.[9]

This question would be reason enough for a tremendous dialogue: Can Communists and Christians respond to all the needs of man? A step which the Communists must take, and in many places are taking, is that of demonstrating that Communism is capable of modification and adjustment to the times. i.e. that it is capable of showing that it will not remain static and petrified.[10]

Among ourselves, Communism cannot pass over the religious fact. Christianity in itself is now valid, and has created values and cultural models. The refusal to dialogue with the Communists is an attitude which in other nations is being reevaluated and definitely overcome.

Whether it is wanted or not, it can be seen that slowly an accommodation between Marxists and Christians is being worked out, in order to fight more effectively, if we are honestly searching for the integral elevation of the immense proletarian mass. The same circumstances will determine the dialogue. The road is long, but that doesn't stop us from starting on it. Camilo established an historical precedent: he looked for understanding through ways distinct from hate and fanaticism. Thus he deeply wounds those who have attitudes of arrogant reaction.

Naturally, there still stands the prescription of John XXIII in the encyclical *Mater et Magistra:* "If, on some occasion, the ecclesiastical hierarchy directs or decrees something in this matter, it is evident that Catholics have the obligation to obey these orders."[11]

The decision of Camilo to enter dialogue with the Communists not only gave an opportunity to his enemies to call him "comrade" but also gave the press a pretext for claiming that he had departed from the initial propositions of the United Front, to become a wolf in sheep's clothing and a traitor to the Church. He had to tolerate all the insults which they could level at his unquestionable good faith with the integrity of a "Christian in service."

It finally came to the systematic and open obstruction of his free expression of his thoughts. When he was going to publish *Frente Unido,* a request was made (without mentioning Camilo's name) to the publisher, El Siglo, to print forty thousand copies. The answer was affirmative. But, as soon as they discovered that it was a question of Camilo's weekly paper, they answered: "Here we can print any kind of periodical except Camilo Torres' paper. We would not even dream of it." And at the same time they had been publishing *Voz de la Democracia,* the organ of the Colombian Communist party, weekly for almost a year.

The Communists in their fight place their emphasis against the North American imperialists. Camilo agrees with them in that he did not want the Cuban to be sugar; the Colombian, coffee; the Bolivian, tin; the Venezuelan, petroleum; the Chilean, copper; the Peruvian, guano; the Brazilian, iron; the Argentinian, leather; the Paraguayan and Uruguayan, wool and tea—for the colossus of the North.

Camilo demanded that the North American should see the inhabitants of Indo-America as human beings, as men. Men who deal with men. He considered this as a necessary point for departure.

But, clearly, the high priests' surrender proclaimed to the four winds that Camilo was a Communist. But didn't *He* sit at the table with publicans and sinners?

Chapter 13

Camilo and the University World

Camilo believed in the students and trusted them. His university activity aroused in them an unlimited capacity for giving without which it is impossible to find an adequate explanation for their enthusiastic mistakes.

He was at the side of the students during the difficult days as a companion in their strikes and their problems—not to stir them up or confuse them but to search for logical and reasonable solutions. When everyone abandoned them during their sit-down strike on the university grounds, he brought them food and other necessities from his own home. It can never be said that he did it for opportunistic, demagogic reasons, or in order to secure support or sympathy; much less out of exhibitionism. He worked in this way in accordance with a principle of human solidarity born of a profound conviction. He was honest, guileless, and disconcertingly sincere.

At the height of the student strike (June, 1962) which broke out in the National University as a protest against the suspension of ten students, the press commented: "Father Camilo Torres showed that he regarded the directives as arbitrary means adopted by the Academic Senate and the Rector for imposing sanctions on those elements who disturbed the normal progress of the classes. In a sermon which he gave last Sunday in the chapel of the University City, Father Torres expressed his dissatisfaction at the treatment given the students who belonged to the Communist Youth; he thinks that 'he who fights for a cause and dies for that cause—even if he is anti-Catholic—must be received in the bosom of the Church.' "[1]

This statement presented the opportunity to Camilo to issue this rejoinder: "Permit me to ask you to include in the next edition of *El Tiempo* on the same page and with the same wide publicity with which the news of my expulsion from the university was published, the following correction: I have never been opposed to punitive measures against illegal acts. The measures taken to punish the university students have not seemed to me to be completely arbitrary. I only asked, in company with the other professors and through regular channels, that the sanctions should be considered and presented in a helpful way and accompanied by objective proofs in order to avoid ideological persecutions, and also to avoid establishing the precedent of punishing only one political sector without establishing proof of their disciplinary infractions.

"On Sunday, June 17th, I did not give a sermon on the strike, nor did I talk about Communists. I spoke on the Holy Trinity, the faith, and evangelical poverty. I would like to know what kind of treatment has been given to the young Communists according to *El Tiempo*. I think the directives of the University have tried to exclude, at least in the formulation of the resolutions, every political consideration from the sanctions."[2]

The newspapers had now published the text of the letter of the Cardinal to Camilo.

"Dear Father Torres Restrepo: In view of these recent events which have taken place in the National University, I have decided that you should definitely withdraw from all activity at the University both as a professor and as a member of any advisory board. May God be with you."[3]

Camilo published the following statement in *El Catolicismo:*

In these last few days I received an order from my archbishop to withdraw from the National University. I was chaplain there, although just nominally. Two of my brothers in the priesthood exercise those functions full time. I also gave one class in the Department of Sociology and I was a member of the Advisory Board. By the will of my prelate, since February of this year, I have been exercising the functions of Dean of the Institute of Social Administration, which belongs to the School of Public Administration, an official autonomous entity, directed by Doctor Guillermo Nannetti. This is a full-time position and my relations with the university were accidental enough. I have renounced these. My prelate, who has the responsibility for the total apostolate, thought that I should withdraw. He would have been able to demand of me that I modify my criticisms and my actions. Nevertheless, he did not do it, because he knew I was acting in good faith. He did not want to violate my conscience, and I am grateful to him for that. Therefore, when he asked me to withdraw, for reasons which it is not my responsibility to judge, he did it according to his own criteria regarding the university problem. He explicitly informed me that he did not want the Church to take sides with me by agreeing that I judged correctly, because that could lead to misunderstandings. Nevertheless, I had already taken a position, and if the Cardinal had supported me, he would have had to drop the attitude which he had decided to adopt.

As regards my withdrawal, I have been permitted to say what I think about the University. Notwithstanding this, it would be very disagreeable for me if my actions were taken as a standard for controversy. I have wanted to adopt a priestly attitude. I have run the risk of appearing to be in disagreement with my prelate. The greatest service which could be done me now would be that of respecting my attitude of obedience, which I chose in deciding to become a priest, and which I would not accept if it were not an integral part of what I consider to be my mission in the world.[4]

As for the plea that "his attitude should be respected," one public organ commented: "Father Camilo Torres is trying to convert the students of the Left into primitive Christians, into soldiers of the New Church and into priest workers. Fraternization with progressive priests is dangerous for the health of both soul and body; and the sensitiveness of many revolutionary students can lead them to be carried away, unconsciously, by the precepts which this Pastor of the new Church sets down. He continues to be the same curate as always, dominated by all the ecclesiastical machinery and at the service of the great landowners, but disguised now as socialist. We must be very fearful of priests with Leftist leanings.

"There are two classical methods for combating revolutionary forces: one is to persecute, to imprison, to isolate through hunger or eliminate by a bullet the more competent opponents. This is the politics of direct persecution, of terror. The other procedure consists in presenting oneself as a nonconformist with the system: it involves at once attacking 'exploiting and decadent capitalism'—as Bishop Botero Salazar of Medellín calls it'—and re-routing the violent fodces of revolution in the direction of educating consciences. The objective is that the capitalists should place their resources—as the bishop puts it—at the service of the poor, and through the divine illumination of their consciences, stop being rich capitalists. This is the politics of the revolutionary conversion of the oligarchy by means of education and divine grace. Anyone who knows the ABC's of the science of society or of Marxism understands that it is not the conscience of itself which determines the conditions of life of a social class, because these material conditions of existence precisely determine both the principles of the oligarchy and the validity of their actions. Their conscience, therefore, cannot be transformed unless the material foundations are first changed. The transformation of their life in the capitalistic class can only be obtained with the abolition of the capitalist system of production. You don't arrive at this point except through a popular revolution. Therefore, let the progressive priests with their pseudo-sciences of society not come to us to tell us that they, with their evangelical teaching, are going to convert the capitalists into combatants of the socialist revolution."[5]

Camilo saw in the students a force which could be directed towards effecting social change, since in every underdeveloped country they offer two qualities which it would be difficult to find together in other groups of society: a relatively high cultural level and a certain liberty, a certain open boldness in the face of the ruling structures and the ruling minority. It is for that reason that the university has played a political role in underdeveloped countries, and especially in Latin America. The cultural level and lack of inhibitions produce states of nonconformity and rebellion in a society whose structures require a fundamental change.[6]

Secure in this postulate, Camilo believed that the university climate would be necessarily propitious. Therefore, he was supported by the students and, convinced of their backing, he launched himself into the battle, despite the fact that certain radical groups regarded him at times with misgivings. They believed him to be the disguised emissary of the oligarchy, and they justified this ridiculous interpretation by reading between the lines of the weekly *Frente Unido*. Others, interpreting the lenient and cautious attitude of the Metropolitan Curia, took him for a spy of clericalism, when "his attitudes at the side of the extremist students—he was involved in each one of their agitations and uprisings—made him appear to the Archbishop as a leader of subversion, instead of a curate devoted to adolescent and troubled souls—the kind of curate they wanted to have in the Church."[7]

At this moment a mutual failing mainfests itself which must be discussed: On the part of Camilo, a certain confident and happy optimism which, in its benevolence, ruled out the cold analysis of the human element, because he judged everyone indiscriminately as good, honest, firm, and sincere with him. On the side of the university students, the doubt, the reserve, the questioning, the delay in accepting Camilo as the leader of great possibilities.

To look at things from another angle, Camilo focused on the university as a structure which had continued to turn its back on the human-social problems of Colombia.

Perhaps the interrogator of Hernández tortured him before he wrote:

La vejez de los pueblos
El corazón sin dueño

El amor sin objecto . . .
Y la juventud?
En el ataud.[8]

Since our university is a faithful or nearby faithful mirror of the country, it appears as a reflection of the predominant political, religious, social, civil, cultural, and economic structures.

Camilo saw it patterned after operative models but without the aid of the social sciences and, therefore, designed for producing that type of individualistic professional who, in the end, serves the interests of the oligarchy, owing to its failure to enter into direct contact with the human elements in the lower strata of the community.

This phenomenon seems to arise from a failure of understanding on the part of almost all our intellectuals. They are cold academicians with no human warmth in their technology. The professional, frozen in such a mold, conceives of man as an anonymous being, a species of unknown qualities who will always follow him. He leaves the university without any deep understanding of the many facets of our problems.

With the academic degree every professional acquires social status. On leaving the university he is equipped with a conformist mentality which permits him to ascend in the social scale; and if he doesn't reach the top, it at least prevents him from sinking. Some think that our university has not succeeded in obtaining the desirable universality and cultural integration because the exclusive groups who control it require a definite kind of professional to administer it in accord with their interests, plans, and conditions. A university thus interfered with can only produce professionals with a strictly limited cultural outlook.

In Camilo's view, the revolutionary is obligated to perfect himself as a technologist or a scientist, with a commitment to carry on his profession even to the ultimate consequences. In following this principle, he inevitably stumbles onto the inhuman conditions in which the people are struggling.

It is the contrast between the inhuman conditions and the consequences of revolution which keeps alive the conviction of commitment to the community in which he has received a degree. This same thing makes him rebel and fits him in an anticonformist mold. In the measure to which contact with what is human grows in him he becomes a better revolutionary, unless his compliance with the status quo converts him into an obstinate conformist.

As Camilo wrote in his message to university students, agitation is important, but its real effect is lost if the organization ends at that point. One of the main reasons that the students' contribution to the revolution is short-lived is their lack of personal and family commitment. Their nonconformity tends to be of emotional origin or purely intellectual. And it terminates with the end of the youth's university career, when he is converted from a rebel into a professional bourgeois, exchanging his integrity for the rewards of the system.[9]

In the political field, the youth of the Colombian university are frequently presented as insincere, as groups characterized by deep antagonisms and suspicions. It is rather as if an artificial structure of nonconformity had been superimposed which is rendered ineffectual through extremism and is incapable of gaining equilibrium owing to the predominance of the emotional over the rational. It is undeniable that students are capable of heroic and generous sacrifice—in many cases of no use because of the absence of a serious and disciplined organization. It seems that every attempt at cohesion is torpedoed by sectarianism or a virulent extreme Left. Extremist positions, when they are irrational, lead to an individual and collective fanaticism from which there emerges with marvelous facility a complete zealous caravan of informers, talebearers, "police," accusers, opportunists, fifth columnists, who make the fighting between groups more inflamed and the continuance in closed circles more prolonged.

Before a crowd of his followers and curious bystanders, Camilo said on the campus of the National University when he returned from Lima: "The revolution is not made by throwing stones at the police or burning a car." And he added: "It is necessary that the revolutionary conviction of the student bring him to a real commitment, even to the ultimate consequences. Poverty and persecution need not be sought. But, in the present system, they are the logical results of a fight without quarter against the thriving structures. In the present system, they are the signs of an authentic revolutionary life."[10]

Camilo spoke with complete frankness of the honesty which an authentic revolutionary proposal presupposes. Perhaps he remembered the words of Fidel Castro when he gave his defense of his position on October 16, 1953: "The first condition of sincerity and good faith in a proposal is to do precisely what no one else does—to speak with complete clarity and without fear. The demagogues and the professional politicians want to perform the miracle of doing well in everything and with everyone, necessarily tricking everyone in everything. The revolutionaries must courageously express their ideas, define their principles and manifest their intentions so that no one is tricked, neither friends nor enemies."[11]

A new train of events which are having negative effects on the university students is the division between the followers of Peking and Moscow. Those of the Mao line are open advocates of armed battle and violence as authentic forms of the revolution. In the opinion of some observers, they lack—sincere though they might be—a realistic vision of Colombia, of our situation and our historical position. They reject what they call "the passivity of the Colombian Communist Party" and take for themselves extremely radical positions. They accuse the followers of Moscow of remaining bound to the traditional patterns of the party, of bad faith, or of an incapacity for revolution, and they think that today it is impossible to organize both the guerillas and the revolution among us.

In their turn, the followers of Moscow accuse the pro-China group of being improvising adventurers, offering as proof the fact that they have not succeeded in organizing a guerilla front, even though they admit to having received considerable financial support. This has enabled them to travel all over the world, cleverly exploiting their patrons.

One day I heard this claim from a young ex-militant Communist: "The party is to blame for the downfall of the armed groups."

"Why?" I asked him.

"Because our comrades are too sectarian. They are static, casuists, dogmatists, very defensive, too mechanical. They are convinced that there is no formula except theirs. The Party draws the line, and the one who doesn't follow it is branded as suspect and he is shut out by any means possible."

"Any other reason?"

"Because they hold key positions among the peasants and workers and don't permit the activity of other groups. They don't want to lose control over anything."

"Anything else?"

"They move in a very limited intellectual circle. Their Bible is *Voz Proletaria.*"

In the press and in public statements it has been said that there is a Communist penetration in some universities which works through clandestine activities or in openly belligerent groups. What do the youth groups think of the Communist Party? What do they say? That there are elements long entrenched in the leading groups which are attached to an internal bureaucracy and uninterested in new values. Clearly, they exclude some very excellent people. They add that the Party has expelled valuable people and withdrawn from intellectuals of undeniable merit. Distrust of the Party has, it seems, roots other than in the simple generational gap.

In estimating every extremist position we should recall the thought of Camilo when he speaks of revolutionary conduct as the people's testimony, commitment, and objective. The people are capable of collective action, and herein lies the strength of the masses. But professional promotion by intelligent men is necessary if the collective dynamic is not to degenerate into anarchy or frustration. The people will always be the guard and the judge of their leaders. They are the guarantors of the authenticity of a revolution and of its constructive application.

For that reason it is essential that all the aspects of our situation be studied, situating Colombia in the context of its social, cultural, historical, economic, geographic, and ethnic universe. The university student is limited by his lack of a precise vision of the realities in our country. Even more, he is not a part of any collective commitment, and this tends to create in him the image of a nation which is unreal and grievously misinterpreted.

Camilo was quite adept at producing among students a really "transforming" mentality, able to eradicate ideas which are firmly established but which lack sufficient dynamism to accelerate effective change. On repeated occasions he analyzed the nature of student nonconformity. He studied its character and pointed out the source in which it must be nourished in order to be persevering and positive. "I know," he said, "that unfortunately this nonconformity is at times too sentimental or produced by frustration and is seldom a rational nonconformity. Therefore, it is important that during the period of studies, the nonconformity become more and more rational, based on research, on science adapted to reality, on immediate contact with the Colombian people and the Colombian reality.

"Despite the fact that in some circumstances we do have reasonable nonconformists and nonconformists in the scientific and technological sphere, we see nonconformity beginning to decay during the last years at the university, when the prospect of being inserted into the social structure enters the student's mental horizon. Then the various needs appear: the need of a patron to open up the way for his protégé in the professional market; of a good recommendation, a good friendship, a bourgeois reputation. We often observe, then, that nonconformity ends with the diploma. This is because neither a true commitment nor an authentically revolutionary mentality has existed in the student body.

"I realize that, in general, the students react against the bourgeois class. But that reaction is neither scientific nor revolutionary, but only formal, external, superficial. The spirit of reaction against the bourgeois class leads them to reject its symbols of prestige: they read different works from those which the bourgeoisie read; they dress differently; they even stop cutting their hair and bathing so as not to look like the bourgeoisie in any respect. I don't think that those things are evil in themselves or prejudicial or opposed to the revolution, but what is serious is that so often the nonconformist who has dressed like the proletariat arrives at the end of his studies harboring in his mind and imagination the ideal of being a professional bourgeois with a magnificent apartment and automobile, and with a tremendous interest in marrying well. Being well-married means finding a woman who has a sufficient income. As all this requires money, an adequate salary is needed, and it is then that he opts for the solution of selling out to the oligarchy, since the larger monetary rewards depend, in general, on the oligarchy. The desire for the revolution terminates there.

"In order to be a revolutionary, one must be ready to suffer hunger and imprisonment, to descend from one's own social status, to live with the workers and, if it is necessary, to take long trips and live poorly. For all this a much more fundamental, much more definite, decision is needed, and therefore it is important that the students begin to be complete revolutionaries with a total dedication.

"It is possible that what the present moment of the country demands of many young revolutionaries is that they abandon their studies and place themselves at the head of the revolution. But it is also possible that for many, this is not required, because of special circumstances or some temperamental factor. That is not so serious because the revolution will need more technologists than those the oligarchy now needs.

"The important thing is the immediate and concrete commitment to the people. I would like to know how many students in Bogotá or in Colombia live with the workers; how many dedicate their vacations to making contact with the common people; how many make an effort to translate into practice what they preach as revolutionaries? In other words, how concerned are the students about understanding the common people? The fact is that in the revolutionary life, going to the common people represents an ascent, and therefore a person must go to them without the paternalism which characterizes the bourgeoisie. Those of us who are of bourgeois extraction will learn more than we will teach, since the poor will reveal to us the misery of Colombia, the oppression in Colombia, the persecution of the workers of Colombia, the common language. If this last would be determined by a majority of votes, it would not be that of the Academy of Languages but the harsh speech of the workers, and it is that language which we must learn and interpret not only in its exterior forms but in its intimate and internal nuances.

"We will mingle with the people in that plan, by committing ourselves to them to the point that if, having made our decision, we begin to fall behind, they are the ones who will oppose us and strengthen our irresolution. Our commitment in the battle demands that we use all our forces for the unification and organization of the lower class until we achieve the final goal, which cannot be other than the seizure of power by the people, cost what it may.

"I believe that the historical moment which is now being lived in Colombia demands of us much more serious reflection on the consequences which our generosity or lack of generosity has; our dedication or our lack of dedication; our decision or our lack of decision; our activity or our passivity.

"I think that at this time, every minute which we lose from our task of unifying the lower class, organizing the lower class for the seizure of power, is a minute we are giving to the oligarchy. Would that each Colombian university student might have deeply implanted in his conscience the mission which providence or destiny bestows today on the university students of America: to light the spark of the revolution and apply it where it should be. But that spark cannot be lit except in the lower class. We know that class will demand more of us each day, and therefore we must go further forward each day because the lower class demands this of us and because it supports our every activity.

"Therefore I want to launch now, as the slogan for the Colombian students and for the revolutionaries of our country and of all of Latin America, the flaming words of Galán: Forward! Not one step back, and whatever must be, let it be."[12]

Now that the thought of Camilo has been explained, it is fitting to ask: What good are sectarianism, extremism, and personalism? They render the organization of the nonconformist university students extremely difficult. Camilo's plans also bring us to inquire if the scientific training, the professional capacity and the preparation on every level are of poor quality in our university? If the answer is yes, then it is interesting to trace the following problem in relation to revolutionary change:

In what measure do poorly prepared professionals constitute a reserve for the revolution? To what extent do the frustrations which they experience, caused by their lack of preparation, convert them into enemies of the existing social order, whose imperfections and injustices are for them only a pretext for the activities they undertake in order to cover up their failures in professional life?

Would the triumph of the revolution mean for those poorly prepared people something like a goal for their frustrated aspirations, converting them into what are commonly called "profiteers of the revolution?" Will they not be thereafter oriented towards purely bureaucratic-administrative positions in the triumphant new regime? What, finally, would be the reactions of those groups of frustrated professional revolutionaries regarding the popular masses, workers and peasants whom they have commanded in battle?[13]

We do not hold that preparation for revolution must be limited to professional preparation. Camilo thought that the professional revolutionary could not be exempted from the obligation of preparing himself more each day, within his sphere of specialization, for a humanization of the culture, in order to precipitate the encounter of the values of technology with the values of the people.

As a document inviting deep reflection, he sends his clearly worked-out Message to the Students, which we have already cited above:

> The students are a privileged group in every underdeveloped country. Poor nations subsidize the few graduates of the colleges and universities at very high cost. In Colombia in particular, given the large number of existing private colleges and universities, the economic factor has become the determining factor in education. In a country where 60% are functional illiterates, 8% graduate from high school, and 1% become professionals, the students are one of the few groups who are capable of analyzing the Colombian situation, comparing it with other situations and offering possible solutions.
>
> Moreover, the university student—in the universities where he can express his opinion and in the schools were there is liberty of expression—has two privileges at the same time: the power to rise in the

social scale by rising in academic degrees and the power to be a noncomformist and manifest his rebellion without this constituting an obstacle to his ascent. These advantages have made students a decisive element in the Latin American revolution. In the agitation phase of the revolution, the work of the students has been very effective. In the organizing phase their efforts have been secondary in Colombia. In the direct fight, even though there have been honorable exceptions in our revolutionary history, their role has not been important.

We know that agitation is important, but its real effect is lost without a follow-up to organize the struggle to seize power. One of the principal causes for the transitory and superficial contribution of the student to the revolution is his lack of commitment in the economic, family and personal fight.

Their nonconformity tends to be emotional (arising from sentimentality or frustration) or purely intellectual. This also explains the fact that at the end of their university career nonconformity disappears, or at least the student rebel stops being a rebel in order to be converted into a professional bourgeois who, to buy the prestige symbols of the bourgeoisie, must sell his conscience in exchange for greater financial rewards.

These circumstances can be the occasion of a serious threat to a mature and responsible response of the students to this historical moment in which Colombia is living. The economic and political crisis has begun to be experienced in its full rigor by the workers and peasants. The student, generally isolated from these, can believe that a superficial or purely speculative revolutionary activity is enough. That same lack of contact can make the student betray his historical vocation; when the country demands a total dedication, the student goes on responding with words and good intentions and nothing more. When the movement of the masses demands a daily and continuous effort, the student responds with shouts, stone-throwing, and sporadic demonstrations; when the popular class demands an effective, disciplined and responsible presence in their ranks, the students answer with vain promises or with excuses.

It is necessary that the revolutionary conviction of the student bring him to a real commitment, even to the ultimate consequences. We must not go looking for poverty and persecution. But in the present system these are the logical consequences of a fight against the existing structures—where no quarter is given. In the present system they are the authentic signs of a revolutionary life. The same conviction must bring the student to share in the economic indigence and the social persecution of the workers and peasants. Then the commitment to the revolution will pass from theory to practice. If it is total, it is irreversible; the professional will not be able to turn back without a flagrant betrayal of his conscience, his people and his historical vocation.

I don't want to dogmatize on the moment of the revolution in which we are living. I only want to exhort the students to make contact with the authentic sources of information in order to determine what the moment is, what their responsibility is, and what the response will have to be as a consequence. Personally, I think we are rapidly coming close to the zero hour of the Colombian revolution. If they "go up to the lower class," without any kind of paternalism and with the desire more to learn than to teach, they will be able to judge the historical moment objectively.

It would, moreover, be sterile and disgraceful if the Colombian students, who have been the spark of the revolution, should remain on its margin for any reason whatsoever—through ignorance, superficiality, egoism, irresponsibility or fear.

We hope that the students respond to the call which their country makes to them in this important moment of their history and that they courageously listen to it and follow it with a generosity without limits.[14]

The "Camilo Torres Fact" requires of the students a reappraisal of themselves, and the first step is not to make of Camilo a cheap pretext for justifying vituperative and useless exploits. Nor have they the right to appropriate him for themselves. "If I situate myself in a specific movement, I disqualify myself for talking with others," he told the students when he returned from Lima. Much less can he be permitted to become a legend, because, as Enrique Dussel says, when human beings or events are elevated to the category of myth, the pressure which they exert on consciences is negative; they are an impediment to creative development.

A minimal program of action in accord with Camilo's desire could be this: To create political centers to analyze and assimilate his thought, in whatever it has that is positively constructive. To work for a frank opening towards dialogue without missionary zeal or bigotry and formalism. To form a new plan with a foundation in reality, so as not to produce the kind of useless actions which take sympathy away from any cause, however just. To do away with that unilateral, exclusive, artificial way of conceiving of students as divided into two unique sectors: reactionaries and revolutionaries—a simplistic scheme much in evidence.

There can be progressive elements which are neutralized by the preponderant sectarian atmosphere, even though, when their time came, they could make very positive contributions to the cause of the revolution.

In addition, the infantile tendency of branding as reactionaries, detectives, or police those poor students who are obliged to earn their living through public employment should be abolished. A sane national purpose should be created without any lapse into Fascist habits. To that end, nonconformity with everything negative and inhuman in our national reality must be sought. This will not be done without studying it, without penetrating it in order to feel, live, and know it. Thus we shall be prevented from falling into this contradiction: knowing what we don't want but ignorant of what we do want. We must put an end to the use of the myth that in Colombia only a gun with ten bullets counts as a pretext for failing to come to grips with our situation through a disciplined use of our cultural and ideological capacities.

Regarding revolution, it is necessary to know: what a revolution is; what is sought in a revolution; whether the only solution is a revolution, understood not as brutal violence, but as progress through channels of authentic, courageous, and rapid transformation; what permanent need the revolution implies for each one.

It is essential for the students to analyze in depth the phenomenon of negativism and immediacy in terms of revolutionary behavior. They must pass from the emotional to the rational if they seek to arrive at effective social action. They must learn to create and preserve, and not destroy anything of positive value. As natural leaders, students must realize that if we should seize power, those who cause division among the students would be the best instruments of the static and inoperative minorities and the worst enemies of any change which might be reasonably considered necessary. Finally, each one must investigate the ethical content of the revolutionaries' principles in terms of these criteria:

Do they over- or under-value man, culture, woman, the lower class, the historical moment, the manifestations of rebellion, the revolutionary action, etc.?

The most authentic message of Camilo for the university youth is this: Be born again! Be born again! Each day, be born again!

Chapter 14

The Worker Movement

When one speaks of the worker movement in Colombia it is necessary to remember, as the jurist Professor Otis Morales Benítez says, that as new economic goals were achieved, paternalism began to disappear among us, and the state ceased to be the passive guardian of social conditions in order to incorporate interventionism into its legal system. In that moment an extraordinary force began to erupt—the right to work.[1] The history of our right to work movement must include the pre-Hispanic epoch lasting until the end of the fifteenth century; the Hispanic period, the sixteenth, seventeenth, and eighteenth centuries, and the national epoch which corresponds to the nineteenth and twentieth centuries. The pioneer in the field of labor legislation in our century was General Rafael Uribe, who as early as 1904 spoke of the necessity facing the country of issuing norms regarding some very important labor questions.[2]

Among ourselves, "the first manifestations in which the workers claimed their rights and the trade union strife was begun, had their baptism of blood, of martyrdom, their prologues of anxiety and worry."[3] The journey has been long and heroic; not a few workers have fallen in defense of their rights under liberal as well as conservative governments. The unions have always fought, with different views, for various interests. Their effort can never be denied as a factor—bloody at times—in the history of the worker battle in Colombia.

The position of Camilo has tremendous significance for the workers of the country. What importance did he attribute to the worker movement? Within the perspective of his theses, his starting point was based on a tradition of sacrifice obligated to serve the rest of the lower class by revolutionary actions. He did not underestimate the more simple and immediate acts in the fight for justice in his anxiety to link them to a wider political orientation. He understood perfectly that the two worst influences—that of the extremists and that of the economists—were corroding the backbone of the worker organization, paralyzing its activities and preventing its development. For the extremists think that the union battle, with its steps of protest and immediate gains, is unworkable and ineffective; and they demand, consequently, an open frontal insurgent action, using all means against the privileged classes. The others, the economists, remain immersed in the simple and primitive economic battle without taking the decisive steps to unite it to political action. Both theses, mistaken and proved to be erroneous through the history of the unions, were succinctly attacked by Camilo, who pointed out that in the struggle which was limited and directed towards immediate advantages, the fact should not be lost sight of that the total and affinitive vindication of the worker could come only with the seizure of power by the majority on behalf of the Colombian lower class.

The Message to the Trade Unionists is nothing less than an expression of faith in the destiny of the workers. We can see in this his concern for the unity which he considered fundamental for bringing the people to effective rather than sterile actions. Let us read it:

Few groups in Colombia have as strong a tradition of fighting and of organization as the laborers, the urban workers. Although the industrialization of Colombia does not begin to have national importance before 1939, Colombian trade unionism, rural as well as urban, possesses a tradition of fighting prior to this date.

The mutineers of Las Bananeras are witnesses of that fight. The government of Alfonso López signals a fundamental step in the organization of the workers and in the Colombian trade union fight. Trade unionism develops as a belligerent and independent force, but soon, under backward regimes, it begins to be weakened by paternalistic, imperialistic elements and strike-breaker puppets of the government. Our ruling class also succeeded in dividing the worker class and after weakening it under religious and political protests, as it had already weakened the lower class with the same pretexts, it resolves to purge it of "Communist" elements in the Congress of Cartagena, i.e. to discard every element not subject to national and North American paternalism.

However, the pressure of the system affected all the workers. The movement of Gaitán consolidated a class consciousness which official violence has not succeeded in erasing in nineteen years of existence. The leaders who had become puppets of the oligarchy became more insolent each day and used always more arbitrary and more violent procedures in order to stay in power.

The National Front accelerated the social conflict when it was instituted as the first class party of Colombia, the party of the privileged class, to consolidate the union of the oppressors against the oppressed, thus launching a challenge to the Colombian lower class to constitute, following the advice of José Antonio Galán, "the union of the oppressed against the oppressors."

The government of the National Front, responsible for three devaluations, increases by 200% the public and defense expenses and tries to repair the fiscal bankruptcy affecting the Colombian people with sales taxes and increased taxes on gasoline, etc. The national strike of January 25 is the culmination of a social pressure imposed on the oligarchy in that they were simply unable to collect these taxes. The system was so disintegrated and corrupt that the parliamentary machinery could not function for either the normal or the extraordinay taxations.

Then dictatorship is installed. They take advantage of a student strike to decree a state of siege which continues, contrary to the constitution, long enough to legislate on economic matters and foster labor demagoguery. The most serious thing about the present system is that not only the workers but the oligarchy is discontented, and this is more serious because when the oligarchy is discontented, the possibility of a coup d'etat becomes more immediate.

When the politicians fail, the oligarchy exchanges them for the military. The military government which now hold power will possibly awaken hope owing to their demagogic methods. Our people have finally been driven to cry with one voice for revolution. Nevertheless, they still lack the knowledge and organization necessary for coping with the deceit which will prevail through demagogical methods after the fall of the government of the National Front.

An interminable series of legal and illegal strikes has begun in our country; all those fights or immediate struggles for justice strengthen the revolution because they unify, organize, and consolidate the consciousness of the Colombian worker movement. The rank and file of all the trade union centers, like many of their leaders, are united around the platform of the United Front of the people. The workers, with the students, constitute the stronghold able to confront the new forms of deceit which the oligarchy will adopt. It is necessary that the workers use their relative financial capacity and their unquestionable organizing capacity in the revolutionary fight and in the organization of the Colombian lower class.

It has been said that the trade unionists are the oligarchs of the lower class. I don't believe it. In reaction against the exploiting attitude of the oligarchy, even those trade unionists who work in monopoly businesses and by that fact enjoy the privileges these businesses have —or at least, many of them—have taken up a frankly progressive and revolutionary position.

It is necessary that the Colombian worker class, in this crucial moment of our history, should dedicate all its efforts to the unity and the organization of the Colombian lower class for the seizure of power.

The individual, partial struggle for immediate advantages must not lose sight of the fact that the total and definitive vindication of the worker cannot come except as a consequence of the seizure of power by the majority on behalf of the Colombian lower class. The unity, organization, and battle for that definitive vindication depend on the unity, organization, and capability of the workers fighting for justice today.

The trade union leaders who fear the platform of the United Front are those who fear unity because they know that the united and organized worker class would harshly demand payment from them for going over to the national and foreign ruling classes.

The working class, like the Colombian people, has been superior to many of its leaders. When the working class is unified at the base, it will bring to bear the necessary pressure so that the rulers who do not want unity or the revolution will be thrown aside by the Colombian people who have broken loose like a torrent to seize power.[4]

Today, the majority of the interpreters of our problem are in agreement regarding the role which the Colombian working class plays. Some go further than others; but all assign to it a fundamental task notwithstanding the small weight it manifests so far in the national political process. It also concurs in the desire for obtaining unity through "unity of action" as a revolutionary form in the present stage, an indispensable instrument for class cohesion, even though the way to accomplish it is not clear.

This desire and this fight have positive aims: to widen the trade union democracy; to do away with bossism of every kind; to abolish, by the simply play of opinion and debate, negative leaders; and to promote by new methods of organization such things as the creation of trade union movements for industry at the departmental and national level. It is a difficult process, accomplished only by a strong nucleus which embodies the best fighting tradition of the workers who have given proofs of heroism and sacrifice and demonstrated in innumerable actions a great capacity for understanding our situation. But they are still not correctly oriented in terms of the intricate problems of our time. Our working class is honest, patient, courageous, capable of giving all when they have begun to grasp the principles which will enable them to recognize and carry out their true role in history.

Actually, the Platform of the United Front rapidly kindled the minds and consciences of many workers belonging to the different worker organizations: the Confederation of Colombian Workers (C.T.C.), Union of Colombian Workers (U.T.C.), and the Trade Union Confederation of Colombian Workers (C.S.T.C.). Camilo branded some elements who had been elevated to high-ranking positions as traitors, double-dealers, opportunists, and adventurers, who exploited those sincere and honest members who were deceived and subjected to the tremendous pressures of the trade union machinery.

Camilo had to express his gratitude to the workers who from the first moment in the political fight gave him unqualified support and accompanied him with wild enthusiasm at numerous meetings. Also, the different unions opened their doors to him in order to hear him, and the Platform was reproduced by the thousands at the initiative of many organizations. This awakened the suspicion of the traitors, who began their attack by denying him access to the trade unions. It was the complement to the siege initiated in the universities, to the blocking of pedestrian areas with barbed wire and armored military detachments done later by political leaders who had supported him in the beginning. All this was done under a single pretext: Camilo was a Communist.

Even now that he is dead, this leader of worker unity and his teachings—this leader who pointed out the merits and the failures of the worker class—are not fairly interpreted. Actually, with his precipitate decision to go to the mountains, Camilo gave an excuse to the extremists, who took him as a standard for confusing Colombian trade unionism. They adopted a position which held back vindictive action, idealizing a false model of an advanced and revolutionary class, with supine ignorance of the fact that class consciousness is not an abstract idea but something very concrete which is born in social practice and grows in the process of the daily battle.

It is a fact, however, that the workers search out the teaching of Camilo with growing eagerness and keep it alive, convinced that his death was not in vain.

Chapter 15

The Way of the Guerillas

In the tropical labyrinthine, mysterious, and hostile jungle of Colombia armed groups of men are in hiding today. They know of the fundamental changes which have been brought about since the rise of violence.

During the past, official partiality and party antagonism subjected an immense group of men to the choice of fighting or dying. Hatred dug deep roots in the soul of the people. Tragedy brought together groups of like ideology and produced the political homogeneity of numerous regions, which, in turn, caused an exodus to the city or to other rural areas. Those who fought in the mountains counted on the support of the members of the party in the towns, who were in charge of the administration of food, medicine, and supplies through a complicated web of information and transport. The combatants were supported both passively and actively by the political directorates. The fight took place between an army which was limited to the tactics of regular war and the peasants who used the system of guerilla warfare. The warlike atmosphere spread throughout the land, except for the coastal region in the north, the western Colombian coastal zone and the extreme south. The troops were selected rigidly by party criteria.

Today things have radically changed because as a result of the plebiscite there arose a type of government based on the alternation in power of the two traditional parties. The immediate result of this was that from the highest official spheres on down, violence was not favored or allowed. Dissidents had access once again to official positions in the armed forces even though all party activity is forbidden while they remain in active service. The political leaders withdrew their support from every armed group, making such a decision clear in public pacts. The political equality in the collegiate bodies and in the official organizations tempered by the passion of the electoral battle. The rebel groups remained subject to the exclusive competency of military justice, whose instrument is the War Councils.

The armed forces progressively sought out the heads of bands who remained as a sequel to the earlier violence, giving them the choice of surrender or death. The elimination of bandit groups freed vast areas where the rural people had been forced to pay with their lives for their unwillingness to cooperate with the violent. The civic-military action developed an active campaign in the affected rural areas, directed towards freeing them from the influence of the anarchists.

Concerning this, Regis Debray reports:

On the material plane, one cannot insist enough on the force of the repressive apparatuses after 1960. On the other side of the coin of the Alliance for Progress there is a military aid to the Latin American governments of a new intensity and nature. A month before Mr. Dillon launched in Punta del Este those optimistic plans destined to transform Latin American into that paradise of gilded latrines whose failure was analyzed by Che Guevara at the same time, Kennedy submitted to Congress in July 1961 "a military program against subversion." According to the New York Times of July 4th, "the program represents a radical modification in military programs for the western hemisphere.

Until this moment, the principal objective had been to equip some aerial and naval units with a view to a joint defense of the hemisphere against an attack from outside. Today greater importance is given to internal defense against subversion." During 1961 alone, 21 million dollars were appropriated for "counter-insurgency teams." The anti-guerilla school in Panama each year sees an unknown number—(it is a military secret but estimated in the thousands)—of young Latin American officials and police pass through its program. Battalions of Colombian counter-insurgency troops, Ecuadorian parachutists, Peruvian commandos, Bolivian rangers, Argentinian police (today equipped with heavy armament) and many other military bodies, highly trained, formed and organized by the North American military missions; today, all those bodies have as their goal the liquidation of an insurrectional force in the interior of the country. But it is in the field of information and infiltration that the North American aid has concentrated its efforts. The FBI and the CIA directly control the local police. In Brazil nobody, except Brizola, who burned the archives of the police of Rio Grande de Sul when he was Governor of that area, thought it objectionable, "when the entire regime of the national bourgeoisie was in complete control," that the FBI and the CIA should seize the secret files of the political police. Argentina, with twenty million inhabitants, has seven bodies of political police, independent rivals of one another. In Venezuela, Sotopal, Digepol, SIFA, PTJ, etc., compete with one another, without counting the agents recruited by the CIA. "Twenty years ago," an Ecuadorian official of military information said with pride, "we were still very naive. When the students took to the streets, we fired over their heads, all of which gave bad results. Today we know that, of the hundred ways to smother a revolution, firearms are the last."[1]

What, then, is the situation of the Colombian armed rebel movements? For the sake of clarity three steps in the development of insurrection must be distinguished: the guerillas of the party type during the period of violence; anarchical banditry as a sequel to the first; the revolutionary stage with strictly political ends, in accord with the modern concept of guerilla warfare. This is what exists today.

Within this last step we must set down some revolutionary designs which are identified with the common purpose of seizing power for the people and finally achieving an authentic democracy, free of North American imperialism. They differ from one another in terms of their attitudes toward the world revolutionary movements—Cuban, Soviet, Chinese—but all insist on profiting from the experience of these movements and using what can be applied to our national reality. As far as methods are concerned, some opt for elections and others for arms as the only way to the revolution.

Among the first we find the Revolutionary Liberal Movement (M.R.L.). This group kept the Left together when, in virtue of the December 1, 1957, plebiscite and the legislative act No. 1 of 1959, it was decreed that only the citizens of the two traditional parties (liberal and conservative) would govern in Colombia until 1974, applying the formula of alternation. The M.R.L. could legally go to the public corporations, as the extreme wing of the liberal party. Reduced to the necessity "of making politics from within," it did not resist personal ambitions. After breaking up into fragments, it lost its prestige with the masses, failed to fulfill its revolutionary plan and ended up by handing over the standards to the old bosses, uniting with the Liberal Party in exchange for bureaucratic positions and occasional benefits.

Among the proponents of armed warfare as the solution to the social contradictions of the country, the MOEC (Worker, Student, Peasant Movement) must be mentioned. It was organized in 1959 by Antonio Larrota, the university student leader assassinated in the north of Cauca. This movement guides its actions and bases its principles on the doctrine of Marxism-Leninism, applied to the concrete practice of the Colombian revolution. It is inspired by the Chinese Peoples' Republic, but it has not succeeded in effectively using its methods of work for the organization of peasant guerillas.

Afterwards we had the rise of the FUAR (United Front of Revolutionary Action) which also posited armed warfare as the solution to our problems. It failed because of the failures of its leaders and militants. Then, the armed movement of Vichada, in which "Minuto Colmenares" and Doctor Tulio Bayer participated, was promptly put down by the government forces.

Today there are two active groups: the Revolutionary Armed Forces of Colombia or the Army of National Liberation, and the

Revolutionary Armed Forces of Colombia (FARC) or the Southern Bloc.

By means of many years of indoctrination in the rural area, the Colombian Communist Party was able to organize peasant nuclei which were never addicted to systems of government inspired and run by the two traditional parties. This fact created a state of tension between the official authority and the agrarian organization. They began to speak of territories which had left the national sovereignty as "independent republics," among which were Marquetalia Rio Chiquita, El Pato and Guayabero.

As a governmental plan for controlling them, the Lazo Plan was put into action. The development of this plan includes several tactical steps. The first is the psychological war which embraces the "civic-military action" consisting of programs of aid to the peasants through army commissions, in order to win sympathy, obtain followers, create webs of espionage and sources of intelligence and take a census of the inhabitants. This work is accomplished with the help of Communal Action, the Peace Corps, and the North American institutions such as Care and Caritas. During this stage, the army prepares its logistical calculations and plans its action against the peasant groups.

The second step consists in the economic and military blockade of the territory, in order to strangle the economy and weaken the cohesion of the peasant organizations. Finally, the army launches punitive aggression, using modern arms and a crushing number of troops.

It was thus that the armed action against the "independent republics" was unleashed, beginning with the attack on Marquetalia, May 18, 1964, in which the combined forces of land and air participated in no less a number than 16,000. Immediately the movements of self-defense were transformed into guerilla detachments under the command of Manuel Marulanda Vélez, Ciro Castaño and Oscar Reyes. The regions were scenes of ferocious wars of destruction—areas leveled, houses bombed, peasants held prisoner or shot, women violated. It cannot be denied that brutal crimes were committed.

The second Guerilla Conference of the Southern Bloc held in

April 1966 created the Revolutionary Armed Forces at Colombia (FARC). The contingents of Marquetalia, El Pato, Rio Chiquito, 26th of September, and South of Tolima constituted a popular army with guerilla tactics, in order to fight for the seizure of power for the people.[2]

It is a frankly revolutionary peasant movement. Its basic programs in synthesis are these: effective agrarian reform; expropriation of properties; industrialization of rural zones; wide system of credit; remunerative prices for agricultural products; protection for the indigenous communities, to which the lands which the large landowners have usurped will be returned.

The Army of National Liberation (ELN) or Northern Bloc was organized in order to wage guerilla warfare as the means to victory but backed up by peasants who had not lost the desire for liberty created by violence and adverse socio-economic conditions. They had a class-consciousness founded on mutual interests and motives at odds with those of the ruling oligarchical group. Fabio Vásquez Castaño and Victor Medina Morón, the creators of the Army of National Liberation, knew that the ruling sector counted on the military as a repressive apparatus and that they would necessarily have to face it, assuming all the consequences. In setting down the essential characteristics of the movement, a clear social and political end is translated into fighting for the people, using the tactics of an openly revolutionary undertaking, constantly intensified as the oligarchy obstinately holds onto its privileges.

The ELN operates in the mountains of Santander in the south and is extended as far as Opón on two fronts: the "José Antonio Galán," commanded by Vásquez Castaño and Medina Morón, and the "Camilo Torres Restrepo," led by Ricardo Lara Parada. The Galán group appeared officially on January 7, 1965, when it took the town of Simacota and issued the following manifesto: "The reactionary violence set loose by the various oligarchical governments and continued by the corrupt regime of Ruiz Novoa-Lleras, has been a powerful weapon for smothering the revolutionary movement of the peasants and has been a powerful tool of domination for the past fifteen years. Education is in the hands of dealers who enrich themselves on the ignorance in which our people are kept. The land is cultivated by peasants who have no place for their dead and who use their energy and that of their families for the oligarchy, who live in the cities like kings. The workers work in hunger for day wages, subjected to misery and humiliation by the great foreign and native businesses. The intellectuals and the young democratic professionals are trapped in the dilemma of whether to give themselves to the ruling class or to perish. The small and middle-sized producers, in the country as well as in the city, see their businesses ruined by ruthless competition and those monopolists of credit for foreign capital, who would gladly sell the country. The riches of all the Colombian people are plundered by the North American imperialists.

"But our people, who have experienced exploitation, misery and reactionary violence, are rising and ready for the fight. The revolutionary fight is the only way open to the people for pulling down the present deceitful and violent government. Those of us who make up the Army of National Liberation find ourselves in a battle for the liberation of Colombia. Both the Liberals and the Conservatives among the people will join together to pull down the oligarchy who run both parties.

"Long live the unity of peasants, workers, students, professionals, and all honest men who want to make of Colombia a country of Colombians! Freedom or death!"[3]

The basic ingredients of their program are: seizure of power by the people; an authentic agrarian revolution; economic and industrial development, including the nationalization of those industries in the hands of the imperialists; housing programs and reform in the cities; creation of sources of credit for the people which avoid the traps of the usurers and money changers; public health and social security benefits for all the people; road-building and transportation programs; educational reform, with free and obligatory primary education and the nationalization of secondary, normal and university education; bringing the lower classes into participation in the economy and the culture; freedom of thought and religion; independence in foreign policy; a standing army subject to the people.

We have a false idea of what a guerilla is because the press, with political and economic interests determined by the oligarchy, persists in disfiguring the guerilla in the eyes of the public, presenting him as a bandit, criminal, rapist, etc. Guerillas today are armed revolutionaries who are deprived of justice by the system which they fight. They are political offenders, not common criminals. They have the courage to fight for their ideas and to defend them even to the point of death. If they appeal to armed resistance, it is because they see no other solution. They are disciplined, organized into groups, many of them from the middle class, sometimes professionals who mix with the peasants from whom they learn many heroic lessons in the pursuit of the common goal.

The life of the guerilla will never be easy. It is full of anguish, danger, the renunciation of every comfort. Being in the mountains is a daily commitment to the risk of death. Not all those who desire it can achieve the honor of being guerilla soldiers. This demands physical qualities which are far beyond the ordinary, uncommon moral fortitude and, in the leader, exceptional qualities which set him apart.

The guerilla is subject to truly basic training. He eats what the mountains produce—roots, palm shoots, tubers, fruits of the forest—and on the interminable marches he quenches his thirst with *liana* juices known only by those most familiar with the wild geography of the tropics. His only food may be *churuco,*[4] shell-fish, armadillos, fish, and sometimes birds when a gun shot would not reveal the place where he is hiding.

He sleeps on beds of straw or leaves for a few hours—or for minutes when the enemy is near. He fords rivers, flees without leaving footprints, lives without leaving any sign of his existence.

As for emotional life, he goes to the mountains, an exile from affection. He leaves mother, wife and children behind. He has no home. He has renounced everything. The "group" makes up his universe. He sacrifices himself to it so that people may be free.

But the first tasks of the guerilla are indoctrinating the rural population and ambushing the enemy. Peasant support is the life of the guerilla. Nevertheless, many times the peasants believe the politicians who deceive him rather than the guerillas who fight for them.

The system is supported by the armed forces which are basically made up of peasant troops who suffer the oppression of this same system and who are obliged to military service by law. They are brought into the army and convinced that their revolutionary brother is an assassin. Once convinced and trained, they are sent to zones where there are "subversive forces" with the assignment to exterminate them. Thus we have peasant soldiers with the mission of destroying those who fight for the peasant on behalf of all the people. When the attack takes place, the soldier trained in anti-guerilla warfare is compelled to face the revolutionary. The revolutionary, free of compulsions, moved only by his mystique of freedom, repels the soldier—i.e., he must sacrifice the soldier who defends the system which the guerilla can never accept. The rulers confront the people with such methods to maintain their oligarchical positions.

There are two messages of Camilo's which clarify many aspects of this problem: that which he addressed to the military and that which he sent to the peasants:

MESSAGE TO THE MILITARY

After having seen in the city of Girardot the power of 40 disciplined and armed men against 4,000 people, I have determined to make a strong appeal to the armed forces of Colombia so that they might be conscious of the historical moment in which we are living and plan how they should participate in the revolutionary fight from now on.

On different occasions I have seen peasants and workers in uniform (where I have never found elements of the ruling class) persecuting and striking peasants, workers, and students who represent the majority of the Colombians. Except for rare occasions, I have not found members of the oligarchy among the subofficials or the officials. Everyone who thinks about the contrast between the majority of Colombians clamoring for the revolution and the small military minority repressing the people in order to protect a few privileged families, must ask himself what reasons induce these elements of the people to persecute their own kind.

It cannot be for economic advantages. All the personnel in the armed forces are very poorly paid. In general, the military are not allowed to take studies which might facilitate a life outside the army.

When they arrive at the grade of major they try to buy a corner house in order to open a store with which they can support themselves when they retire. I have seen generals and colonels taking positions as teachers of physical education in high schools and as insurance salesmen. The salaries of those in active service are low, but they are more than those of the retired, who receive neither medical attention nor any other economic advantage. Nevertheless, we know that one third of our national budget is allocated to the armed forces. As is obvious, the war budget is not used to pay the Colombian soldiers but to buy the junk which the United States sells us, for the maintenance of materiel, and to increase the internal repression in which Colombians kill their own brothers.

Perhaps the reason the soldiers join the army is their dedication to the laws, to the Constitution, and to the Fatherland. But the Colombian fatherland consists principally in its men, and most of these suffer and do not enjoy power. The constitution is constantly violated when they do not give work, property, liberty, or participation in power to the people who should be, according to the Constitution, the ones to decide public affairs in the country. The Constitution is violated when a state of siege continues after the causes which were the pretext for its declaraton have ceased. Laws are violated when citizens are detained without a warrant for arrest, when mail is withheld, when citizens are prevented from traveling on the streets, when the telephones are controlled, and lies and tricks are used to persecute the revolutionaries.

Perhaps it is necessary to inform the soldiers more about where the Fatherland, the Constitution, and the laws are, so that they might not think the Fatherland consists of twenty-four families whom they now protect, for whom they give their blood and from whom they receive such poor remuneration.

Perhaps the principal reason the military continue to be the arm of the oligarchy is the lack of opportunity in the other fields of human activity in Colombia. The military must understand that when the revolution triumphs, the economy will be planned, the schools and universities will be opened to all Colombians, and they and their children will have the opportunity for remunerative employment and liberal careers. As long as the reactionary enemy continues there will be an army for the defense of the privileged minorities and not for the defense of the people. The sacrifices which they make, then, will be to build up the country and not to destroy it.

The honor of the armed forces will not then be stained by the caprice of the oligarchy and lackeys who have the armed forces at their service. We will no longer see three-star generals destitute because they had spoken of structural reforms and pressure groups. We will no longer see generals from the middle class thrown out as smugglers with a public scandal while their superiors in the upper class or those related to the Colombian oligarchy succeed in keeping their smuggling hidden, smuggling which is directly against the interests of the country and against the national sovereignty.

Soldiers: The United Front promises you it will unify and organize the common people to seize power. Don't fail to join in the battle when we give the mortal blow to that oligarchy which oppresses all Colombians, which oppresses you as well as us.[5]

At this point the press accused Camilo of inciting the army to rebellion.[6]

MESSAGE TO THE PEASANTS

As the census indicates, the peasant population has diminished. Even though those who live in centers with populations over 1,500 are considered as urban population. In reality that is not so. We can still say that the majority of the Colombian population is rural.

Besides numbers, the most important thing is that the greater part of the national income is produced by the peasants. Ninety percent of the exports are agricultural (coffee, tobacco, bananas, sugar). Without agriculture, we would not be able to import the machines or the food which we need. Unfortunately, the peasants, like all others in this system, serve the few. Those who manage the Federations (of coffee, cotton, bananas, tobacco, etc.), the United Fruit, and those who run the banks (especially the Bank of the Republic) receive most of the revenue. The revenue which the government earns is used for paying employees and to buy old weapons to kill the peasants who have given the money to buy them.

The contrast between the economic and social importance of the peasants and the treatment which they receive from the present system is an open scandal. The violence has been principally among peasants. The government was the initiator of the violence: from 1947 it produced it at first with the police, and afterwards, since 1948, with the army.

The liberal oligarchs paid the liberal peasants and the conservative oligarchs paid the conservative peasants to kill one another. The oligarchs didn't even receive a scratch. When that oligarchy didn't need them any more, it declared them bandits, hunted them down like wild beasts; and then when it murdered them, it published the photos of their bodies on the front page in the press, boasting of this triumph obtained in the name of peace, justice and legality.

That governmental violence financed by the oligarchy afterwards taught the peasants many things: it taught them to recognize in the oligarchy their true enemy. First it taught them to flee; then it taught them to defend themselves; and then it taught them to attack in order to obtain what the oligarchy obtained with violence: farms, harvests, cattle, power. The system did not give them these things. Quite the contrary! The peasants have the lowest salaries, the smallest number of schools, the worst homes, the fewest possibilities for progress. When they finished with the notorious rebel leaders, the peasant press remained in the hands of the same landowners.

With the repressive politics of the United States imposed on them, the Colombian rulers could not permit "suspicious" zones even though they were peaceful. The army needed to increase its importance in order to show that it was necessary and to increase its budget.

The government says that the peasants began the violence. The peasants say that it was the government. In France, intellectuals of every persuasion, after having investigated, say that the peasants are right.

I want to challenge the government to ask, if it dares, an investigating commission from the United States, consisting of neutral nations (e.g. Egypt, India, and Chile), to judge the cases of Marquetalia, Pato, Guayabero, and Rio Chiquito. We are aware of the resemblance of the landing of the "Marines" in Santo Domingo to the landings of the Colombian army, directed by the North American military mission in the "independent republics."

These landings will continue. Yesterday it was Rio Chiquito; tomorrow it will be Sumapaz; the day after tomorrow in Ariari and Llanos. The army begins with civic-military action and ends with bombings; it begins by pulling teeth and ends by shooting bullets. The peasants already know that the military brings bread in one hand while in the other a dagger is concealed. The "dependent Republic" of Colombia will continue to obey the North Americans until it destroys with blood and fire the other, independent republics of Colombia. The

North American legislature has decreed it. Our peasants already know what they must put up with. They already know what they must prepare for. They do not easily enter into an adventure, but they will not run away from this fight. Already the oligarchy, with the state of siege, has arrested people in the public plazas. It already pursues them with machine-guns in closed areas such as Medellín. When they make life impossible for us in the city, we must go to the country. And from the country we will not be able to be driven into the sea. There we will have to resist. For that reason the peasants must be prepared: organizing now the commandos of the United Front in groups of 5 or 10; purging the areas of traitors to the cause of the people; making collections of food and clothing; preparing outselves for a prolonged fight and not allowing ourselves to be provoked, nor presenting resistance when the conditions are not favorable for the people.

The oligarchy will continue to strengthen the peasants' conviction that they must support the revolutionary forces. Why have they not finished with the guerillas of Simacota? Only because of the support of the peasants.

When the oligarchy continues in this way, the peasants will have to give refuge to the urban revolutionaries, the workers, and the students.

For the moment they must be united and organized to receive us so that we might undertake the long and final battle.[7]

The army thinks that the guerilla problem is under control and that the armed forces will be able to liquidate it soon, and therefore the squadrons continue to be reduced as much as possible.[8] The commander of the Fifth Brigade, Colonel Alvaro Valencia Tovar, thinks that they have the necessary instruments for the eventual elimination of the guerillas, checked already by not having succeeded in obtaining their objectives. Far from growing, he says, they have diminished in power, combat ability, and force. Military experience thus judges that the guerillas cannot be controlled unless isolated.[9]

Objectively, the army will not be able to eliminate the present forces in the immediate future. To claim the contrary is not to recognize the real conditions to which the anti-guerilla warfare is subject. There are still guerillas; they still exist and this cannot be denied. Can other guerilla fronts rise up? The press of the country protested (January, 1967) because I had responded affirmatively to that question. Such a possibility was fully denied. Nevertheless, on January 9th *El Espacio* announced the appearance of a new group, the "Camilo Torres," supporting the information with seven undeniable photographs.[10]

On the 11th there was a communication that a band was pillaging in the zones of Borbur and Otanche and another one was around Cajamarca in Tolima.[11] In the meanwhile, men from Tirofijo passed through Ariari attempting, it seems, to open up a new front.[12] The assaults on Vijagual (Santander), La Perdiz (Huila) and Las Coloradas (Valle) were causes of concern at that time. For reasons of security the government ordered the arrest of the leaders of the various revolutionary movements on March 10, 1967. The Minister of National Defense, General Gerardo Ayerbe Chaux, clearly admitted the potential for guerilla warfare in the country.

Since March 1967 guerilla movements have appeared in Brazil and Bolivia, and those in Guatemala and Venezuela continue. Recently (October) the press informed us of the rise of insurrection in Chile.

How did Camilo interpret the guerilla problem? To answer, it is necessary to look at the conflict in himself and with the guerillas.

"What has been called 'the violence,' that civil war which has continued for twenty years in our country, is basically an unorganized, empirical, unconscious change of structures. The external structure of the country continues to be the same. But in all these years, the peasants have changed—that is, the great majority of the Colombian population. Take the example of the 'independent republics.' From the right and from the left, there are some who deny their existence. The truth is that it is not important whether they qualify as republics or not. But there has risen a new power in those regions, parallel to the central power, embodied in the guerilla leaders, supported by the peasants, and all this has generated a new attitude in the peasants towards all the institutions existing previously: property, the State, the Church are now no longer seen as unmovable elements of existence but as subjects of possible changes in which they feel they have a growing role."

As for the guerillas, he judges that "they are much more than a police problem. They are a social problem which goes to the very roots of the country. Therefore, moral qualifications do not serve for condemning the guerilla warfare. It is the same as the army: we cannot approve it or condemn it with abstract moral qualifications. We must see what ends are served by the guerillas or the army. When all the channels for rising socially seemed to be closed to the peasants and the oppressive structure of Colombian society remained unmoveable, the guerillas came into the open, for good or for evil, as new channels for rising, and as a result of their existence hundreds of thousands of peasants became conscious of the fact that they are human beings capable of deciding the history of Colombia, for the first time. Those who condemn this phenomenon in the name of social conservation must first explain why the old structure could not satisfy that necessity. The guerillas created a new power parallel to the conservative-liberal power of the State, as a result of which by good methods or bad, but imposed by necessity and by the incapacity of the ruling classes to accept changes, great peasant masses rose up, confident in themselves, in their own forces, in their sense of human dignity and in their capacity for decision and self-government. A consciousness has been growing within the peasant class which has been unifying nationally in a form unknown before and which constitutes a powerful pressure group for profound changes. Therefore, I have said on another occasion that what is called 'the violence" constitutes the most important and profound socio-political change in the life of Colombia from the time of independence up to today."[13]

It is undeniable that there were a number of underlying factors, which, placed in action again through constructive channels, could be used profitably with revolutionary ends. It was not overlooked by Camilo that in the present active groups a phenomenon of political consciousness was operating which evolved from political party pretexts into the battle for social justice. He considered as positive factors of the old guerilla conglomeration, the capacity for organizing, the detection of natural leaders, the development of discipline, the community sense, the mystique of war, the topographical knowledge of the country, the experience acquired, the adaptation to the milieu, the rebellion against injustice and what could be called an incipient class consciousness.

He believed that the peasants had achieved a sufficient realization of their subhuman situation and that he could very easily direct them towards a movement to achieve justice by simply showing them possibilities and ways.

He thought that the farmers had passed the stage of political antagonisms (negative, individualistic motivation) in order to integrate themselves in a common desire for justice (positive, pluralistic motivation) and that such a thesis, assimilated by the masses, gave validity to the theory of pressure from below as a decisive factor of transformation.

But he did not succeed in establishing direct contact with the leaders, nor in motivating them; nor was there instruction, nor could the old staffs be strengthened again. Neither did he pause to think of the effect produced in the centers of violence by the psychological war promoted by the Regular Forces of Colombia through such efficacious instruments as civic military action and community development, even though these were transitory and discontinuous accomplishments.

Proof of this is that some leaders gave in to the temptation of the high price and were converted, in exchange for gifts or benefits, into informers or immediate collaborators of the Armed Forces, under the pretext of re-establishing the constitutional order weakened by the political persecution which began the past violence. Only those groups with a long-standing political sense, like the Communists or the People of ELN, understood the scope of Camilo's thesis and thus expressed it in written documents.

Camilo stumbled onto the large mass of people with an as yet embryonic social political sense: the reluctance of the peasants to take up arms again if they were not victims of political persecution; a strong tendency for self-defense locally, directed towards protecting an incipient agricultural economy; the present state of peace on the roads which facilitated the reconstruction of family life for the present; the rural conformity before the superiority of the military forces; the submission of the peasants to the influence of the traditional bosses, a leftover from our semi-feudal customs; the negative reaction which anarchical factions stirred up, proceeding from the old guerilla groups; the prestige which the old political leaders recovered, even though it was precarious, before the electoral campaign.

It is frequently said that in those armed groups, elements trained in Cuba are fighting. One testimony is enough. "Cali.—A patrol of the police yesterday afternoon captured 7 members of the Army of National Liberation, in the mountains area of Ginebra. Among those detained was Hernando Galeano, trained in Cuba, in guerilla warfare. . . ."[14]

Opposed to every possible revolutionary design coming from the peasants, there are at present two factors: (1) All the guerilla commandants of the late violence were eliminated, as also the rebel leaders of the armed groups who remained active in the sphere of anarchy and crime, on the border of legality. (2) The surviving liberal ex-guerillas, whose dynamic motivation was political, think that no liberal peasant should promote armed rebellion or even assume such attitudes passively towards the government, since this is the last period in which, in accord with the plebiscite, a liberal President will have the exercise of command.

Doctor Lleras Restrepo must hand over power to a conservative President. When this has been done, a belligerent liberal party should arise; because otherwise, conservatism would take possession of power in order to enthrone a long period of hegemony. Absurd? Perhaps, but the liberal peasant masses thought that way. Therefore the liberal guerillas support the anti-guerillas, or they belong to them, as an adequate way of smothering any outbreak of rebellion against the government.

This fact helps us to understand why the groups of a Communist or neo-guerilla type are confronted with the hatred belonging to long ago. Many brand them as traitors. These others are simply with "their" government because of party concern. Where have they suppressed political motivation to act on behalf of methods with a social content?

And what has happened? The peasants are confronted with elements of their own social group involved in this duality of conflicts: those for and those against the government. The first, used or supported by the armed forces, search for legal establishment and collective peace; the second are helped by the revolutionary groups. This has an immediate consequence: men still fall in the mountains and on the roads of Colombia, but on a much lesser scale, certainly; however, the rural exodus to the cities and towns is less frequent and smaller than in those days of the greatest violence. The victims continue to be the peasants. They seem to be under a curse: to die or to emigrate to other regions, to the urban centers or to the mountains.

As with Camilo himself, so with many. But the case of Camilo is exceptional. Why did Camilo become a guerilla?

It is important to review what went before:

He posited as his central thesis the necessity of the seizure of power for the people.

He launched an advanced Platform. With it he looked for the unification of the Left as an immediate possibility for accelerating change, but he did not find a true response.

He tested the capacity for reaction of the masses to economic-social announcements.

He evaluated the possibilities which could succeed by legal means and saw himself hindered by the repressive methods of the system.

He mobilized the people into enthusiastic multitudes to break the state of siege.

Harassed by the official repression which obeyed the orders of the ruling oligarchy, he judged that the only solution was armed warfare.

He was obsessed by the idea of bringing to the groups who had risen up a new, reasonable instrument for their coordination and fixing the immediate and remote goals which should be obtained.

He presumed that many students would follow his example. He felt that their wild revolutionary fervor was expressing itself in immediate and sterile reactions.

He also judged that the military repression would move many people to the mountains as guerillas.

On July 5th it was known by the press that Camilo was resting in a home in the country.[15] When he returned with great secrecy to his house in Bogotá I called him, and I found him completely fatigued, and with good reason.

After long pauses, questions, silences, he told me: "You know, don't you? I come from an interview with the guerillas of Chucurí. I have walked a lot. I am impressed by the life of those boys, by their decision to fight, their organization, their conviction. I found in them the same ideals I pursue with the United Front. They want the unification of the peasants without religious or party differences, without a desire to fight revolutionary elements of any sector, without caudillos. They are identified with us in the proposal to free the people from the oligarchical and imperialist exploitations and not to lay down their arms as long as the power has not passed over to the people. In agreement with their objectives, they accept the Platform of the United Front."

"Are you thinking of going to the mountains?" I asked him.

"No," he replied. "But if it comes, it comes."

I tried to show him, in a very long conversation, the pros and cons, the hard reality of guerilla life, the environment, the difficulty for him in adapting to it, the anonymity, the catastrophe which it would mean for the movement if he abandoned it without having responsible leaders at all levels—the calamity which the omission of the organizational step would involve.

Camilo raised various objections. And he concluded: "I would have to go if the people needed me there."

"But, would you do it?"

"Frankly, there is much to do. You are right. . . ."

August 9, 1965, a patrol of the Artillery Battalion No. 5, in the vicinity of Hoya Ciega, captured José Dolacio Durán Nova; he had with him documents in which details on the "Army of National Liberation," its components and leaders, organizers, revolutionary activities and goals were given. The 24th of the same month, agents of the intelligence section of the Brigade of Military Institutes arrested six citizens in Bogotá on whom were found communications intimately related to the documents captured in Hoya Ciega.

Because of this the Army of National Liberation was blamed for the following crimes:

(1) Capture of the Santander town, Simacota, on January 7, 1965; (2) assault on the Police Station of Popayal, municipality of Rionegro, Santander, February 5, 1965; (3) assassination of Florencio Amaya Ramírez in the Bucaramanga clinic of the same city, July 3, 1965; (4) explosion of a high power bomb in the building of the Ministry of National Defense, July 27, 1965; (5) assassination of the agent of the National Police, Luis Ernesto Báez, in a public bus in Bucaramanga, July 25, 1965; (6) assault on an army patrol in Cruz de Mayo, municipality of San Vicente, August 15, 1965; (7) retention of fire arms and confiscated explosives in Bogotá, August 24, 1965.

From the confiscated letters it seems that Camilo was given the name of Alfredo or Afredo Castro with a view towards attracting him to the movement, in order to capitalize on the popular sympathy which he enjoyed. It was presupposed that Alfredo would join the guerillas. In a letter dated August 7th in Llano it is said of him that he has to think of someone to replace him as the director of *Frente Unido*.

In another communication it is arranged for Camilo (Alfredo) to be trained by them, to be observed, to be accompanied on all trips. Was this pressure so irresistible that Camilo was unable to resist joining them? Certainly not! It is barely established that he corresponded with the leaders of the Army of National Liberation.

Among some very personal papers of Camilo, I stumbled upon some letters which verify this point. The first, dated July 6th (1965), proves that he traveled to San Vicente on the 5th at night, after a reception given him upon his return from Lima. According to what I have been able to check out, he went up to the town cited, did not find the contact agreed upon; when he had finished his writing, the guide sent by the guerillas arrived. Camilo set out on the road, taking the letter with him. Surely this was the document which served as the basis for the conversations. It is easy to deduce that its contents forced Camilo to remain in the mountains until he was convinced that he had been the victim of a series of deceptions, of false promises, and that he was moving in an unreal world. Once more advantage had been taken of his openness. Here is the text:

"Tuesday, July 6, 1965

My dear companion Helio:

Only upon my arrival from Lima did I know of your wish that I come so that we might coordinate the legal action with the underground action. I still have the opportunity to do much legal work before finally coming. I think I must resist as long as it is possible for me. As my immediate work, I am agitating in all the cities of the country, forming groups of urban supporters who are for the present studying and distributing the Platform of Popular Union. (I will send you the copies which they published in Lima and are distributing through Latin America.) These same groups established the network for distribution of the periodical *Colombian Revolution* which will be distributed in the entire country (500,000 copies) addressed to workers and peasants. The situation could not be better. The trade union sectors are also ready to support armed warfare. It is the same with some sectors of the middle class, the university students, and even sectors of the upper class. There are possibilities of division in the Army. I have had the first contacts with a general and two colonels. A military chaplain informed me that 'all the colonels and those below this rank are with me.' Of course this has to be treated very delicately, committing them very carefully even though it could be the end for all of us. The popular fervor is extraordinary, and it is necessary to take advantage of it in a truly revolutionary way. Depending on what you think, it seems to me that the most important jobs are:

1. To strike sure and continuous blows, widening the base more each time;

2. To try to coordinate actions with the other groups and principally with the MOEC, the Vanguard of the MRL, the New Party, ORC, Young Christian Democrats, and P.C. (all have prepared groups);

3. Creation of urban groups;

4. Purchase of a printing press and hiding it (the financing is practically complete);

5. To obtain the division of the army.

6. If the rest happens, to plan a march on the cities for the seizure of power. In this last case I would unite myself to you only after having succeeded in obtaining the neutrality of the army. If

this is not obtained, then I would unite myself with you when the legal work begins to be too difficult for me. This depends on the repression, but I figure two or three months more.

At the present moment I believe that every minute I lose in the legal battle is time that I lose in the revolution. Tomorrow, Wednesday, I have a large group in Cali which I pleased before. Therefore, if the contact doesn't come, I will return to Bucaramanga. I understand that my trip to Lima prevented the peasants in Bogotá from coordinating things better. We will continue to communicate with one another through them. I would like to know your opinion on my plans. I do not aspire to be the leader but to serve until the end. I was visiting your family trying to explain to them the total Christian meaning of our fight. They are well. Very much with us. I believed that they were consoled when I left. Your mother told me that she was praying for the cause. If you decide on coordination with the other armed groups, I offer you the contacts I have with all those I think are good enough. When you think that I am more necessary here than outside, I ask you to tell me. I will consult with the others about it, and I believe that what I decide will have in mind the triumph of the Revolution. Tell all the companions that they have all the Colombian and Latin American people and the poor of the entire world behind them and hoping in them. I hope to have the honor of finding myself among you as soon as it is necessary.

Accept a sincere hug from your brother and unconditional companion in the War of National Liberation,

Alfredo Castro

P.S. We hope to be able to publish in the periodical the news of INSURRECTION in order to have national public opinion informed. The periodical is also practically financed."[16]

The second letter is dated July 22, 1965:

"Dear Brother and Companion Helio:

The revolution continues to go forward in a truly stupendous way. The popular sentiment seems unanimous: Cúcuta, Ocaña, Convención, Rio de Oro, Bucaramanga. I have tried to explain the processes and foresee the future everywhere. In every place (although not in Bucaramanga) a coordinating committee of the United Front has been set up in which those aligned in political groups are the minority. With the "Comrades," as always from the very beginning, there have been difficulties because of their desire for control, but it seems that they are learning little by little. They have helped us much. I have continued to insist on the necessity of forming basic committees, first in order to discuss and publish the platform, afterwards to publish the periodical and then to form regional committees and a national committee. The National Committee will give the assignments to the United Front for the seizure of power. I have tried to explain it by showing that in a state of siege, for example, we cannot take a plaza or a city with a demonstration. Power is taken when the peasants can control a plantation, a large farm, when they control a region, a highway, a factory, a city. As you will see, all these plans lead us to realize that formation is necessary. As you will also understand, I would not have made all these plans if it were not for knowing what you have done and are doing. What I learned in the mountains has always been a stimulus, an example, and a secure help in this whole campaign of agitation.

In each city I have also left one or two persons who will help with the secrecy as we had spoken about it. It is clear that they need a test, but something is better than nothing.

The periodical will continue to be directed by me. Manager, Israel Arjona; Assistant Director, Julio Cortés; head compositor, one of the linotype trade-unionists. About *X*. . . . I need your decision soon. I don't see clearly. He can accompany me constantly as political advisor. It would be very good for him to dedicate himself to the administration of the periodical in order to control that more. It would be very good to have a bodyguard from the ELN. I am very pleased with you and with the ELN for the magnificent collaboration and effectiveness in Bucaramanga and the outing at Santander. As administrator. . . . would help me to obtain the offset and to mount the publications apparatus for which I can't really rely on anyone. The finances are now in the hands of. . . . For the offset we already have the money. The finances are not very good. I think we have $70,000 (outside of that for the offset). I will leave the secret contacts to. . . . Please give me all the suggestions which you think are necessary. I will always accept them as from a brother and companion in the Liberation of Colombia. Regards to all the companions. Remind them of the hope which all of you signify and the moral foundation which they represent for us. If they need. . . . , even though we need him, we will send him to you. I hope you are taking care of yourself. Your companion and brother,

Alfredo"[17]

Here is the third document (August 7, 1965):

"Cherished Helio:

I received your letter of July 8th and it pleased me very much. Since my last letter I have been to meetings in El Valle, a good part of the coast, and finally at Medellín. In each city we have left behind trained committees of the F.U.; some very good, others regular, and what is much more important we have always found someone for that which interests us, the war—for those to support it and participate actively in it. The exposition of my personal thesis on abstention, which the enemies understand to be the thesis of the F.U., has provoked a brutal reception on the part of the leaders and has permitted the rise now of the first enemies within the government opposition (López and Anapo). I did not try to neutralize the clergy, which is now important, but I had a very long chat with Rojas, with the result that at present their opposition is not so deep. We must, naturally, test it. . . . knows them all personally, which will also be very important afterwards. The brutal repression directed by the Church in Medellín has also provoked very important reactions in our favor; the open support of the trade union, student organizations, etc., could now be sensed. Parliamentarians were naturally the most discussed; but I tell you that. . . . has just left the MRL to work full-time with the F.U., and that Ruíz Novoa lost even more prestige for wanting to take advantage of his support for his dissident branch of the M.D.N. As was expected, the round table with Zalama was something I consider useless even though several of the assistants have found that he left it in a very bad state. Within one hour we left with . . . . and . . . . for Villavo, and it is possible that other companions might travel there by land tomorrow. The periodical is always out on the 26th, and we already have enough brigades for its distribution; I will be in Bogotá that day and I will personally organize one of the brigades. For the periodical (legal aspect of the F.V.) we have obtained a small office, which, although it is lacking in any luxury, has the great advantages of being cheap, legalizing the F.U. and assuring easy contact with all the people, which was very important. Naturally those lizards flock there like flies, but you know as well as I do that very soon they will retreat and that in the moment of the first danger they will disappear by themselves. The work nucleuses of non-aligned people are already being formed, and from the 23rd to the 28th (i.e., between Villavo and Tolima) I will devote myself principally to the work in the slums, above all in those which already have an embryo of a F.U. committee. For the Offset I will tell you that. . . . is going to sign a contract. He will work with. . . . in order to learn how to handle it and he will run the apparatus fulltime. . . . failed me in the sense that he cannot help us with more than 10,000 for the offset and the F.U. is not in condition to help. The finances are bad enough, but I am not overly anxious.

I am completely in agreement with all the points treated in your letter and it is truly the path we are following. Your decision regarding. . . . is marvelous; I sincerely believe that he is the person indicated to accompany me. In Medellín, especially, his presence at my side was very useful.

We spoke for a long time with. . . . about the security measures, and I believe that today everything will be organized. As far as. . . . in relation to. . . . I am in agreement with you. The first is already working but. . . . will have a long chat with him.

I am writing you on the run today. When I return from Villavo I will have more time to be able to fill you in on all that is being done. Especially regarding the organization, the important contacts, etc.

As regards the comrades, the old "pacos" are giving me a hard time. Until now, I have privately shown them that I don't like their activity, but I think that within a short time I will have to do it publicly; with the necessary tact, of course.

Tell Doctor. . . . that we await his works for the periodical.

A hug for everyone.

Last news: . . . . would like to travel with me; what do you say?

Is your offer to travel firm?

Alfredo"[18]

The logical explanation of the previous letters becomes clear by comparing them with those which figure in the following campaign against the Army of National Liberation. These deserve to be studied before a final judgment is given. Camilo could be summoned before the War Council at any moment because of these confiscated documents. Only the most opportune moment to strike was patiently awaited. But even though this could be alleged as a powerful reason, it was certainly not the cause of his decision. One afternoon of that same month of August he commented: "I am a guerilla on commission here in the city."

What impact did the calamity of the October demonstration produce? He had instigated it through the weekly *Frente Unido*. Enthusiastic messages began to arrive from all over. He visited the poor neighborhoods of Bogotá and spoke with the workers and the leaders of the progressive movements. The students were organized. It was to be a colossal event—100,000 persons would enter the Plaza Bolívar and the adjoining streets in an orderly parade. At the moment of truth, the result was disastrous. The armed forces were informed and took measures. The promised self-defense did not materialize when the troops blocked the main plaza.

At the last moment meetings were called, but very few participants arrived. Some troops which were previously informed divided the demonstrators. Some clashes were reported. Camilo was struck, and was saved only because they hid him in a building in the center of the city. To sum it all up, it was a complete fiasco. Was he the victim of a double-cross?

A little later he undertook new excursions. When he returned from the second to last one, they presented him with a tentative organizational scheme. He thought it was marvellous, and it was agreed that when he returned from his next trip of agitation through the cities, the proposed plan would be put into effect. What actually happened is that it all remained in the planning stages.

At the time, Camilo said, "The day the oligarchy begins to make me offers to betray the people, the possibility for war in the city will be finished and I will continue it in the country." And they did make him offers: the Cardinal, to go to Louvain; the Rockefeller Foundation, a scholarship in the United States; the ANAPO (Alianza National Popular) asked him to support their nominee in exchange for an embassy in any part of the world. In the government some suggested that he be placed at the head of the opposition in exchange for laws and decrees to precipitate rapid social transformation. Camilo did not give in. A little later a friend informed him, "Be careful, because in the Ministry of National Defense steps have been taken to bring you before the Council." In support of this, a few days later, they made known to him a list compiled by the Intelligence Service, with thirty names of activists in the United Front who would be apprehended soon.

In August, he was advised that he would be "attacked by any means possible, including eliminating him." In the face of this turn of events, three choices were open to Camilo—to seek asylum in an embassy, to remain in the city in the absolute certainty that they would murder him in jail or during a demonstration, or to go to the mountains.

Convinced of the necessity of an authentic revolution and that his work in the city was finished, he resolved to give the final proof of his total commitment and he went to the guerillas, thus signalling armed warfare as the only effective way to take power away from the oligarchy. He did not communicate his decision to many of his closest friends. I received only this message, "Regards from Camilo; he has gone to the mountains." "He has sentenced himself to death," was my response. Every morning from then on I asked myself, "Will it be today?"

A friend of his, a serious man, truthful and responsible, has directly submitted for this book some very interesting data. It is my judgment that his testimony reflects the truth.

On October 18, 1965, at 5 P.M. Camilo said to him: "I cannot remain here any longer. The army already knows everything. It knows of my connection with the Army of National Liberation. I don't want to let them kill me as they did Gaitán on the Carrera Septima. They will have to kill me in the mountains. They killed Gaitán in the city, and his death did not point to any solution. If they kill me in the mountains, my death will show the way. The army is not so stupid as to put me in prison, because I would be more dangerous to them there. I have become a problem for them."

At 7:50 in the evening he was seen meeting with many people in the offices of *Frente Unido*. They were waiting to take him to a gathering in one of the neighborhoods of Bogotá. At a particular moment he called aside a friend—from whom I have heard this—and said, "Come with me when I leave."

They left and took a taxi. Camilo told the driver to take them to the military hospital. On the way he picked up another person. When they arrived, Camilo dismissed the car, entered the entrance hall on the ground floor and asked in the information office for a fictitious sick person. In five minutes he returned to his two companions and they left the hospital grounds on foot and came to Carrera Tercera. While they were waiting for a taxi, Camilo said:

"This shouldn't be a puzzle to you. I came here to check that no one was following me."

A fine drizzle was falling on the city. Camilo said very little; he didn't seem worried but was more silent than customary. When finally, they got a taxi, he said to the driver: "Carrera Septima at Calle seventy-two, please."

The driver, when he recognized Camilo, told him that the people had great confidence in him. Camilo replied: "Rest assured that I will not fail them."

At the corner they left the car and went down Calle 72 to Carrera Octava. They walked to Calle 70. Camilo seemed even more tranquil, walked slowly, and seemed euphoric. On Calle 70 they returned to Carrera Septima. There they saw a car parked.

Camilo stopped and said in a low voice "You two are the only ones I trust at this moment. I am going to the mountains. The time has come. The army knows everything. I hope we will meet there some day."

He at once embraced one of his friends and said to him: "It is always a great adventure to think that we could be there seven or ten years." Then he embraced the other.

Immediately, he went up to the car where two persons waited for him—one, the driver, the other in the back seat. The car headed north. It began to rain harder. The two friends watched him pull away from them, and one of them exclaimed: "Oh hell, this Camilo is a very brave man." They returned in silence to the offices of *Frente Unido,* where many continued to wait for Camilo, to go with him to the meeting scheduled for that night in a worker neighborhood.

What did Camilo take with him? Really nothing material. But instead something which was the reason for his life: faith in the people, hope in his people.

Why did he choose the zone of San Vicente de Chucurí and no other? Located towards the center of the country, close to the petroleum workers, people of very clear democratic conscience, a scene of violence in the past and the seat of a guerilla group made up of elements of a higher cultural level than that of the simple peasants, it held the possibility of contact with insurgent forces from Venezuela, or Colombians. These are factors which perhaps helped him make his decision.

There he fought with the Army of National Liberation. He joined it so that the sons of those who wished to give their lives might have an education, a home, food, clothes, and, above all, dignity; so that future Colombians can have their own country, independent of North American power and of the exploitation of the oligarchy. He had said this in his message of January 17, 1966.

Chapter 16

The Hour of Witness

A little before October 18, 1965, the day on which Camilo went to the mountains, he said to the reporters: "I have to take a long and painful trip. I don't know if I will return to Bogotá. We revolutionaries must be prepared to give all—even our lives."[1]

A presentiment? At times we prophesy our end without realizing it. He had now handed over his plea and his ideas to the conscience of the reactionaries. Events would give them their exact answer and confirm the justice or injustice of his acts.

In the beginning of 1966, Camilo's last pronouncement reached the daily papers:

"From the mountains, January 1966

Colombians:

For many years the poor in our country have waited for the call to battle in order to launch the final attack against the oligarchy.

In those moments in which the desperation of the people has reached the extreme, the ruling class has always found some way to trick the people, to distract them, to appease them with new formulas which always amount to the same thing: suffering for the people and good living for the privileged class.

When the people asked for a leader and found him in Jorge Eliecer Gaitán, the oligarchy killed him. When the people asked for peace, the oligarchy spread violence in the country. When the people could no longer put up with violence and organized the guerillas to seize power, the oligarchy invented the military coup to trick the guerillas so that they would be betrayed. When the people asked for democracy, they were again tricked with a plebiscite and a National Front which imposed on them a dictatorship of the oligarchy.

Now the people no longer believe. The people do not believe in elections. The people know that legal avenues are exhausted and that only the way of force is left. The people are desperate and resolved to gamble their lives so that the next generation of Colombians might not be slaves. So that the children of those who now wish to give their lives might have education, houses, food, clothing and, above all, dignity. So that future Colombians can have their own country, independent of North American power.

Every sincere revolutionary must recognize the way of force as the only one which remains. Nevertheless, the people await leaders who, with their example and their presence, will give the call to battle.

I want to tell the Colombian people that this is the moment; that I have not betrayed them; that I have passed through the plazas of the towns and cities campaigning for the unity and organization of the people for the seizure of power; that I have asked that we dedicate ourselves to these objectives even though it may mean our death.

Now everything is prepared. The oligarchy wants to organize another farce of elections, with candidates who renounce and then accept, with bipartisan committees, with movements of renovation based on ideas and persons who not only are old but who have betrayed the people. What more can we expect, Colombians?

I have involved myself in the armed battle. From the mountains I will continue the fight with arms in hand until power is conquered for the people. I have joined the Army of National Liberation because I have found in it the same ideals as in the United Front. I have found both the desire and the fulfillment of a unity which has a peasant base, without religious differences or traditional parties . . . without any desire to battle the revolutionary elements of any other sector, movement, or party . . . without *caudillos*. It is searching for a way to free the people from the exploitation of the oligarchy and from imperialism. It will not put down its arms as long as power is not totally in the hands of the people. In its objectives it accepts the Platform of the United Front.

All of us Colombian patriots must place ourselves at the service of the war. Little by little experienced guerilla leaders will arise in all the corners of the country. In the meanwhile we must be alert. We must collect arms and munitions, seek guerilla training, talk with the more experienced, bring together clothes, food, provisions and drugs in order to prepare ourselves for a prolonged fight.

Let us perform small works against the enemy; in this way we will assure victory. Let us prove to them what revolutionaries are. Let us throw out the traitors. Let us not fail to act, but let us not be impatient. In a prolonged war all will have to act at some time. What is important is that the revolution finds us ready at that precise moment. It is not necessary for everyone to do everything. We must divide the work. The militants of the United Front must be the vanguard of initiative and action. Let us have patience in the hope and confidence of final victory.

The battle of the people must become a national battle. We have already begun, but the journey is long. Colombians, let us not fail to respond to the call of the people and of the revolution. Militants of the United Front, let us make our objectives a reality.

For the unity of the people! Until death!

For the organization of the people! Until death!

For the seizure of power for the people! Until death!

Until death because we have decided to persevere to the end.

Until victory because once a people gives itself completely it always obtains victory.

Until final victory for the objectives of the Army of National Liberation!

Not one step back! Freedom or death!

Camilo Torres Restrepo"[2]

What followed? A series of fatal events converged. When he went to the mountains Camilo became a very dangerous threat to the continuation of the prevailing "order." Because of his leadership qualities, there was a very great possibility of polarizing a considerable guerilla contingent which, spread out in strategic places, could give the impetus to an arduous and difficult fight. This could have such grave consequences as the country being invaded by the North American Marines, as in the case of Santo Domingo.

When asked about Camilo's decision, President Guillermo León Valencia replied to the reporters: "He is a bandit." Lieutenant Colonel Rivas Farero, the Commandant of the Tenerife Battalion, quartered in Neiva, had said, referring to Camilo: "If he raises his head, he will be knocked down." This matches the tactics in use where the guerillas were concerned: "Either they come over or they die."

On January 17, 1966, the following story appeared in the press:

ARMED FORCES BATTLE THE ARMY OF NATIONAL LIBERATION

The armed forces of the nation recently determined to engage in battle the so-called Army of National Liberation which has been operating in a definite region of eastern Colombia and to which the ex-cleric Camilo Torres went a few days ago.

It was officially revealed that the high military commands and the commandants of the Army Brigades met in the last week of December to analyze carefully the situation with which we are faced by the action of this new extremist force.

The appearance of the Army of National Liberation reaffirms the revelation made last November 5th by the Minister of National Defense that a new type of political violence was growing in the country which was clearly and definitely of Communist direction.

In the meeting of the military high commands, after the report of

Colonel Alvaro Valencia Tovar, Commandant of the Fifth Brigade with headquarters in Bucaramanga, they arrived at the conclusion that this Army of National Liberation does not represent any serious danger for the stability of the country. It was deduced that the organization is directed by extremist elements with the definite goal of imposing the Communist revolution by means of force. Special measures were adopted in that meeting to prevent the activities of the extremists from erupting in other regions of the country. It was agreed to seal off the entire zone between Gamarra (Magdalena) and San Vicente de Chucurí (Santander).

The military spokesman also indicated that civic-military action will be intensified in the region and that the Armed Forces will remain on the alert in order to avoid new incursions of the Army of National Liberation.[3]

On February 1st the following item appeared in the press under the heading "Study of Public Order":

Drastic means of preserving public order were studied in a meeting of the National Defense Council. As regards the ex-priest Camilo Torres, it was stated that the Armed Forces lacked information concerning his whereabouts.[4]

In the meantime, in the mountains, Camilo went in search of his destiny. Without doubt he thought of a different Colombia; of an army advancing from the mountains to re-establish justice through violence; guerillas answering his call to arms in waves; of a change of structures to enthrone a new order; of the advance of the people on the roads of liberty.

Thus obsessed, he would look at this beloved country raked from the south to the north by the harsh geography of its three mountain ranges, giant arms which divide the heart of the country, whose highest peaks reach heights of 5,800 meters and then open up into valleys, altiplanos, and plains with the most varied climates. Cold plains; green hillsides perfumed with the flowering of the coffee plantations; crests of basalt which defy time; thundering waterfalls; plains where rivers sleep in back-waters where men and centuries walk without anxiety; and everywhere the golden hope of the grain, the lightly etched cornfields, the defiant green banana shoots, the sugar cane whose leaves shine like swords under the sun and the peaceful pastures with their marshy lands where the boa sleeps lazily and the alligator lurks with insatiable appetite, and beyond that, the immense, mysterious, devouring jungle.

Colombia the beloved, land of contrasts, with white snow and the blossoming of bright fresh flowers; devout and mystical in the Andean mesas, inspiring song in the souls of men. Colombia of the airplane and the mule and the nomadic tribe; soothing in the enchanting pleasant tones with which the common language is spoken; learned and literate in the upper class, still unlettered in a great percentage of the poor class; congenial in its people, heroic in the daily honest toil of the workers whose backs are burned by the tropical sun. Colombia growing with its bursting population—women pregnant with the hoped-for fruit of life, even when their children will never see the light because of the mothers' undernourishment. Colombia, on whose ground the feet of young girls and the galloping hooves of the centaurs of emancipation pass with equal confidence.

Colombia burdened with underdevelopment but in search of potential riches; with too many people who are housed in the slums of cities where industry is accelerated with violent rhythm, who work day and night with unquestionable honesty; with 800,000 rural families coming to the large cities in serach of a "dorado" still far away; with a responsible government, persisting in a peaceful transformation through democratic channels, confronted with international economic pressures and difficult national commitments; with a handful of Quizotes who dream from the jungle of an integral change, called criminals by others but by themselves guerillas, for them a synonym for the actors in an historical drama.

Within all this Camilo is a point of reference. The mild-mannered teacher dedicated at one time to subtle study in his room; surrounded by books whose diversity indicates that they belong to a man of very considerable culture; gentlemanly in his manners and a pleasant conversationalist when he plays with his great mental agility or subtle and serious when he speaks as a scientist in speeches, seminars, and round tables or as a skilful debater in conferences of a social or political nature. There he was the young man of the upper class, educated in Europe, who drove recklessly on his motorcycle or in his car to arrive with unrepentant tardiness at the next conference; the priest whose white hands shone with the glittering gold of the chalices. Now he is Camilo Torres Restrepo, no longer the professor, no longer the bright intellectual, no longer the gentleman of the distinguished salons, no longer the priest but the militia-man lost in the jungle, without any comfort, without electric light, without newspapers, without cultured dialogue, harassed by mosquitoes' stings.

Camilo was tall and robust with a noble, even elegant, appearance. He had fair skin and a good build, clear dark eyes and long, graceful hands. His full lips emphasized the pleasantness of his appearance. The simplicity of his manners never lost the mark of his good breeding. He was intellectually restless and gave the impression of a rebel, although he was basically humble. He had constantly to fight physical fatigue. His was a nervous temperament, easily moved to impatience, but just as rapidly he would regain his calm. He was inclined to be caustic in arguments, in which his mental agility served him well. His social behavior was uncomplicated. He had the good fortune to be naturally frank and the misfortune to be naive. He was adamant in his convictions when he considered them reasonable. His profound sense of justice made him instantly and deeply sensitive to human problems. He had an outward peacefulness which revealed the inner strength of a compelling and decisive personality.

Perhaps the blood of some bellicose ancestor made him desire a triumph won through immense trials. We can see the stamp of our old political leaders who left everything to go to fight behind their rebel standards.

Once in the jungle, it would have been fitting that Camilo's mission should be to instruct small, newly arrived groups, very far from the line of battle and with all the safeguards necessary to preserve life. To be involved in active fighting was a possibility which should have been avoided by all means possible. Why did he commit himself?

According to all trustworthy accounts, he arrived at the group in arms and demanded that he be subjected to a training course just like any other guerilla. He washed his own clothes, he cooked for his companions, he took guard duty, he received military instruction, he learned how to handle arms, and he promoted political formation in some areas around them. In a very short time he earned the first positions. No one could prevent him from participating in the action which cost him his life. He wanted to obtain his own arms from the enemy. To all the arguments they gave him, he responded, "Do you all think I came here to be treated as useless baggage? Or that I am not capable of fighting? Or that I have less courage than you? Do you think I am less energetic than you are? Either I am treated like a guerilla or this is no place for me. I have to run the same risks you do."

When they insisted that he should not go, he became furious and told them: "Either let me fight or shoot me." Going against the orders of the leaders, he marched to the ambush. For the first time he participated in an act of war.

How is this explained? The power of conviction which Camilo possessed was so often overwhelming. Those who sought to oppose him lost to his immense influence over his companions, his courage, his integral concept of friendship, his conviction of commitment and his honorable rendezvous with death. He was in the mountains and he knew that at any moment there he could be surprised by the burst of gunfire. And in the mountains he remained facing heaven, Colombia, this Indian and mulatoo America—face to face with the conscience of free men.

The circumstances, the form, the details, the accidentals are not important. In people such as Camilo, the transcendence of their destiny begins with death. It happened on a Tuesday, February 15, 1966, at 10:30 in the morning. The first news came through on the 16th:

> In the foot paths of the Andes, district of El Carmen, jurisdiction of the Municipality of San Vicente, troops of the Ricaurte Battalion made contact with a group of bandits of the so-called Army of Liberation. Men fell on both sides: four soldiers and five bandits, one sub-official and one soldier wounded. . . . There are peasants who testify

that Father Camilo is also found there. They pick out a new person who looks much different from the rest of the group.[5]

The first military communication:

> The Commandant of the Fifth Brigade makes known to the citizentry that in the place called Cañón del Pilar, Patio de Cemento, on the way to Riosucio and three and a half hours from the district of El Carmen, municipality of San Vicente, on today, the 15th of February, at approximately 11:30, there was an encounter between armed bandits and troops of the Brigade who were fulfilling missions of rural security. In this action, one of our patrols was ambushed. One official, one sub-official, and one soldier were wounded and four soldiers were killed. The army patrol reacted immediately, killing five of the bandits and capturing all the weapons they were carrying, including three long-range weapons. The troops in the area will continue in their search.
>
> The Fifth Brigade will continue to exert all its efforts to cover the peasant areas and offer them the security which is indispensable for the preservation of order and the free exercise of honest work.
>
> Colonel Alvaro Valencia Tovar,
> Commandant of the Fifth Brigade.[6]

The radio begins to announce the news at 11:00 A.M. An atmosphere of tension is created. *El Vespertino* carries the news in large headlines: "Extra! Camilo is dead." *El Espacio* also: "Camilo Torres is dead!"[7] The citizens, anxious for details, grab up all the papers and one question is on the lips of everyone: How did Camilo die? Popular fantasy runs wild before the unexpected events. But as the reality hits them with all its brutal force, confusion slowly gives way to certainty or to a close approximation to the truth, a process which starts with rumor, supposition, the absurd, and ends in the evidence.

This explains why the following versions of the death of Camilo circulated:

1. The Army had the peremptory order to kill him, as he was the most dangerous enemy in the mountains since, given the prestige which he had, he could create a very grave situation for public order.

2. Camilo was captured, and when he was being led to military headquarters a fanatical enemy of his killed him.

3. Camilo was held for days in the prison of El Carmen, from which he escaped one morning at four o'clock. A soldier saw him and shot and killed him. When they realized who it was they had killed, they invented the ambush.

4. The military brought Camilo to the mountains. They faked the assault and killed him. Thus they fulfilled their assignment to kill him.

5. Camilo wanted to leave the guerillas. Those in the Army of National Liberation betrayed him, placing him in the line of fire. Such is the information given by *El Tiempo* in Bucaramanga: "Not long ago the news spread that 'Father Camilo' was fed up and was going to escape from the organization. In order to keep him, they committed him to an ambush of the army on the road. Then two soldiers were killed. It seems that it was the first baptism of blood for the ex-priest."[8]

6. The Communists killed Camilo because they were interested in exploiting him as a revolutionary incentive, in order to harm the prestige of the government, the oligarchy, and Yankee imperialism.

7. Some inhabitants of the petroleum zone related: "A group in arms plundered a camp. They didn't kill anyone. They took away drugs and some kitchen equipment. The head of the camp immediately informed the Army, testifying that it seemed that Camilo was with them. Two patrols pursued them, making contact, and in the encounter Camilo died."

8. In Pamplona, during the War Council towards the end of 1966, it was discovered that the army patrol was assaulted by the group where Camilo was. The sergeant, a man very experienced in anti-guerilla warfare, already wounded, feigned death, and when Camilo advanced shot him. Two bullets hit him: one in the shoulder and the other in the stomach, necessarily mortal. Taking advantage of the confusion, the sergeant entrenched himself and, helped by some companions, killed those who tried to take out the body of Camilo.

When they searched him they found letters in French and English and in his sack a pipe and some books. These were the indications which helped Colonel Valencia Tovar suspect—in addition to the physical description—that this was Camilo. It also transpired that the soldiers, in an understandable reaction, when they gained control of the situation, had struck the body, not knowing who it was.

9. Military Communication No. 007:

The Commandant of the Fifth Brigade reports to the citizenry the following: Because of the ambush which an armed group of about 25 men produced Tuesday, February 15th, against a patrol of this unit in the place called Patio Cemento of the district of El Carmen, municipality of San Vicente de Chucurí, we have the results which were given to the public. Five men who were shot down by the patrol have been identified where possible, even though their identification has not been definitive:

(1) Camilo Torres Restrepo

(2) Aureliano Plata Espinosa

(3) Salvador Afanador, alias "Saul" or "El Tuerto," who participated in the assault at Simacota and who was the person who was the cause of the death of the first agent of the National Police who lost his life at that time.

(4) Paulino Rodríguez Sandoval, alias "Policarpo," who actively participated in the assault on Simacota.

(5) This man has not been identified.

Among the arms recovered by the troops who participated in the action there was found the M-1 .30 caliber rifle which was carried by one of the soldiers who died at the hands of the bandits in the assault on Simacota, January 7, 1965. This rifle, with the number 5.188.554, was found in the hands of someone later identified as Camilo Torres Restrepo. It has been technially proved that it had been fired moments before its capture.

The bodies of the persons enumerated in this list were buried in a place located within the general area where the armed encounter, to which reference has been made, occurred.

Bucaramanga, February 17, 1966

Colonel Alvaro Valencia Tovar, Commandant of the Fifth Brigade[9]

10. Guillermo Joya Zuñiga, correspondent for *El Espectador* in Barrancabermeja, reported for *El Vespertino:* "When we arrived at the headquarters (El Carmen) they told us to wait, as the bodies would arrive at any moment. Several members of the DAS (Departamento Administrativo de Seguridad) accompanied me as well as some personnel from the fingerprint lab who came to take the fingerprints of the dead men in order to fully establish their identity.

"It was two hours later, approximately, when the five bodies arrived at the headquarters aboard an Army truck. They came on some improvised stretchers of rustic wood, rope, and army canvas. Groups of soldiers were taking the bodies down one by one and placing them in a row in the patio behind the headquarters. The second one was Father Camilo Torres. Once the corpses were placed there, the technicians of the DAS were given the task of taking their fingerprints. In the meantime a great number of curious people, mostly peasants from the region, and the local curate tried to find out what was happening. . . .

"All five wore olive green military uniforms and campaign boots and had cartridge belts and holsters for their revolvers. Next to the bodies, the soldiers brought the arms which they had captured: two rifles, two revolvers, a large number of bullets and a homemade bomb. They also brought in two sacks which contained some canvas, medicines, and a pipe belonging to Father Camilo.

"I heard it said that the patrol which was on inspection in the zone of El Carmen had received an order to return to headquarters, since up to eight o'clock Tuesday morning they had not found any sign of the rebel groups who were said to be operating there. When the patrol arrived at the place called Patio de Cemento, it was surprised by a group of more than twenty guerillas. Among them there was a woman who wore blue jeans and who carried a rifle which she began to fire against the Army patrol. This first attack left four dead and two wounded. The soldiers who were not hurt prepared to repel the attack.

"According to the soldiers, five of the guerillas advanced to where the soldiers lay dead and wounded. One of the guerillas—according to them, he was Camilo Torres—was preparing to finish off Lieutenant González, who lay on the ground. On seeing this, one of the soldiers nearby fired his rifle several times at the person trying to kill the lieutenant, killing him instantly. The other soldiers also fired against the four who were with this one who they say is Father Camilo.

"The other guerillas stayed hidden behind the shrubbery. Suddenly, the woman who wore blue jeans appeared and fired in the direction of the hidden soldiers. She managed to get to the body of a soldier who was carrying a machine gun and she took it. When she began to run, a bullet fired by one of the hidden soldiers hit her hand. Nevertheless, the woman continued running and hid in the forest."[10]

11. Carlos Chacón Soto, reporter for *El Tiempo,* wrote for his periodical:

"The place where the battle developed is located two and a half hours from the hacienda El Centenario, which is as far as it is possible to go in a car. There is a large house which is used as a school for Riosucio. From there on you have to go on foot or on a horse, and there are only thatched houses or simple farms inhabited by old families who cultivate cacao or coffee. The road is all broke up and very difficult to travel.

"Patio de Cemento is the only level place that exists in that sector. It seems to me that it is the remains of an abandoned heliport which could have been constructed in the first stage of the violence which raged in San Vicente during the times of Cabo Florido.

"A few meters' distance from Patio de Cemento, within a sheltering grove of cacao, the bodies of the five members of the so-called 'Army of Liberation' were found; they were in a row at a distance, one from another, of one or two meters, and fifty meters from the Sucio river bed. All were found behind the trunks of the trees. About five meters beyond, the bodies of the four soldiers were found almost in a pile, and little further away the three wounded, including Lieutenant González. Alarcón.

"The incident developed in this way: Camilo Torres and his companions had already seen the first army patrol, probably at Patio Cemento, which the troops had to pass through if they wanted to continue their inspection. When they entered the cacao orchard, they were surprised by a volley which immediately killed four and wounded three. Some minutes of silence followed while those who had done the firing stripped the bodies of their arms.

"At that moment the rebels approached the dead and wounded soldiers. A soldier who was uninjured and near the wounded lieutenant, feigning death, suddenly got up and fired his machine gun against the group who were approaching. The shots hit Camilo Torres and four of his companions, while the others fled into the deeper forest. The Inspector of El Carmen, first sergeant of police Jaime Quintero Herrera, removed the bodies at 5:30 in the evening."[11]

12. The following version seems to be the closest to the truth:

"For days before, the guerillas had followed the steps of the patrol. The ambush was well prepared, as they knew the terrain well and had other strategic advantages. The military detachment was in two groups. The lieutenant marched in the second squadron, at a distance of some meters from the vanguard. When this group entered the area, the guerilla leader fired his Madsen and four soldiers fell. The others were dispersed while the battle intensified. Camilo tried to pick up the rifle of a soldier who had fallen a meter and a half from him at the most; in his first attempt he was wounded. The leader asked him if he was wounded and Camilo responded: 'They hit me but I can still move.' The leader yelled to him 'Retreat! Get back!' But Camilo, in a second attempt to get the arms, was shot again, and this time fatally. One of the combatants tried to recover the body and was brought down. The same thing happened to a young peasant who crept through the zone of fire to where Camilo lay.

"Two more guerillas fell in the skirmish. They were shot by a sergeant, a veteran of anti-guerilla warfare, who managed to get into an advantageous position. In the meanwhile, the lieutenant had begun an encircling operation, but he was stopped by a guerilla group. He fell wounded close to Camilo.

"The combatant who carried the grenade was told several times to throw it, in order to dislodge the sergeant, but for unexplainable reasons he didn't do it. It is known that he deserted that same night.

"When they realized that the operation was a failure and it was impossible to recover the bodies, the surviving guerillas crossed the river Sucio and fled to their camps."[12]

13. The Army of National Liberation issued the following statement:

With deep sorrow and increased rancor against the oligarchical classes, the Army of National Liberation reports to the Colombian people, and to the revolutionaries of the entire world, that the death of the great revolutionary priest leader, Camilo Torres Restrepo, occurred on February 15th of this year during a battle between our own forces and punitive detachments of the traitor army of the National Front.

In this encounter our heroic soldiers courageously fought the official forces, causing numerous dead and wounded, confiscating several long-range weapons and various military equipment and repulsing once more the attempts at total annihilation by the official army. Nevertheless, we had the irremediable loss of five courageous patriots, among whom fell the irreplaceable Camilo, together with other injured companions who tried to rescue him from the danger zone.

This new crime of official violence is the result of the punitive action against the magnificent forces which our people have raised in order to throw off the hateful yoke of the oligarchy and North American imperialism, seeing themselves obliged to sacrifice their best sons on the altar of the country's interests.

Camilo died as a hero, conscious that leaders must set an example. He never accepted a safe position for himself. He knew the risks of war and he accepted them, convinced that his death might spark the fire which the Colombian people would begin to direct against the government forces which sustain the system of injustice and ignominy.

We who will attempt to be legitimate heirs of his thinking and human greatness wish to place his sacrifice in perspective before the masses. We have many things to learn from it. His life was clear and pure. He united the scientific conception of revolutionary war, as the only effective way to develop the fight for freedom, with his profound Christianity, which he extended and practiced as a limitless love for the poor, the exploited and oppressed and as a complete dedication to the battle for their liberation. He died in the work of guiding the people to the seizure of power, but he only died physically. His body was outrageously treated by the government assassins. Proof of that are the facial bruises which appear in the photos of the press. The people will make them pay for this act of miserable cruelty.

But his thinking grows more important with his martyrdom. The justification of his theses takes progressive hold of the conscience of the workers. As a tribute to his memory, we will make the popular unity, on which he insisted so much, a living reality as soon as possible. Thousands of peasants, workers, students, professionals and dedicated men will replace him in the ranks of the ELN with their physical and moral presence. Our force will grow in strength, guided by the great spirit of Camilo. His rememberance has filled our hearts with fighting spirit and hatred for the mercenaries of the oligarchy. Our people will grind into dust those responsible for the death of their great leader. Joined to him we will redouble our eagerness for the fight until death because, as Camilo taught us, "a people that fights until death will always obtain victory."

Peasants, we will seek a basic unity, with a peasant foundaton, without religious or traditional party differences, reinforcing the battle units of the ELN.

Students and Intellectuals, your fight will cease to be sterile when it is closely bound to the forces of the guerilla fighters.

Workers, the final decision of the social freedom battle which is shaking the country is in your hands and your organization.

Officials, subofficials, and soldiers, stop your repressive action. Don't be the assassin instrument of the oligarchy and of your anti-national government. Don't stain your hands with the pure blood of those who, like Camilo, seek only to give our country dignity.

Priests, take the martyrdom of Camilo as a sublime example of a love of neighbor which gives all and asks nothing in return. Become a part of the people in the fight against their oppressors!

Finally, let us call on all popular organizations to energetically demand, even to the point of forcefully taking away from the clutches of his murderers, the body of our beloved leader. Let us make of his tomb a national monument.

For the unity of the people, even to death!

For the organization of the people, even to death!

For the seizure of power by the people, even to death!

From the mountains, February, 1966 Army of National Liberation (ELN)

Fabio Vázquez Castaño,
Victor Medina Morón[13]

Some have been infantile enough to assert that Camilo did not die and that it was only a trick. But his death is certain. It was "the fatal encounter of a man in arms engaged in battle with the forces of order." The official certification of the body of Jorge Camilo Torres Restrepo reads as follows:

February 19, 1966

N.N. of 35 years of age, tall and muscular. He had long hair and a red beard. At the general inspection of the body there was found: (1) circular wound of one centimeter in diameter in the surface of the left shoulder, made with a bullet of heavy caliber; the bullet left by the shoulder blade; (2) equal wound in the left side; the bullet followed a trajectory from above down and from the left to the right, and left through the right ilium. This wound was necessarily mortal. Autopsy by Dr. Rafael Calderón Villamizar, Head Legal Doctor, Office of Legal Medicine of Bucaramanga[14]

The certification of death is as follows:

Third Notary of Bucaramanga, No. 473. Name: Jorge Camilo Torres Restrepo. February 24, 1966, the citizen Sigifredo Grisales G. advises the notary of the fact of his death. He gives as the hour and date: 10:30 A.M. February 15, 1966. He says that Camilo was 37 years old and was born in Bogota and that he died in "Patio Cemento" (Municipality of San Vicente, Department of the South of Santander.) Notary: Dr. José Maria Philla Prada[15]

Here is the report of the DAS:

The body is that of Camilo Torres Restrepo who, according to the archives, was born February 3, 1939 [sic: it was in 1929]. 1.80 meters in height. Citizenship card No. 653 of Bogotá. In September of 1954 he presented a certificate of good conduct in order to travel to Belgium as a student. He did not have any police record. Report No. 1.039; Bogotá.[16]

This sad chapter must close with the question everyone asked—where was Camilo buried? In a place located within the general area where the encounter occurred according to the communication of the Fifth Brigade. But, where?

Someone said, in Bogotá, that he saw the body of Camilo in the command post of the Armed Forces, where a small group of some diplomatic missions had been invited before whom (with the body present) an official reported on the details of the death. "This is macabre! It isn't even seen in the Congo," said the informant.

In any case, his body will be found some day. In the meanwhile, the following documents throw light on the efforts which have been made in that direction:

"Minneapolis, Feb. 22, 1966

Doctor Pedro Gómez Valderrama, Minister of Government
Bogotá, Colombia

Mr. Minister:

In order to prevent my presence in Colombia in these days from being taken as a cause for disturbances, I have decided to remain permanently outside the country. Nevertheless, I am still very interested and consider it my duty to obtain a guarantee that my brother Camilo Torres Restrepo, who died on the 15th of this month, has obtained Christian burial. I understand that for reasons of public order it is necessary to keep hidden the place where Camilo was buried, but I also think it is necessary to have the assurance that the authorities know the exact place where he was buried so that once it is thought prudent, we, his family, can transfer the body to a place of our own choice.

I would be grateful to you, Mr. Minister, if you would send me as soon as possible a letter giving me assurances as regards the two points enumerated. Your word will be sufficient guarantee for me and I will not require on this occasion that you tell me the place of burial but only the assurance that this is known and that this information will be guarded in such a way that it can be used in the future to find the remains.

Since I know that, owing to possible bureaucratic complications, the consideration of this letter could be indefinitely postponed, and since for me and for my family as well as for the many friends of

Camilo this is of the utmost importance, if within a reasonable time I do not receive your response, I will have to consider that you can not give me the guarantees I ask and then we will make plans in accord with the situation.

Without anything else for the moment, I remain, Mr. Minister,

Sincerely,
Fernando Torres Restrepo
Professor of Neurology
University of Minnesota

Copies to: His Eminence Luis Cardinal Concha
Father Gustavo Pérez"[17]

"Bogotá, D.E., Feb. 26, 1966

Doctor Fernando Torres Restrepo
1300 Mount Curve Ave.
Minneapolis 5, Minnesota

Dear Doctor:

Today I received your letter of Feb. 22nd, in which, after communicating to me your decision to remain for the moment outside the country, you ask for a guarantee that your brother Camilo Torres Restrepo has had a Christian burial and the assurance that the authorities know the exact place where he was buried so that when it is considered prudent his family can transfer his body to a place of your own choice.

I understand very clearly your justifiable desire, and for that I hasten to give you an answer with the information which I have in relation to your inquiry. I have spoken with the Minister of National Defense to whom I have transmitted your petition, and I have asked him for the reports of the case. Only the Army knows the exact place of burial. The Minister of Defense authorized me to give you full assurances that the tomb is in a place perfectly known by the Army and that the moment the considerations of public order which you generously recognize in your letter have disappeared, his remains will be given to the family in accord with your wishes.

The National Government as well as the Armed Forces are

deeply grateful for the generous and admirable attitude which you have assumed in this sad problem. I wish, then, to express our appreciation and give you assurances that the information on the exact site of the burial of your brother will be rigorously protected so that the remains can be transferred in the future.

Sincerely,
Pedro Gómez Valderrama
Minister of Government

Copies to: His Eminence Luis Cardinal Concha
Father Gustavo Pérez
Ministry of National Defense"[18]

"Bucaramanga, April 19, 1966

Doctor Fernando Torres Restrepo
1300 Mount Curve Avenue
Minneapolis 5, Minnesota

Dear Doctor:

I am very grateful for your kind letter of the 11th of this month and for the noble expressions which distinguish it. They are an unmistakable sign of a character which I have had the honor to know only through letters which reflect its excellence, but one I hope to admire at closer range when the circumstances make a personal meeting propitious. For me this will be very pleasant.

I do not personally know the place where the provisional tomb of Camilo is found, but I have carefully registered the place from the moment in which he was buried, and that information is in the safe of the Brigade Command, under my immediate control. Now, and in fulfillment of your desire, I have ordered a copy which I will keep in my possession, foreseeing the eventuality of a transfer. This copy will be at your disposal the moment it is possible to fulfill your just wish to transfer the remains to the place of your choice.

I will personally make an inspection of the site, in order to be exactly informed on the details of its location, and in this way to be better able to fulfill towards you and towards Camilo this duty of consideration and friendship.

I wish to repeat at this time for you and your very worthy

family, my expressions of human friendship in these sad circumstances which have harshly taken his life.

Once more I am at your disposal in this Command, and I ask you to accept my firm sentiments of admiration and friendship.

Very Sincerely,
Colonel Alvaro Valencia Tovar"[19]

"Bogotá, December 14, 1966

Doctor Carlos Lleras Restrepo
President of the Republic
Mr. President:

Almost one year ago the Catholic priest Camilo Torres tragically fell in some place in Santander, according to public information. The Armed Forces buried the body, and since then in no way nor before any authority, directly or indirectly, as the mother of Father Torres and in exercise of the lawful right which that condition should bestow on me, have I petitioned for the remains of my son. This was because of the special circumstances in which his death came about. These circumstances could have been the reason for invoking the needs of public order against such a transference.

However, the passing of time has brought it about that, in my judgment and surely in the judgment of the government over which you preside, such reasons are no longer valid and that, on the contrary, the right which I have is more solid and more indisputable in that I can and should reclaim from the Colombian Nation the handing over of those remains, whose sentimental value, you can well judge, is immense for me.

That consideration, and the intimate conviction of reclaiming what is mine, united to my status as a Colombian citizen, move me to make use of the right which Article 45 of the Constitution sets down for formulating respectful petitions to the authorities and asking you, as the first authority of the Nation, to do what is necessary so that they may turn over to me, in the place and the date you think convenient and opportune, the remains of Father Camilo Torres.

I have permitted myself to direct this petition to you, Mr. President, since according to decree No. 2733 of 1959 'it is the primordial duty of all functionaries or public agents to make effective the exercise of the right which Article 45 makes sacred, through the rapid and opportune resolution of the petitions which, in civil terms, are presented to them and have a direct relation to the activities in their charge.'

For the rest, I refer to the terms mentioned in paragraph 2 of article 4 of the same decree, which prescribes that, 'when it should not be possible to resolve the petition within 15 days from the date on which it was received, the interested party will have to be notified and the reasons given for the delay and at the same time the date set on which it will be resolved,' so that if you are the competent official, resolve my petition in definite terms, either conceding or denying that which is sought, or in the absence of that, send it to the official who has responsibility over this particular case, advising me accordingly, all in conformity with the disposition of article 6 of the decree mentioned before.

I have invoked the right of petition as I believe that would have been the legal means used by you, Mr. President, if you were found in circumstances similar to mine.

You have been a righteous man and I have complete confidence that you will recognize and protect my right, which is that of all the women of Colombia and which consists in enveloping with our heart that which once was part of us.

Mr. President,
Isabel Restrepo de Torres"[20]

As of this date, this letter has not been answered.

The following is a letter of Senora Isabel Restrepo de Torres to Pope Paul VI:

"Bogotá, August 21, 1968

Holy Father:

I present myself to Your Holiness as the mother of the priest, Camilo Torres Restrepo.

The universally known case of my son, Camilo Torres Restrepo, reflects a situation of misery, oppression and exploitation suffered by a majority of our people. It demands a radical change in the economic, political and social structures of our country.

Camilo believed that his mission, as a Christian and a priest, could not be fulfilled without a revolution to liberate the poor, the peasants, the workers and the intellectuals—indeed, all the oppressed classes. As a consequence, he became a revolutionary and opted to involve himself in the armed struggle. This painful course was imposed on him by the violence practiced by the oligarchical classes of my country.

Camilo never preached violence for its own sake. He consistently stated that the ultimate decision belonged to the ruling classes. If they were disposed to peacefully abandon their privileges, the struggle could be peaceful. But if, as they have demonstrated, they were obstinate in trying to maintain themselves in power, the people would have no other means to defend themselves except armed struggle.

Camilo proclaimed the urgency of liberating the country from imperialist domination. He believed that there could be no basic structural change without freeing ourselves from imperialism, which is an inhuman and unchristian form of domination.

In essence, Camilo's thought coincides with what Your Holiness later proclaimed in the encyclical, *Populorum Progressio,* which impressed the entire world with its profound social significance.

Because of his courageous and constant preaching of these principles, my son Camilo Torres Restrepo was sacrificed somewhere in the Colombian hills. Like all those who prophesied and sowed the seeds of the renewal of the Church, my son had to suffer misunderstanding, personal attacks and calumny.

I do not pretend to make a defense of my son to Your Holiness, who are so profoundly human, whose wisdom has penetrated and pointed out the inequalities which exist between the various sectors of Christianity. I realize how difficult it is to make my mother's voice penetrate the lofty dignity of your office but it is significant that it is precisely Colombia—the homeland of Camilo Torres Restrepo, the priest sacrificed for the defense of his humble people, who suffer hunger and thirst for justice—that has been chosen for such a grandiose celebration as the International Eucharistic Congress.

I have suffered this rude shock in silence, without asking any more consolation than that the body of my son be returned to me, in order to render it the pious tribute which the Church itself prescribes for her dead. I ask that his remains may repose with mine in a consecrated place.

Why am I denied this elemental right which I have again and again begged of the Colombian government? I do not know, but it is certain that the body of my son lies ignored in some hidden place in Colombia. My sorrow grows in the face of the cruelty of this overwhelming injustice.

Holy Father, forgive me for disturbing the peace of your visit to Colombia with my sad request but I am certain that with your intercession I shall obtain the supreme and ultimate consolation of recovering the remains of my son, sacrificed on the altar of the purest ideal: the restoration of the doctrine of Christ.

In hopes of your benevolence, I remain your daughter in Christ,

Isabel Restrepo de Torres"

Chapter 17

Torn Garments

In the mountains, the life of Camilo could be snuffed out at any moment. Friends and adversaries had this feeling, almost this certainty. Would his death unleash in the masses a reaction as brutal and as devastating as that of April 1948 when the popular leader Jorge Eliécer Gaitán fell assassinated? Why was another deplorable massacre not produced?

Gaitán created a mystique of the masses, but he did not succeed in giving them a sense of concrete action directed towards the seizure of power. Therefore, when he died, the anarchy went beyond every attempt at channeling energies towards positive means.

Camilo revived the hope of the people, but he was unable to found historically either a strongly progressive Christian movement or, if not that, a movement with deep roots in a socialism anchored in our national reality. Then too the bloodshed of April 9, 1948, was too sorrowful a memory for the people in addition to being meaningless and sterile.

The inconsistency of Camilo's movement, his organization barely in its infancy, the responsible groups only outlined, the general confusion which spread with his abortive determination to go to the mountains, the impact of the violence still too real—all of these were no foundation for an abortive, spontaneous, dominating, irresistible overflowing of popular emotion. The stupor was intensified by a sensation of impotence which paralyzed every violent reaction.

Moreover, the news of the death was given officially after every means necessary for safeguarding public order in the country had been adopted. In Bogotá and the principal cities an intense patrol was organized as the best means of precaution.

It is interesting in view of future studies to observe the reactions in the different groups.

STUDENT CLASS:

In the National University flags were flown at half mast. In some buildings of the White City black crepe appeared. The reaction was no more than small disturbances on the streets adjacent to the University grounds. As always, stones thrown at cars. The students were on vacation. The police energetically put down the isolated outbreaks of disorder which occurred on the Avenida Jimé nez de Quesada. Two reporters suffered the wrath of the rioters without serious consequences.

In Popayán, five hundred students of the University of Cauca marched, shouting, "Down with the Government and the oligarchy!" Some stones fell on the building of the daily *El Liberal.* The head of the editorial staff was cut slightly. In Bucaramanga thirteen commercial establishments and the Santander Radio Station were stoned. In Medellín there was a rampaging crowd which sacked some stores. New incidents were reported in Cali and Bogotá on the 23rd.

THE PRESS:

El Tiempo editorialized, on February 18th, "On the Death of Camilo Torres Restrepo":

"Unfortunately his very vocation of service, which was generous and unselfish in him, carried him to extremes, and first led him to a separation from the priesthood and then to change his cassock for the clothes of a guerilla, in a country where today such activity lacks all justification and even all revolutionary significance. Blinded by a certain romantic halo which surrounded him, he dared to walk on the edge of the abyss and thus his existence was brought to an end. He was thus tragically frustrated, since many good and noble things could have been expected of him if he had not provoked this useless holocaust."

Further on, the same daily adds:

"If Torres had been violent and imprudent when he wore ecclesiastical robes, it was much worse when he wore the clothes of a peasant. When he arrived at Lima the ex-priest began to sound like a long-playing record played over and over again at a high rate of speed."

El Espectador editorialized on the death of Camilo in these terms: "When at the beginning of this year the 'Proclamation of Camilo Torres to the Colombians' was known and it was shown by incontrovertible photographic documents that Camilo Torres Restrepo had taken up arms against the legitimately established order in Colombia, we permitted ourselves to observe—in an editorial commentary—the following, which today takes on special meaning since it has been announced that he died in combat with forces of the Army of Colombia, in San Vicente de Chucurí, Santander:

> The development of the facts has demonstrated that there was no such advanced priest, either of the modern type or of special sensitivity. There was simply (in Camilo Torres) a convinced Marxist in religious habit. Nothing more and nothing less. Therefore, Camilo is today at the side of the armed squadrons, following the way which the Marxists of the Peking line—in a special way—have shown their followers.

"Everything in the course of the life of Camilo Torres, who as a priest, increased his flock with misguided sheep and wolves in sheep's clothing; who as a pastor rebelled against his own hierarchy and abandoned his religious dress in order to proclaim the revolution and mobilize the people behind his destiny and his ideas; who took up arms and went into the jungle and proclaimed himself leader of the insurrection—everything in the life of Camilo Torres, we said—led inevitably to the finale which is certainly very sad. Because it is sad that the life of a man of brilliant intelligence, of definite character, of culture, is interrupted in the middle of his career, in circumstances in which no one can say, without tremendous injustice, that violent interruption could have been avoided. . . ."

On page 4-A they reproduced the complete article which the Cuban Pardo Llada published in *Bohemia.* This was commissioned and paid for by the reactionary forces in order to cause havoc in Colombia. We read there: "Camilo Torres—with or without cassock—has been converted into a species of red priest, like Father Bolo of Peru, a declared militant Communist, or the vanished Father Sardiñas of Cuba, the chaplain of the Sierra Maestra, who if he did not take off the cassock, dyed it green in order to match the uniform of Fidel Castro."[1]

El Siglo, among other headlines, wrote: "Camilo Torres had renounced a position of 4,000 pesos in order to become a red guerilla."[2]

In the section *Here in Bogotá,* Arturo Abella wrote: "The death of the ex-cleric Camilo Torres closes a modest chapter of our national history. He sincerely believed that he could be a *caudillo,* that he could repeat the exploit of Fidel Castro, that he could be the 'providential' man of the revolution. His writings, his social programs, could be Communist or Marxist, or whatever you wish, but in every case they were utopian.

"He was given more importance publicly than he deserved in reality. A certain influence with the people was due to that publicity. His social mission could have been fulfilled completely within his priesthood, with more influence and higher destinies than that of a *caudillo* without a cassock. He wanted something else. We must allow him the gesture: he pledged himself completely to his ideal. Crazy? That is for the wise to decide. Perhaps unadapted and badly formed. But the chapter is closed and there is nothing more."[3]

El Espacio reacted against the inhuman language employed by the very conservative Christian daily "of the working man": "It will not have passed unnoticed by Colombians who read yesterday morning in the daily *La República,* the headline with which this periodical registered the death of Camilo and in which they called him a bandit. Really, without it being our intention to justify the subversive conduct of this ex-priest—because we early on condemned it—the headline of the conservative daily does not correspond to the life of Camilo Torres. He was not a bandit, an expression which, according to the dictionary, is used to mean thief or highwayman."[4]

El Signo, at the same time, commented: "We cannot call Camilo Torres a bandit. All that can be said of him—insane, unbalanced, naive, disoriented, deluded—does not include bandit—because he really was not one. In his abnormality he took the way of the mountains; contemptible if you will, but he does not deserve the name bandit."[5]

Voz Proletaria, the organ of the Colombian Communist Party, announced the death of Camilo in this way: "The death in combat of Camilo Torres Restrepo, Catholic priest, revolutionary and guerilla, has shaken the conscience of the Colombian nation. The people are pained by such an unfortunate event. All the popular forces of the country—political, student, workers, peasants—express their vigorous protest against this crime of the oligarchy, the vassal of Yankee imperialism, and they lower their flags in mourning before his unknown tomb, hidden in some place in the mountains of Santander, the land of the people.

". . . The oligarchy, with inhuman sadism, has wished to gloat over the corpse of the rebel priest. It has not covered his tomb with flowers, as the people want, but with low insults, cowardly and treacherously hurled, like pebbles. But the reaction must be silent before the reality. They cannot deny the value of Camilo's high example. They cannot hide the fact that he is an authentic guerilla, a popular and just man, and never a bandit. The myth of 'banditry' has been interred with Camilo. And as an artist said in the Spanish Civil War, 'Fascism does not bury bodies but seeds!' "[6]

El Catolicismo editorialized: "The Church, aware of her true mission in the world, has always held an unequivocal doctrine as far as relations with temporal things are concerned, particularly with political activity. Conscious of the fact that its role in the midst of men is essentially of the spiritual order, it has wanted its priests to abstain from involvement in party fights; and if there have been some few exceptions to this traditional norm, they have had the approbation of the respective bishops each time. On the other hand, as far as the laity are concerned, it wants them to take part in politics in their own name, bringing it to the Christian sense of justice and charity, and always rejecting the systems which promote fratricidal violence.

"Unfortunately, this was not the line of Camilo Torres. His prelate, with good reasons, never permitted him, as a priest, to involve himself in the political and revolutionary actions which were not proper for the clerical state. Afterwards reduced to the lay state by his own petition, he opted for armed rebellion, which is not the way to promote a Christian politics. These are the facts which all know. Whatever he may have thought inside himself, the answer which he has given to those questioning him about his own conscience is something we cannot judge because only God scrutinizes hearts.

"Before the deeply sorrowful fact of his death in circumstances known by everyone, we cannot lament less the mistakes which led to the frustration of a life which was called to serve the Church and in the Church the poor and oppressed. It comforts us to know that God is love and that His love is infinite."

ECCLESIASTICAL CIRCLES:

His excellency, Rubén Isaza Restrepo, Coadjutor of Bogotá, commented only,

"Naturally, it is a sad thing."[7]

Monsignor Victor Wiedemann, Vicar General of the Archdiocese of Medellín: "It is evident that we must all lament the death of Camilo Torres and recommend his soul to God, who is the only one who can judge the man. He knows all the intimacies of his heart.

"But for things as they appear, it is evident that everything has happened as people of right judgment had expected. Unfortunately, Camilo Torres little by little was destroying his work as a pastor of souls although he was vested with the sacerdotal character and continues to be a priest for all eternity.

"As chaplain of the university, he had some anxieties which he succeeded in overcoming and which were well viewed by the Church and admired by his superiors. Later he was falling into the temptation of wanting greater prestige, and for this he wanted to accomplish works in the university which were no longer in accord with the mind of the Gospel of Christ nor with the exercise of his properly sacerdotal ministry.

"He thought only of the material, leaving to one side everything related to the spirit and eternity. His superiors called his attention to it. Through lack of obedience in the priest they were obliged to take him out of the university and give him another field of the priestly apostolate in which he did not feel satisfied, even though he had at his side the poor and the needy whom, according to his judgment, he should favor and support.

"For this reason, though still in the exercise of his ministry, he launched ideas which led to revolution and which were not in complete accord with the norms of the Church since the performance of works which are of temporal character, and especially politics, does not correspond to the priesthood. Disgusted with the manner in which they proceeded with him because his superiors wanted to prevent him from going from fall to fall, he preferred to be reduced to the lay state; i.e., to renounce the exercise of the priesthood in order to dedicate himself as a layman to politics.

"And so he took off his cassock and began to work in politics. In the beginning he had the illusion that all would rally to him and his political platform would be accepted in all social spheres. He began to work with university students, with workers, and with the distinct political sectors into which our society is divided. But his surprise was great when he saw that through his erroneous methods, everyone was little by little abandoning him. The students no longer rallied to him; those unhappy with politics were disconcerted when he spoke to them of those not affiliated in political camps for his campaign, because they told him that if only those not affiliated with some political party should rally to him, his movement would end up a fiasco.

He didn't believe it and continued straight ahead. He visited cities and towns, and in the beginning they followed him; but when they saw that his accomplishments were nil, they rejected his movement. Even the periodical which he founded became a fiasco. And thus it was that this man, disillusioned, resolved to go to the mountains to conspire now directly with arms against the legally constituted government, in order to implant by force the theses which he had preached.

"Thus he placed himself outside the law and was treated like a bandit. This is very sad, but it had its logical consequence in death because the legitimate forces could not tolerate his method of procedure.

"One thinks that because of the many difficulties which he had in his home life and social life Camilo Torres incurred some mental unbalance which led him to the catastrophe, but we hope that our Lord, in His infinite goodness, has pardoned him his errors and through His mercy saved his soul."[8]

Father Carlos Pérez Herrera, Press Secretary of the Archdiocesan Curia of Panama and Pastor of Santa Ana, said: "Free men of America have the right to lament the death of Father Camilo Torres Restrepo which occurred, according to the dispatches of the UPI, in a battle with the regular army in the mountains of Santander. Father Torres believed in insurrection as the only way to redeem a people hungry for bread and thirsty for justice; and like the Mexican clerics, precursors of emancipation, Camilo has paid for his rebellion with his life in a sacrifice which will be appreciated in its just dimensions for generations to come.

"To be silent before the death of the recently sacrificed Colombian priest would seem to be the most prudent thing in order to avoid nasty epithets and bitter criticism. But silence would be hypocritical and lacking in courage.

"In history we frequently have the case of soldiers who change the uniform of the soldier for the religious habit. To exchange the habit of the cleric for the uniform of the guerilla is less frequent. Father Camilo sought from the ecclesiastical authority the release from his ministry in order to launch the fight against misery from an angle which until now is reserved for political revolutionaries.

"Then he abandoned the city in order to fight in the mountains next to the guerillas. If it had been possible for us, we would have reminded Father Torres that clerics are not military men nor do we know military strategy.

"Mistaken or not, Father Camilo embraced as an idealist the warlike projection of his social apostolate in the uneven fight between the public forces at the service of the oligarchy and a handful of idealists who raised the standard of justice for the people. Mistaken or not, Father Torres left the newspaper conflicts and his university conferences in order to try to obtain in the mountains that which he could not obtain from the pages of his periodical or in the academic halls. Mistaken or not, Father Torres preferred to be called a Communist rather than remain silent before the lack of social sensibility of a society which is resisting the Christian message of justice and charity. Mistaken or not, Father Torres has opened up a high road on which many idealists who seek justice will walk. Therefore, before the remains of the visionary who dreamed of a free people, healthy and productive, we are reverent, humbly asking God for eternal rest for the priest, the guerilla, the patriot who has fallen wrapped in a blood-stained banner on Colombian soil."[9]

The Franciscan priest, Eduardo Arango Trujillo, on the Radio Juventud, made a violent attack on the systems of government and the high ecclesiastical authorities, who he said had in effect murdered Camilo Torres from the very moment in which they had thrown him out of the Cardinal's Palace, and then had hunted him like a rat, closing off every avenue of escape. He also said that every country should keep the name of Camilo Torres before its eyes, since Christ preached love and pardon and now only hatred and death were practiced. Then, after a series of strong criticisms of the hierarchy of the Catholic Church, he ended his speech in honor of the ex-priest Camilo Torres by saying that he (Arango) would very soon probably be persecuted.[10]

From Father Agustino José Tejada, Ecuadorian: "This young priest of thirty-seven renounced his sacred office and began a revolutionary fight which was suggested by a noble ideal—the redemption of the poor. His priestly soul was scandalized by the tears and misery of the proletarian class of his country; and without stopping to consider the wisdom of his means, he identified himself with Communists, incorporating them into the life of the guerillas. We can do no less than deplore his premature death, in anonymity, for a humanitarian cause and in lamentable disagreement with his hierarchical superiors."[11]

When the church of Veracruz where Camilo had been a curate was asked for permission to have services for his soul, someone responded that they could not authorize the liturgy there, for "Camilo had died like a common criminal."[12] The services were celebrated February 23rd in the church of San Diego, thanks to the kindness of its pastor, Monsignor Simón Peña. At the request of the Christian Democrats, a Mass was celebrated at Ibagué with a great number of laity in attendance. In the parish of the Vigil in the State of Mérida (Venezuela), a funeral Mass was said for Camilo, with ten priests present. In Paris a Mass was concelebrated by Colombian priests in fraternal charity for the soul of Camilo. In the Cathedral in Cuernavaca, Mexico, funeral rites were celebrated for Camilo with the full approval of Bishop Méndez Arceo. In Louvain, Canon Houtart and Father Alberto Rodes participated in the rites.

GOVERNMENT CIRCLES:

The Minister of Justice, Francisco Posada de la Peña, said: "He put himself outside the law, and he had to suffer the consequences."[13] The Secretary General of the Presidency, Doctor Guillermo Isaza Mejía: "It seems to me that any person who begins such activities must end up in this way."[14]

WORKER AND TRADE UNION GROUPS:

Tomás Herazo Rios, former member of the Communist Party, from which he was expelled, a member today of the Confederation of Colombian Workers (CTC) commented for the Press: "The death of Camilo Torres does not surprise us, because everyone who stands up against the public force must run that risk. He was a guerilla and was against the Army."[15]

Antonio Días, executive secretary of the Union of Colombian Workers (UTC), said: "Really, it is a shame that the ex-cleric Camilo Torres should have been chained to the fortunes of those who have sacrificed lives of innocent peasants and who, being an intelligent man as he was, should have ended his life this way."[16]

The Trade Union Confederation of Colombian Workers (CSTC) declared that "in the name of its 170,000 members, it expressed its most outraged protest for the cowardly assassination of the illustrious priest Camilo Torres Restrepo, at the hands of the armed forces, which have been converted into the principal instrument for the punishment of the people, at the service of the oligarchical interests. Deaths such as that of Camilo Torres enlighten the conscience of millions of Colombians, in respect to what is the fight of our people, to the heroic path which they will have to take, to the methods of cruelty and violence enforced by the ruling classes under the direction of the North American military mission."[17]

THE POLITICAL PARTIES:

Only one party, the Communist, officially set down its position, in this document: "The Communist Party of Colombia publicly expresses its grief at such an unfortunate event which deprives the revolutionary forces and the Colombian people of a national leader and popular fighter.

"Father Camilo Torres had been incorporated into the revolutionary group called the Army of National Liberation, convinced that it was the best way for the emancipation of the people from oligarchical exploitation and imperialistic oppression.

"He died in combat against the forces of reaction, and this makes him worthy of popular homage. The masses will remember the name of Camilo Torres with respect and emotion. He gave his life for the immortal cause of the Colombian revolution and national liberation.

"The Communist Party lowers its flags before the memory of this brave and conscientious fighter. His name will serve as an example for the young revolutionaries of Colombia."[18]

CULTURAL CIRCLES:

Alberto Zalamea declared for the radio program "Advance": "The circumstances in which Camilo Torres disappears make his death more sorrowful and unpardonable. He followed his way with purity and courage, but that way was mistaken, as is demonstrated today. Colombian youth suffers as new frustration. It is that of hoping that the tragic error of Camilo Torres might help young people meditate on the real perspectives of the Colombian revolution.

"That example of Camilo shows to what extremes of desperation the unjust system which we suffer is pushing the new generation. Oh, that his sacrifice might help all of us meditate on the concrete and real, essentially political path which Colombian youth must take; they must be conscious of their historical responsibility, apart from adventurism which is advocated by irresponsible persons who afterwards abandon their protagonists to misery and death. What are those who advocated the adventure of Camilo saying today? What are those saying who pushed him to his death? Those of us who fight that political error bow our heads, in any case, before this new sacrifice of Colombian hopes."[19]

Jose Gutiérrez, psychiatrist, in the article already cited, thought: "Politics does not consist of evading difficult themes but in speaking of them with frankness, even when one can appear undiplomatic or 'unpolitical.'

"Is this the case of the death of Camilo Torres Restrepo? Who is not aware that it is complex and that, speaking frankly of him, there would necessarily be sentiments of sympathizers, adversaries, believers and sceptics who knew him intimately and who were solely concerned for their public image of the political priest?

"He could not fight against the bohemian romanticism which is in every young person of the upper class who becomes a nonconformist full-time. And therefore, he was unable to find paths of nonviolence in order to give greater effectiveness to his proposals.

"That which he should have given to the epic of the reconstruction of Colombia never arrived—his moral and scientific authority—since he died like the simple hero of a novel.

"Those of us who have judged that the structure of a society such as the Colombian society urgently needs change, moralization, modernization, and stimulation, now know that in order to respond to the cry for new direction, we revolutionaries must guard in our leaders and in ourselves the feeling of authority. Because he who does not feel authorized is not authentic and therefore energetic, renewing, and productive.

"Camilo, with all the authority of his investiture, of his knowledge, and the magnetism of his personality, never felt he was authorized. And therefore he could not contribute to the social and moral reconstruction in Colombia which is what we call revolution."[20]

Juan Pablo Ortega, conservative journalist, wrote: "The end of Father Camilo Torres is sorrowful and deplorable. To judge at this moment, before his abandoned and destroyed body, the inner value of his behavior is useless and unchristian. We must respect the conscience of individuals and especially in this case which had such a melancholy and dreadful end, when he who has suffered should have merited another destiny and another tomb.

"I knew Camilo Torres in the first years at school. He belonged to a little older group; nevertheless, in many escapades of infancy and youth I was with him; I was in his house; I knew his youthful anxieties and the preoccupation which he had, as do all at that stage in life, about the future. He was happy, always ready for a party, without complications, a bit loquacious, but with many friends around him.

"Perhaps he could not overcome the confusion, in one of those mistakes from which the human being is not exempt. He could be a misfit or suffer a psychological crisis, situations from which the will is not exempt.

"It is not, then, the time to exploit his memory with cruel recriminations; nor with passionate vehemence. In full youth, Camilo Torres, fighting against the law, in conditions which were not fitting for his intelligence and much less for his priestly character, fell at the hands of the army. Let us hope that he has found the peace which he never found in his short and tormented life. He was not an ex-cleric nor a bandit as some, now that he is dead, have wanted to brand him. The chapter of his life is closed, but it remains for Colombian history to judge him, when the circumstances are more favorable for a calm and objective judgment."[21]

"The Rebel" is the title which the jurist and academician Doctor Bernardo Gaitán Mahecha gave his commentary on Camilo. Some of it is here transcribed: "In the times in which we live, ideals frequently succumb before a selfish and cowardly life. In these days, anyone who has taken on the task of speculating on the sad social episode which was the life and death of the priest Camilo Torres cannot limit the subject to a mere individual interpretation, to a simple vital event of one person and forget everything else; that is, the amount of responsibility which falls on each man in a drama which penetrates to the very womb of the nation and is born of the entire society, satiated with blood, injustice, and misery.

"What is inevitable and certain is that there exists a deep process of rebellion whose powerful dynamism is twisted or frustrated at times in the lassitude of those who choose the ordinary path of ascent and end up by becoming accomplices and helpers of a totally arbitrary and unjust state of things. In their servility, from holding economic power they end up devoured by it. Some in their rage throw rocks left and right without any logic or reasoning, but only with the plain ferocity of nonconformity. A few brave men who, as in the case of the priest Camilo, place the rifle on their shoulder, judge that the only way to produce change is through armed action and violence.

". . . The priest Camilo may have proceeded badly when he chose a violent method; mistakenly, when his rebellion erupted in an armed action, cruel and unjust for the soldiers and peasants but representative of a voice which does not conform with what exists and which does not find any possibility or hope that it can be changed by ordinary methods. Violence will not be silenced until the manner of thinking is modified, and it changes the mercantilist, utilitarian, and selfish ideology of the ruling class; until the subhuman conditions in which the majority of the people live are modified; the social sense of the rich is created; those politicians who make of politics a lucrative profession are finished; governmental improvisation is destroyed; administrative corruption is finished; more is produced and better distributed. The Colombian rebellion fights for all these things."[22]

Gonzalo Canal Ramírez, journalist and publicist, spoke this way about Camilo: "The circumstances of the death of Father Torres are morally unacceptable. But in his death, we must distinguish between the death of a revolutionary rebel bearing arms and that of a bandit. Father Camilo did not die as a bandit but as a revolutionary. In his history there is no record of common crimes. His thought, mistaken as to procedures and some points of his program, was widely disseminated by Camilo in the press, the radio, the university and the public square, and in all the organs of expression to friends and enemies. That thought of his did not preach common crime but violence as a political weapon, which is another crime but of a different quality, especially in this country where so many men who have also preached it have been raised to illustrious places both in the past and today. The difference is in the fact that these violent men whom we have made respectable men—even though we owe them thirty-five years of violence—were not capable of dying for what they believed, and Camilo was. There is another distinction: those violent men honored by us worked on behalf of traditional political interests; Camilo—even though he was as mistaken as they were—worked on behalf of new social theses.

"The reproachable attitude of Camilo does not deprive him of grandeur in his act of dying. To give your life for your ideas (even though those ideas are not ours) and to give it to science and conscience, has always been great. Not to acknowledge it contributes to the greatness of the victim and weakens the opposite cause.

"The eternal priestly character is one thing and the canonical norms which regulate and organize the exercise of that profession are another thing. Camilo, when preaching violence as a political instrument and total socialism of the State as a program, separated himself from the essential fundamentals of the philosophy and the procedures of the Church and fell into a lack of fidelity to his ecclesiastical commitments. But Camilo publicly asked to be relieved of them by his superiors, suspended in his external priestly activity and laicized regarding religious dress. The Church, with surprising rapidity—not frequently its style—gave him a suspension from his duties and laicization regarding dress. With that Camilo was separated canonically from priestly activity and the ecclesiastical hierarchy, but in no case did this extend to his priestly character. One could speak of an ex-cleric but not of an ex-priest."[23]

Martin Amaya, a priest reduced to the lay state, confronted the hierarchy once more and said: "The hierarchy is to blame for the death of Camilo, not consciously and deliberately, but unconsciously for not adopting a humane and Christian attitude such as that of Jesus Christ when he abandoned the ninety-nine good sheep in order to search for the one who had been lost and for adopting an inquisitorial attitude of sanctions, threats, and moral pressure.

"I think that the way the hierarchy has approached our problem, Camilo's and mine, was precipitate and typically inquisitorial. In my case I was condemned without having been given a hearing; and in the case of Torres, the Cardinal, against the prescriptions of Canon Law or ecclesiastical legislation, hastened to declare that Camilo would never be able to return to the priesthood, even though one is a priest forever. I think that this helped to precipitate Camilo's spiritual crisis. The hierarchy is to blame for the death of Camilo. I consider it anti-Christian, for example, that Monsignor Victor Wiedemann has made offensive allusions to the intimate life of the deceased priest."[24]

We transcribe some opinions of Victor Aragón, a columnist of the conservative daily, *El Siglo:* "I was one of the first to lament the unfortunate decision of Camilo Torres when he unexpectedly abandoned the activities which were progressing with brilliant success in civic battles in order to involve himself in armed action which was beyond his competence. It was not right for a pure intellectual such as Camilo to change the irresistible force of his thought for the gun which any clown can manage and which this delicate dreamer, of pure conscience, was incapable of raising against a human being. And certainly not to kill off a wounded adversary! In that tragic moment of his life, Camilo lost the flaming sword, the sword which comes forth from the mouth of the Word in the Apocalypse, and he threw over his shoulders the shadow of a gun of which he never made use, which only served to make his remains more heavy in the tomb which was awaiting him.

"And now after his youth was cut short in an adventure and the torch of his brilliant soul was extinguished, it is not important whether the road he took in his restless anxiety to reach his goal was wrong or right, nor do the material circumstances in which his sacrifice could occur change the diagram of his suffering and glorious career. In that career, so brief that it will be difficult to understand his biography in the future, there is one stage of interior fire such as the fire which devours the tinder, in which his whole personality experienced an irresistible impulse which took him out of his usual surroundings and made him, immediately, a military commander with the materials of a philosopher. I had the opportunity to know him and to enjoy his friendship before there was offered up in him the transfiguration which was to carry him, in a Wagnerian act, to the death of Siegfried in the cross-road of a path of goodness and love. We shared political anxieties and deep philosophical interests in the university, in conversation, in the seminars, and in the interchange of books and concepts. But while my life was calm, his was a torrent.

"To try to clothe him, after death, with the skin of the Communist bear is a vain effort to make him look like the enemy while he was simply a spirit convinced of the value of his own ideas. Even though he may have violated the ordinance of custom when he abandoned the procedures of legalized proselytism and proceeded by the short-cut of rebellion, the arena of his combat was not that of arms but of intelligence.

"He had to confront forces too powerful for the belligerence of ideas whose power is not seen except after years. Socrates opposed concepts to magistrates and soldiers, the executors of injustice who vanished like light cinders while his ideas continue invincible and eternal, and yet Socrates had to drink the poison which the oligarchy of Athens sent him."[25]

Hernando Giraldo, columnist of the liberal weekly *El Espectador*, published this commentary: "The historic frustration of the priest Camilo Torres constitutes a sorrowful blow for this generation. The young revolutionary died of excessive idealism. Such was his faith in the revolutionary ideal that he was incapable of containing his overflowing eagerness to accomplish it immediately. Naive and good, he didn't know the meaning of intrigue. For this reason he was rapidly depriving himself of those arms which could be useful to an intellectual and so to die carrying arms which could not be useful to his idealism, culture, or intelligence.

"I am sure that if something drove the romantic priest to launch himself in a warlike adventure it was what he, in his impulsiveness, would judge the cowardice of the companions of the revolution. So sound were his proposals that he could not even see that he was acting in the most conservative country in the world where even the revolutions are planned in meetings of governing boards. When in June of last year I talked to Camilo Torres for the first and last time I had hope that he was the man to organize a renewal movement within the reactionary Colombian clergy.

"In the place where the idealist Camilo Torres died, Humberto Castellanos, Eugenio Alarcón, Luis Navarro, and Guillermo Patarroyo, four humble soldiers who also had the ideal of saving the country, fell. The distinguished young man, belonging to the upper middle class, died fighting against the social structure which supports his class. On the other hand, the four sons of the soil died defending the social order of the bourgeois class from which their unexpected adversary came. We Colombians must bow our heads before the romantic gesture of these five idealists, who had to be killed in the same place where there should have been the fraternal embrace."[26]

Gilberto Vieira, Secretary General of the Communist Party of Colombia, wrote: "All Colombian patriots are moved by the tragic end of the revolutionary priest Camilo Torres, who was one of these exceptional personalities who succeed in expressing the needs of an entire people and who rise up courageously against old and tottering social structures.

"Camilo Torres is a new martyr for our people, even though the petty editors of *El Tiempo* try to deny him that glory. A martyr is someone who suffers or dies for beliefs, convictions, and causes, according to the classical definition. But we are talking of a martyr who fell fighting. And therefore he is a hero, if by that we understand 'a visionary of action' according to the concept of the Uruguayan José Enrique Rodó.

"Father Camilo undertook the revolutionary battle with complete sincerity and unlimited self-denial. His proposal was to unite all the popular forces in order to accomplish the Colombian revolution through a wide United Front.

"Inexpert and generous, Camilo believed that all those who joined his movement were likewise sincere. He was hindered, moreover, by the presence of opportunistic elements who were destroying the unity he preached, and he did not know how to direct his movement toward a consistent politics. Anti-Communism subtly disguised, even among the ultra-revolutionary groups, helped to destroy the formation of the United Front.

"The martyrdom and glorious end of the Catholic priest Camilo Torres will never be forgotten. His example will be productive and his sacrifice will show the grandeur of the Colombian guerillas to those who are vainly engaged in ridiculing them as bandits."[27]

To complete this chapter, we will transcribe four documents which will complete the picture of the reactions to Camilo's life and death.

1. Lucio Dugán, perhaps the most authoritative columnist of the Liberal daily, *El Espectador,* wrote: "Even sadly mistaken people merit the most profound respect. The person and the life of Camilo Torres are not now a proper theme for empty discussion. The feverish passion which he put into the battle for the social order in which he believed and of which he dreamed led him to the end which today moves all of our hearts. Camilo Torres was certainly not a bandit. Neither his protest nor his open defiance of the law and of established institutions originated in the fear that the law would be applied to him, or in the desire to preserve through

disorder the impunity of crime and vice. All of us know that this ardent, rebellious, vehement man was a pure man and that the revolution he preached was a conviction which had so taken possession of him that he did not hesitate to leave everything to give himself without any reserve to achieve it. It is probably that those who invited him to follow it, or those who followed him, did not think as he did. The idealist always goes before the pragmatist. The pragmatist remains in the rearguard to make sure that the lighted fire is well spread so that it can be converted into an advantage for the great enterprise at the opportune moment. The history of all revolutions is the same, those which are frustrated as well as those which triumph, those which are no more than an adventure or a heroic episode—it is always the same. Trotsky was the victim of Stalin. Many of those who went to the French guillotine believed that the people would not again permit the use of the guillotine, particularly against those who were the promoters and authors of their liberty. Camilo Torres had an intelligence and a sensitivity sincerely mobilized to seek a better world and his memory is respected and has dignity because there was in his acts a purity which is only comparable to his sad mistake. The better world which he looked for was not that for which he offered his life. But his sacrifice has a grandeur of spirit which no one would dare to deny."[28]

2. Doctor Fernando Torres Restrepo, brother of Camilo, was emboldened by his dreadful sorrow to write: "Camilo Torres is dead. There are many who weep for him today because he had many friends of every nationality and in every social and economic sphere. Nevertheless, only a handful of friends can feel the great, deep and constant pain which I am feeling. The fact that he was my brother was only an accident of life which served, nevertheless, for knowing him better and over a longer time than other friends of his, so that there was born and grew between us a friendship without reserve and without limits, full of comprehension, love, mutual respect and admiration. Ours was one of those friendships about which no one speaks and on which much is written, but which are rarely found in real life. No one and nothing will be able to repair the loss of my best friend.

"Camilo Torres is dead. I don't know how long his memory will live in those who loved him and admired him. I do know that the duty of his true friends is to prevent his image, his death and his body from being an object of vulgar and sensational demonstrations promoted by those who saw him in life and think of him after death only as a means for creating disorder and for achieving their own ambitions.

"Camilo Torres died in the battle for what he considered just. He should be considered a soldier fallen in battle or a martyr for an idea. It is not important that some of the methods he employed are considered wrong. He is one more who has fallen in an eternal battle but one for whom we cannot blame any person or any institution. His adversaries also suffer death and we cannot accuse them of being assassins. Camilo was a victim of the universal violence which is seen every day in the entire world and which has tormented Colombia for many years. Let us not allow the image of Camilo to be obscured by increasing that violence and the number of Colombian dead, using his name as a standard.

"I want to appeal to the true friends of Camilo with my only claim being that I am one of them. I do not, for one moment, want to abandon the cause he started. On the contrary, I think that we must continue the fight for the betterment of our people as the only basis for the survival of our country. But I want to make them see, with the perspective which distance gives, that they would not benefit that cause by producing riots, disorders, and crimes without objective.

"Only a few would take advantage of this, those who are always ready to exploit the masses in order to obtain their own ends, which are completely distinct from the ones which Camilo pursued.

"I want to appeal to the students whom Camilo loved so much. I appeal to them since I was one of them; since I have dedicated a great part of my life to university teaching, and especially because I have known how to interpret Camilo as few others could do, I ask the students to maintain their expressions of sorrow on a tranquil and decent level and that those who have believed in the cause pursued by Camilo, continue the battle, but that they do not let themselves be guided by the false or the naive who think they see an opportunity in the death of our friend for destroying what exists without anything with which to replace it.

"Let us allow the moment of sharp pain to pass by and let us hope that, together with a pain perhaps deeper but less acute, calm might return to our mind, before deciding to do something which would then weigh down our consciences, because instead of enlarging the image of our beloved Camilo, we would diminish it. Let us render our dead friend a final tribute of human understanding and worthy and serene sorrow."[29]

3. The journalist Aníbal Pineda, a great friend of Camilo, wrote in the magazine *C.N.P. Repórter:* "Our world is more depersonalized each day. It is a world in which the individual is flattered, tricked, seduced, complimented, black-mailed. The man of our epoch has been molded in order to fulfill the needs of super-efficiency, totally devoid of human warmth. Standardization has come to politics, thought, and culture. Any man, not made for super-efficiency, who strays from the path which the majority has followed is called crazy or hopeless. But this touch of insanity is necessary for charismatic people. Desperation is not for them. It is a characteristic of dead social classes which crumble, as someone said, when they embrace the causes of evil and are incapable of fighting.

"The lack of ideals of our modern society begets the ideal. Perhaps it was the idealist philosopher Hegel who explained the creative force of the ideal as a consequence, in its way, of the tenacious rejection which it encounters in crude reality.

"This sociologist, priest, professor, and martyred politician had the qualities we enunciate. He has passed to history, perhaps with an epitaph which could rank him a great American thinker, because of his very anxieties and passions—life is stranger than the novel, reality than fiction.

"This desperate anxiety of man to reach his own capacity, creates and destroys. It has left him, finally, the exalting sensation of reaching the stars. Because for a man to conquer those planes and even other more elemental ones of the daily semi-barbarous world of efficiency which surrounds us, he must give all; he must understand and love his reason, respect the reason of others, even though limited by a tradition which frustrates individual and collective solutions, and subject to doctrinaire and social controversies. A man is thus the symbol of an epoch.

"It is inconceivable that a man destroy his heart and brain, which are filled with dreams of human redemption. But this is the way it was because tradition is implacable, a sedative, ineffectual in its movement through history.

"This man who confronted tradition, taught with fervor—with the same fervor he had in his religious exercises—new truths which even he, researcher and sociologist, did not succeed in explaining. He captured the ideals and the vigor of those who surrounded him in the classrooms and the streets. Thus he grew and became invulnerable, protected by the tender affection of his friends and also—why not say it?—silently surrounded by his enemies. In a few months he succeeded in moving the multitudes who waited for him as an apostle.

"No one or nothing can hold him back after that. His faith enlightened and increased, he redoubles the attack. He changes tactics. Other victorious tracks are fresh in America. Everything is possible, he says, We are right. We must give the example, he adds.

"And off he went alone. He found friends in the interior, in our tropics where only radio messages and reconnaissance groups of the army can reach. Just as he began his political rise, he died. All of this didn't surprise him, for he didn't think of immediate things but of the immense issues of social justice. Flowers do not cover his tomb, those which would fit the priest and professor, the friend. Lianas, deep moss and the enervating atmosphere of the tropics wall him in.

"So certain is his case that it will soon be examined in the light of psychological theories in order to measure the scope of his human and ideological projections, because a rebel priest, a guerilla priest, is a human complexity.

"But the earth is full of these men. They are the men who appeal to the novel in order to explain life, because scientific rigor, at times, is too slow to experience truth. Victim of his reason, victim of Latin America, he dreamed of a land full of flowers and smiling children. He was a victim of agrarian reform, the chief problem of our convulsed continent.

"And we say it without political passion. It pains us that a good man, full of ideals—perhaps, for some, full of idealism—falls under the machine gun.

"Nothing has changed in the meanwhile. Rivers follow their course as they are accustomed to do. But man thinks. And like the rivers, he follows his course, always forward. A small mound remained behind in the jungle. It is the body of a dreamer, or of a redeemer, or of a leader. It is not the body of El Cid who won battles in the feudal world. It is a human weight which sinks more into the earth each day, into the difficult problems of the modern world, of our America. Will it be possible for a dead man to move future multitudes? We believe this because the people needs and creates its own mythology: yesterday, to defend itself from the wolf, today, to defend itself from man."[30]

4. Tristán de Athayde, one of the most accomplished exponents of philosophical and social thought in Indo-America, a Catholic of unquestionable orthodoxy, speaks of Camilo in terms which must be transcribed in their totality: "When reading the tragic news of the death of the young priest Camilo Torres who, just a little while ago, became a guerilla without ceasing to be a 'sacerdos in aeternum' and lost his life fighting in the Colombian mountains, there came to my mind a scene I recall not for the first time. I refer to what occurred in one of the banquets which the association of North American Catholics, The Knights of Columbus, hold in Washington each year for the Latin American diplomatic corps. The North American speaker was Father Ellis, author of an excellent biography of Cardinal Gibbons, who awakened in that book a lively polemic on the present condition of Catholic thought in the United States. . . . What comes to mind is the discourse given in that ceremony by a Latin American, the ambassador of Colombia in the OEA, who the following day left to take his new position as Ambassador to the Holy See. The speech of the eminent Colombian began thus: 'The two values which we must defend, above all, in our days, are Capitalism and Christianity.' He put capitalism in

the first place, perhaps in order to give the place of honor to Christianity. Until today the phrase has not passed my lips. And now, reading the news of the tragic death of that young guerilla priest, also Colombian, the phrase of the ambassador went to my stomach producing real nausea. That ambassador embodies precisely what is not Christianity.

"That young priest, so dramatically sacrificed in the atmosphere of fanaticism which envelops our century, is undoubtedly a sublime flower of Colombian Catholicism and represents an indelible character of the new Christianity; I would even say that he is a martyr of the new Christianity although I may be exposing myself to bad interpretations, for I know well that we should use the word martyr only with exactness of those pouring out their blood or giving their life for the Faith. But in the end, what else did that young man do if he didn't die for the Faith?

"He opted for a procedure which I never tire of fighting, and which is the use of violence even in defense of truth. In considering him a martyr of the new Christianity I don't want to justify his method in any way. We must fight for the Kindom of God by means of meekness, love, tolerance, reason, patience, and especially prayer and nonpaternalistic charity. But we must also do it by means of sacrifice.

"When the majority of those who, with the vanity of the peacock, proudly exhibit their plumage, and even, in certain religious seminaries, insolently repeat the phrase pronounced by the ambassador, then we must recognize without vacillation that, in changing the cassock for the guerilla's rifle, those young men who gave their blood in defense of the Faith and of their fight for the redemption of modern society deserve admiration.

"He proclaimed the necessity of an honest and frank understanding with the guerillas who are not simply 'instruments of Communism,' and much less bandits but, in the majority, patriots who have been rebelling against an unjust, anachronistic, and untenable social structure and among whom we find that sublime flower of this new generation.

"One day he lost patience and pulled the trigger. At another time the 'Chouans' and 'Carlist' fathers of Spain, the 'Miguelistas' in Portugal, and even the 'Cristeros' in Mexico did the same in order to defend the 'return to the past,' monarchical absolutism or a theocentric conception of the Church. All those who offered their lives for noble ideals occupied a place of honor as martyrs of Christianity. Today the Camilo Torreses and others like him do the same, also calling on Christ, but in the name of the Future. They sacrifice their life and give their young blood for a new Christianity. We can disagree with their methods as we do with the Chouans, Carlists, Miguelistas, or Cristeros, but no one can deny that they are the purest, the most noble, the most authentic exponents and martyrs of the new Christianity, and that Christ is not of the past but of the future."[31]

Chapter 18

Presence and Destiny

Camilo, a priest and a guerilla—who understands him? How can we understand the blessing which ends in curses? Will his work continue or is it only the fleeting testimony of a martyr and hero? Within the Church, is he something significant or merely an adventurous insurgent?

It is certain, writes Marinello, that the Church has offered—and not only during the initial period of evangelization—a good number of admirable individuals. They were present during the Conquest, during the colonial period and after independence. When we recall them, their names are numerous: Pedro de Córdoba, Antonio de Montesinos, Sarmiento, Las Casas, Marroquin, Pedro de Gante, Motolinía, Vasco de Quiroga, Julián Garcés, Zumárraga, Francisco Solano, Mogroviejo, García Peláez, Francisco de Bustamante, Espada y Landa, Félix Varela . . . The first petition for the independence of our people, the *Letter to the Spanish*

Americans, was the work of a Jesuit, Juan Pablo Vizcardo. Miguel Hidalgo and José María Morelos illustrate to the fullest degree revolutionary action against the colonial power. Their denunciation of the "total havoc and destruction" was eloquent, courageous and at times heroic. Those pious priests—again let us appeal to the testimony of José Marti—were then the only protectors of the oppressed poor. But Marti also tells us that very soon "the scene belonged to the pompous official or the official who threw out in disgrace the good bishop who came to him to seek laws for the Indians without any armor but his friar's robe, with no fear but that of not being courageous enough. It is with real blows that those Christians received these bishops who would sanction crime with religion."[1]

Many believe that Camilo can be explained only as absurd. It is, indeed, certain that his personality contained many contradictory and baffling facets. He possessed great intelligence and a generous heart. Perhaps he thought more with his heart than with his mind. His culture is undeniable, but he sacrificed it in favor of a commitment to the impossible—or, at least, the apparently impossible. He spoke several languages, but he learned to speak the people's tongue with perfection. In spite of his bourgeois background he did not walk proudly among the poor. He was well-connected in high society, but he chose the company of the disinherited. Even as a professor, he had sufficient humility to learn from his students. He could have prospered in high clerical positions, but he rebelled against the very advantages it would offer him. He was a cleric, but he knew how to be a man.

To avoid compromises he opted for clear positions. He rejected numerous invitations to banquet with the great and powerful in order to sit down at table with the publicans and sinners. He could have preserved himself from discord, but he mixed with nihilists and the constantly argumentative students.

According to Christ, the poor belong to God. Camilo held that Christianity must be translated into effective charity toward our neighbor. This is the idea that animated his *Message to Christians,* written to tell them that they are obliged to promote the revolution: "The convulsions produced by the political, religious and social developments of our days have possibly brought much confusion to some Christians. In this decisive moment, we Christians must be firm regarding the essential foundations of our religion. In Catholicism the principal one is love for neighbor. 'If you love your fellow man, you have carried out your obligations.'

"In order to be true, this love must search for effectiveness. If the beneficence, the alms, the few free schools, the few housing projects—everything that has been given the name 'charity'—does not succeed in feeding the majority of the hungry, or clothing the majority of the naked, or teaching the majority of the illiterate, then we must search for effective means to bring about the welfare of the majority.

"The privileged minority which holds power is not going to look for such means because, generally, effective means will oblige the minority to sacrifice its privileges. For example, in order to see to it that there is more employment in Colombia, it would be better for them not to take their capital out of the country in dollars but rather to invest it in sources of employment. But as the Colombian peso is devalued day after day, those with money and power will never prohibit the export of money because in this way they escape the consequences of devaluation.

"It is necessary, then, to take power away from the privileged minority in order to give it to the poor majority. This, done rapidly, is the essence of the revolution. The revolution can be peaceful, if the minority does not give violent resistance.

"The revolution, therefore, is the way to obtain a government which will feed the hungry, clothe the naked, teach the ignorant, fulfill the works of charity, of love of neighbor, not only occasionally or in passing, not only for the few but for the majority of our neighbors.

"Therefore, the revolution is not only permitted but is obligatory for Christians who must see in it the only effective and complete way to achieve love for all. It is certain that 'there is no authority except from God' (Romans 13.1), but St. Thomas says that the concrete assignment of authority comes from the people.

"When an authority is against the people, that authority is not legitimate and is called tyranny. Christians can and must fight against tyranny. The present government is tyrannical because only twenty percent of the electorate supports it and because its decisions come from the privileged minority.

"The temporal defects of the Church must not scandalize us. The Church is human. What is important is to believe that it is also divine and that, if we Christians fulfill our obligation of love of neighbor effectively, we are strengthening the Church. I have left the duties and the privileges of the clergy, but I have not stopped being a priest. I believe that I have given myself to the revolution out of love of my neighbor. I have stopped saying Mass in order to realize that love of neighbor in the temporal, economic and social sphere. When I have accomplished the revolution, I will again offer Mass, if God permits. I believe that thus I am following the command of Christ, 'So then, if you are bringing your offering to the altar and there remember that your brother has something against you, leave your offering there before the altar, go and be reconciled with your brother first and then come back and present your offering.' Matthew 5:23-24)

"After the revolution we Christians will know that we established a system which is directed towards love of neighbor. The fight is long; let us now begin."[2]

Camilo's attitudes were always authentically Christian. One example is the following dialogue: one day I told him "In the jail there is a political prisoner dying of hunger and tuberculosis. They won't let anyone in to see him. We must do something." That same afternoon he went to the jail. In a long conversation with the prisoner he realized that their faiths were not in agreement, but he gave him what he had, lifted his spirits and encouraged his hope. When we met again, he told me, "What power the cassock has in Colombia! They let me in immediately and paid me great attention. I went through the entire prison. I heard some prisoners' confessions . . . and I realized the absolute abandonment in which those men are."

Another day I told him that a deposed politician who was dying needed a quart of blood for a transfusion. The next day he told me, "What a good man that Communist is!" I tried to explain that I hadn't known he was a Communist. He stopped me. "Christ gave his blood for the Communists too."[3]

Such actions, and his eagerness to find solutions within contemporary technical data, caused some to look on him as "the priest with the crazy ideas." Soon every dunce could call him 'Camiloco.'

They accused him of scandal and of leading many astray. They caluminated his morals, and to make it worse they pretended to testify against him out of charity. They called him dissipated, but he lived on the grace of God.

He baptized the son of a Communist "Christopher" and the first-born of a Christian family "Lenin de Jesús." He held that "in order to understand the poor today, it is necessary to become one of the proletariat, because those who now determine the direction of the world are the proletariat." He called the poor "my lord" and he called Christ "el Patron."

He earned some money, but he lived very poorly in order to pay for the lodging of poor students, to give medical assistance to the needy and to help evicted families. When the taxi driver he was riding with went to him to confession, he gave him as a penance to "drive carefully, because you are responsible for the life and safety of your passengers." Many political impostors who flatter the people, but really loathe them, wear a halo of fictitious virtue. But Camilo was anointed with democracy and died in the odor of damnation. One day he preached: "There are so many vain women in our high society who are evil; while, on the other hand, many 'fallen women' will enter the kingdom of heaven."

He said to a poor man, "Your situation is not consonant with what is Christian. Moreover, there are many Christians with possessions which in justice belong to the poor because they are the fruit of avarice and usury." He did not justify misery; rather he wanted to live in a hovel in a poor neighborhood. Every Monday he took what he needed from the wardrobes of friends to give to a family of exiles. I checked on this and discovered that because of this help the mother and two daughters were freed from prostitution. But he did not give alms to beggars, because he said that this held back the revolution. He stated that the living standards of some priests affront the hunger of the people, but that there are many curates as poor as anyone, while some have haciendas like any oligarch.

He asserted that the revolution would be violent if the oligarchical minority, overcome by the majority of the people, unleashed violence rather than handed over power. For such people, it is a sin to speak of revolution. They said that Camilo preached violent revolution. He said, "It will be violent, if. . . ." They said, "Torres is a violent revolutionary." To prove his point, he stands with the demonstrators during strikes and allows himself to be struck down.

He wanted to bypass all organizational apparatus. For this reason he did a number of things that seemed strange in our environment: he refused to take advantage of the sacro-emotional value attached to the priest's cassock by many Colombians; he was willing to live outside the law; he passed from nonviolence to violence; he frustrated his intelligence, his youth, his culture by taking a short-cut to death. All this appears senseless to those with a narrow view of Camilo, who refuse to face his complications.

Camilo was like a meteor, moving with such speed and power that it is impossible to chart. He belongs among the heroes, liberators and martyrs who defy logic and rationality. What we must deal with is the antithesis of two opposing viewpoints: ours seems absurd to him, his seems fated to disaster in our eyes. As a result, many will never be able to understand, much less justify, his actions and his end. The explanation is precisely his identification of his life with his ideals. It is this which has made him a portent, a prophetic event which has entered into every facet of the life of Colombia. The poor and oppressed know him; but so do the tyrants who oppress them. The wretched and those who practice paternalistic charity without love feel his influence. Patriots and opportunists, Christians who live the Gospel and hypocrites, the sectarians of Right and Left, Christians and Communists—all feel his influence. Camilo is a condemnation of all that is not authentic: pseudo-revolutionaries, pseudo-democrats, pseudo-Christians, pseudo-interpreters of the Second Vatican Council, pseudo-militants, pseudo-poor hiding behind fictitious vows of poverty.

The heart of Camilo's influence and condemnation is in his Christianity. He is a Christian because he saw man integrally and accepted his complications. He was a negative person, and he willingly accepted man in his historical reality. He did not side with man the angel against man the devil; he did not accept only economic man, or man the savage, religious man or man the atheist. His philosophy was expressed in this way: "Man is life. What is life? The love of God among men and the effective practice of love among men. This love which is life has different expressions for different men and different times. At this historical moment it must be expressed among us in terms of technology and the society in which we life."[4]

Camilo applied a contemporary conception to contemporary man, to the man of today, the society of today with all its complexity, in the full conviction that we have entered a new era, a point of departure in history which presupposes an adaptation of institutions. Not to be less than modern man was his desire. His life, his deeds, his attitudes were an invitation to be a part of this modern world, to understand the present. Therefore, his position was very advanced, what he would call a "progressive position." This word in Camilo's language must be understood as a "position of transformation" as opposed to an "attitude of conversation."

His universalist attitude is another reason for understanding that Camilo was a Christian. He understood the transcendence of dialogue and therefore he searched for the sources of any significant unrest in the cultural, economic or social field. For this reason his positions were never negative, escapist or exclusivist.

He is a fact which moves us, though we are in groups characterized by a crude, inhuman and dehumanized sectarianism. The sectarian does not dialogue, he condemns. He does not respect the opinions of others, he lashes out. He does not admit the slightest honesty in another viewpoint. He is characterized by the "guarded position," by lack of confidence, by suspicion. His theses are absolute, Olympian, haughty. He understands only the interests of his own group, the techniques and theses of his party. He does not admit any reasoning contrary to his own, because he considers himself the exclusive master of reason. This leads him to see the course of human liberty from only one angle. This posture makes him mentally unilateral. All of this also leads him to ethical Manicheeism: Only I think correctly, my adversary is in error; only my group and I are good, all others are bad, detestable. Thus, since he does not understand another's reason, neither does he accept his neighbor's error. He falls on him implacably with the fury of a vengeful deity. Since man, however, is both truth and error, greatness and misery, heroism and weakness, the sectarian is unable to interpret or understand man. His interpretative unilateriality is rooted in what we may call pseudo-orthodoxy.

Within a revolutionary context nothing has been, nor is, so harmful in Colombia and America in general as the sectarianism of the revolutionaries. The unity of the Left is a myth, so long as it is not free from the sectarianism which dominates and paralyzes it. Many of our Leftists must begin the revolution by overcoming their own sectarianism. Otherwise, they will never be anything other than simple, underdeveloped agitators.

The present tendency of the world is towards the union of forces for the common good. This is not only an abstract concept but a positive and practical value for all. Many of our Leftist revolutionaries have not understood this. This is why Camilo demanded dialogue as an absolutely necessary basis for action. He did so because he understood the times. He had a global concept of the problems. Therefore, he wanted to gather all the parties of the Left around his platform as a minimal basis of understanding. Did they respond? No! They continued in their sectarianism. Camilo subjected them to a trial by fire, and they could not stand up to his absolute honesty.

Thus we can see why they abandoned him. The decisions to abandon him were always justified by a number of "reasons." In the attempt to exonerate their own consciences and image, they usually added "fundamental." Thus stated, it sounded very good—"fundamental reasons." With such a pretext every treason was justified. But Camilo did not appeal to "fundamental reasons." He called for an opening to dialogue on the part of all and addressed to all.

What we must understand is that Camilo's ideas are more transcendent than he himself was. We must give to Camilo a universal dimension, a universal meaning, because he was a symbol of rebellion against the oppression of the people. We must at the same time defend Camilo from fanaticism, sectarianism and "canonization." Every group wants to carry away his body. That is the error. They want to take his body, not his ideas nor his meaning. The reactionaries claim Camilo's body to bury it a thousand feet deep and impede his historic resonance. The revolutionaries demand Camilo as their property in order to disfigure him. And the canonizers?

"In the life of great revolutionaries," wrote Lenin, "the oppressor classes subject them to constant persecution, hear their doctrine with the most savage rage, with the most furious hatred, with the most immoral campaign of lies and calumnies. After their death, they try to convert them into inoffensive canonized icons, surrounding their names with a certain aura of glory in order to 'console' and trick the oppressed classes, castrating the content of their revolutionary doctrine, dulling the revolutionary edge of this doctrine, degrading it."

Listen well to that. It is not right to make a myth out of Camilo. Nor is it right to wrap him in the banner of opportunism. The only flag worthy of him is that of his own exact dimensions, of his own greatness. It is not right to carry him to glittering altars nor to exhibit him at fiestas—nor at the noisy meetings of fanatics. You, Christian; you, Communist; you, nationalist; you, democrat; you, unbeliever; you, student; you, socialist; you, worker; you, peasant; you, man—do you understand Camilo?

The dialogue which he demanded had a human foundation. He did not intend to discuss abstract theology (every group has its own theology or at least its own mythology) but rather to concentrate on the necessity of interpreting and understanding man.

Such dialogue cannot treat only political dogmas. It has to be established among progressive groups who desire an integral social transformation. It must be stimulated by the urgency of socioeconomic change, the mechanics of accomplishing it, the instruments which make it viable, the ultimate consequences it will have. It must be a dialogue uniting men in action, not a hare-brained crusade or mere meaningless apologetics.

What other reasons are there for understanding why Camilo was a Christian? why he was not a pretender? why he believed in his commitment but avoided fanfare? why he would not accept wretchedness?

Because he was loyal to his convictions, not an occasional revolutionary. He was authentic. He had the courage to face the exploiters with absolute honesty. He was an idea in action and he knew how to be consistent. His was a loud cry for justice. His was the courage to expose himself to frustration at the hands of the people. He had the audacity to shout aloud that there was some truth in all the various systems and that we must encounter one another in that truth.

Every man is the consequence of his own vocation. If he is absolutely faithful to it, his personal destiny is soon converted into the necessary sacrifice. Camilo was the result of his vocation, poured out in a total offering. He was an unheard-of case. Colombia produced him, gave birth to him. It gave birth to what was unheard-of. Now it gives him to America, to the World, with the certainty of inevitable resurrection. Camilo has not died. He is the symbol of the new America. With him *hope* is born.

Notes

CHAPTER I

1. *Frente Popular,* organ of the Frente Unido (United Popular Front) movement, I, No. 1 (February 15, 1967), pp. 4, 5.
2. Julián Motta Salas, *Recuerdos del Ingenioso Hidalgo* (Imprenta Departmental, Neiva, 1950), p. 115.
3. A. Porot, *Diccionario de Psiquiatría* (Labor, Barcelona, 1962), p. 408.
4. Carlos Castro Saavedra, "Despedida," *El Tiempo,* February 1966.

CHAPTER 2

1. In statement to the press, June 24, 1965.
2. Camilo Torres Restrepo, "El Hombre Bidimensional," a conference given in the auditorium of Radio Sutatenza, Bogotá, September 1963.
3. *Idem.* in: CIDOC (Centro Intercultural de Documentación), Sondeos No. 5, Cuernavaca, Mexico, May 1967, p. 203.

4. In "El Hombre Bidimensional."
5. Vicente Andrade Valderrama, S.J., "Quien es responsable de la tragedia de Camilo Torres?" *Revista Javeriana,* March 1966, p. 179.
6. Fr. Enrique Acosta Rincón, letter to Fr. Vicente Andrade Valderrama, Bogotá, April 7, 1966.
7. François Houtart, "Camilo Torres en tant que prêtre," *Le Cercle,* a publication of Colombian Students at Louvain, pp. 14, passim.
8. Vicente Andrade Valderrama, S.J., *op. cit.,* p. 179.
9. Fr. Enrique Acosta Rincón, letter already cited.
10. Camilo Torres Restrepo in a lecture on the importance of an economic progress for the apostolate in underdeveloped countries, presented at Louvain (Second International Congress of Pro Mundi Vita, 1964), published by Editiones del Caribe, Bogotá, 1965, under the title *La Revolución Imperativo Cristiano.*
11. *El Tiempo,* June 27, 1965.
12. *El Tiempo,* September 2, 1965.
13. *El Pais* (Cali), August 2, 1965.
14. Camilo Torres Restrepo, "El Sacerdos es un Brujo?" CIDOC, Sondeos No. 5, p. 63.
15. Hernán Zambrano, "Mi Amigo Camilo Torres," *Revista Inquietudes,* II, No. 8, April 1966, p. 7.

CHAPTER 3

1. Camilo Torres Restrepo, "El Problema de la Estructuracion de una Autentica Sociologia Latinamericana," p. 10. A report presented in *Journadas Latinamericanas de Sociología.* The citations are taken from Camilo's original.
2. *Ibid.,* p. 1, passim.
3. Orlando Fals Borda, "Desarrollo y Perspectivas de la Sociologia Rural en Colombia y La America Latina" in *Memoria del Primer Congreso Nacional de Sociología* (Iqueima, Bogotá, 1963), p. 155.
4. Camilo Torres Restrepo, "Los Problemas Sociales en la Realidad Actual,"*Fondo Universitario Nacional: Reforma Universitaria* (Empresa Nacional de Publicaciones, Bogotá, 1957), pp. 158 and passim.
5. Idem, "Un Sacerdote en la Universidad," *El Catolicismo* (Bogotá), June 28, 1962.
6. *Idem,* "Informe General del Instituto de Administratión Social" (a mimeographed report). ESAP, 177-65/IAS-86 (May 13, 1965), pp. 1 and passim.
7. *Ibid.,* pp. 5 and passim. (Although the dollar sign is in use in Bolivian currency, these are not, of course, American dollars. At the present

rate of exchange, $1.00 United States is approximately 15 Colombian pesos. Ed.)

8. Camilo Torres Restrepo, Personal Documents, No. 25.
9. *Ibid.*, No. 26.
10. Prades, "Camilo como Sociólogo." A conference published by the Colombian students at Louvain, *Cercle* (1966), p. 8.
11. Camilo Torres, "La Violencia," *Actas del Primer Congreso Colombiano de Sociología,* pp. 97-98; *Cristianismo y Revolución,* No. 4 (Buenos Aires), March 1967, p. 11.

CHAPTER 4

1. Cited in *Documentos Politicos,* magazine of the Colombian Communist Party, No. 61, Bogotá, August 1966, p. 67.
2. J. L. Martin Descalzo, "La Renovación de la Iglesia Eterna," *El Tiempo* Dominican Lectures, February 5, 1967, p. 7.
3. See the Encyclical, *Populorum Progressio* of Pope Paul VI, Second Part, Nos. 44, 56, 57.
4. *Documentos Politicos,* No. 58, p. 125.
5. *El Tiempo,* January 6, 1967.
6. Acción Cultural Popular, Sintesis Gráfica de los Grandes problemas de Colombia, Bogotá, 1962.
7. *El Tiempo,* July 13, 1966. Report of the Bank of the Republic, November 1966, p. 465.
8. *Voz Proletaria,* January 26, 1967, p. 4. Consejo National del Trabajo para una politica de empleo. Bogotá, 1966, pp. 12, passim.
9. International Financial Statistics, October 1966, p. 86.
10. United Nations Report, *El Financiamento Externo de América Latina,* New York 1964, p. 53.
11. "Controlaria General de la República," *Economia Colombiana,* No. 82, p. 35.
12. *Mensaje,* No. 115, p. 663.
13. *Mensaje,* No. 115, p. 666.
14. "Comunismo en la Iglesia?" *La Hora* (Bogotá), May 1965.
15. Maurice Duverger, "La Influencia de las Fuerzas Políticas en la Administración Pública en los países en proceso de desarrollo," *Documentos de la I Conferencia Latinoamericana sobre la Administración Pública en los Países Desarrollados,* I, p. 18. ESAP, Bogotá, 1963.
16. Second International Congress, Pro Mundi Vita. Camilo Torres, *Programmation Economique et Exigences Apostoliques* (Louvain, 1964), pp. 215 et passim.
17. *Frente Unido,* December 18, 1965, p. 1. Author's note: Message to the

Oligarchy and those directed to the Political Prisoners and to the United Front of the People were certainly not written by Camilo. It appears that he only gave the ideas. They were written by some of his collaborators. The difference in style can be seen at first glance. However, he did not renounce them, even though they appeared under his signature.

CHAPTER 5

1. Ignacio Silone, *El Pensamiento vivo de Mazzini,* 2nd ed. (Losada, Buenos Aires, 1945), p. 135.
2. *Ibid.,* p. 80.
3. Bernardo Gaitán Mahecha, "El hombre rebelde," *El Siglo,* February 20, 1966.
4. Oscar Maldonado, "Camilo Torres," *C.I.F. Repórter,* Vol. 5, No. 4.
5. Arnold Toynbee, *America and the World Revolution* (1962); J. Comblin, *Naçao e Nacionalismo* (Sao Paulo, 1965), pp. 134ff.; *Situaçao social de America Latina* (Latin American Center of Research in the Social Sciences, Rio de Janeiro, 1965); "Revolución en America Latina," *Mensaje,* 115 (1963); "Reformas Revolucionarias en América Latina," *Mensaje,* 123 (1963); C. Furtado, *A Prevoluçao brasileira* (Rio de Janeiro, 1962); C. Mendes de Almeida, *Nacionalismo e desemvolvimiento* (Rio de Janeiro, 1963); F. Houtart, "Service social et transformation social en 'Latin America,'" *Service social dans le Monde,* 21 (1962), 122-129.
6. Jaime C. Snoeck (Doctor of Theology from the Angelicum, Rome): "Revolution and Christianity," *Concilium,* Vol. 2, No. 15, May 1966, pp. 25, passim.
7. Camilo Torres Restrepo, "Conferencia a los Obreros," *Vanguardia Sindical,* July 23, 1965.
8. Camilo Torres Restrepo: Personal Documents, No. 18.
9. *Mensaje,* 115, December 1962, p. 593.
10. Snoeck, *op. cit.,* p. 35.
11. *Mensaje,* 115, p. 593.
12. *Ibid.,* pp. 590-593.
13. *Vanguardia Sindical* (Bogotá), July 23, 1965.
14. "Two-Edged Sword" was the name which appeared on the Cardinal's letter.
15. *Mensaje,* 123, pp. 481, 482, 484.
16. William Fulbright, *Old Myths and New Realities* (New York: Random House, 1964, A Vintage Book), pp. 35-36. Cf. Hernando Agudelo Villa, *La Revolucion del desarrollo* (Roble, Mexico, D. F., 1966), p. 137.

17. Ignacio Fernández de Castro, *Teoria sobre la revolución* (Taurus, Madrid, 1966) p. 25.
18. *Ibid.*, p. 163.
19. Camilo Torres Restrepo, "Un sacerdote en la universidad," *El Catolicismo* (Bogotá), June 28, 1962.
20. *Mensaje,* 115, p. 592.
21. *C.N.P. Repórter,* 2, May-June 1964, pp. 13, 9.
22. *El Siglo,* October 1, 1967, p. 5.
23. *La República,* June 16, 1965.
24. *El Tiempo,* June 16, 1965.
25. *El Vespertino,* June 19, 1965.
26. *Ibid.*, June 21, 1965.
27. *El Tiempo,* June 21, 1965.
28. *La República,* June 21, 1965.
29. *El Vespertino,* June 28, 1965.
30. *El Espectador,* June 4, 1965.
31. *El Nacional* (Barranquilla), August 6, 1965.
32. *El Espectador,* August 11, 1965.
33. *Muchedumbres,* September 6, 1965.

Chapter 6

1. *Frente Unido,* I, No. 1, August 26, 1965. Author's Note: Texts with some additions appeared later. It has been impossible to determine whether Camilo had had advance notice of them. However, he did not disown them.
2. *La República,* June 23, 1965.
3. *Biblioteca de Autores Cristianos, commentarios a la "Pacem in Terris"* (Madrid, 1963), p. 162.
4. *Etica Social* (Bogotá, 1964), p. 70, passim. Work developed by Father Adán Londoño, S.J.
5. *Frente Unido,* October 14, 1965, p. 8.
6. Stefan Zweig, *Sternstunden der Menscheit.*

Chapter 7

1. Personal Documents, No. 2.
2. Cf. Letter to Bishop Isaza (no date). The original copy signed by Camilo was consulted.
3. Hernán Jiménez Arango (Priest, Doctor in Canon Law), reported in *El Tiempo,* September 11, 1966.

4. *Cidoc Informa* (Cuernavaca, Mexico), Vol. III, No. 14 (July 15, 1966), p. 249.
5. In "El Clero, Una Especie que Desaparece." CIDOC Doc. 67/19. Reprinted by the magazine *Siempre* (Mexico), July 12, 1967.
6. In "Encrucijadas de la Iglesia en América Latina" (no date). Cf. Sondeos No. 5, p. 312.
7. "La Violencia y Los Cambios Socioculturales en Las Areas Rurales Colombianas." Cf. the minutes of the first national congress of sociology already cited, (Ch. 3, n.3); pp. 137 and passim.
8. Interview given to *La Patria* (Manizales), reprinted by *El Tiempo,* May 22, 1965.
9. *El Siglo,* June 22, 1965.
10. In "Encrucijadas de la Iglesia en América Latina." Sondeos No. 5, p. 315.
11. *Ibid.,* p. 319.
12. "Comunismo en la Iglesia," *La Hora* (Bogotá), May 1965.
13. "Hablan los Curas Rebeldes," *C.N.P. Repórter* (Bogotá), August-September, 1965.
14. In a letter to Bishop Isaza (already cited).
15. Informaciones Catolicas Internacionales. No. 255, January 7, 1966.
16. Taken from *Cristianismo y Revolución,* reprinted by *Reconstructión,* VI, No. 34 (Medellín), February 1967, pp. 3 and passim.

CHAPTER 8

1. See the declaration of the Cardinal, May 28, 1965.
2. Camilo Torres Restrepo, Personal Documents, No. 2.
3. *Ibid.*
4. *Inquietudes,* No. 5, p. 24.
5. *Ibid.,* p. 25.
6. Camilo Torres Restrepo, Personal Documents, No. 1.
7. *Inquietudes,* No. 5, p. 27.
8. *Ibid.,* p. 27.
9. *Ibid.,* p. 35.
10. Camilo Torres Restrepo, Personal Documents, No. 3.
11. *Inquietudes,* No. 5, p. 40.
12. Camilo Torres Restrepo, Personal Documents, No. 4.
13. *El Siglo,* July 7, 1965.
14. *El Espectador,* August 15, 1965.
15. *El Espectador,* September 24, 1965.
16. In *Frente Unido,* September 30, 1965.
17. "Camilo Torres en tant que prêtre," *op. cit.*
18. *Mensaje,* No. 147, March-April 1966, p. 120.

CHAPTER 9

1. *El Espectador,* June 15, 1965.
2. *Ibid.*
3. *Ibid.*
4. *El Vespertino,* June 15, 1965.
5. *El Tiempo,* June 15, 1965.
6. *Ibid.*
7. *El Pais,* June 21, 1965.
8. August 4, 1965.
9. *La República,* June 21, 1965.
10. *El Espectador,* March 15, 1965.
11. *Ibid.,* Sunday, June 20, 1965.
12. *Ibid.*
13. *Ibid.*
14. *El Pais,* June 22, 1965.
15. *El Colombiano,* June 22, 1965.
16. *La República,* June 22, 1965.
17. *El Tiempo,* June 22, 1965.
18. *El Tiempo,* June 23, 1965.
19. *El Colombiano,* June 25th and 26th, 1965.
20. *El Espectador,* Sunday Magazine, June 27, 1965.
21. *Occidente,* June 28, 1965.
22. *El Correo,* July 4, 1965.
23. *El Espectador,* July 8, 1965.
24. *El Tiempo,* July 10, 1965, and *El Espectador* of the same date.
25. Occidente, July 11, 1965.
26. *El Correo,* July 25, 1965.
27. *La República,* August 8, 1965.
28. *La Patria,* August 10, 1965.
29. El Colombiano, August 12, 1965.

CHAPTER 10

1. *Frente Unido,* I, No. 1 (August 26, 1965), p. 1.
2. Ricardo Valencia, "Los no Alineados: El por qué repudio a los partidos," *Frente Unido,* I, No. 4 (September 16, 1965), p. 5. Emphasis added.
3. *Frente Uuido,* I, No. 7 (October 7, 1965), p. 7.

CHAPTER 11

1. *El Espectador,* Sunday Magazine, July 4, 1965.
2. *Frente Unido,* I, No. 1 (August 26, 1965), p. 6.

3. *El Tiempo,* June 18, 1965.
4. *Semana al Dia,* June 18, 1965.
5. Jaine Niño Dies, "Responsable Nacional, La Democracia Cristiana y Camilo, February 2, 1966," *La Gaceta,* III, No. 13 (March-April 1966), p. 28.
6. Camilo Torres Restrepo, *Personal Documents,* No. 6.
7. *Frente Unido,* No. 5 (September 23, 1965). Editorial, p. 8, "Un Nuevo Camino."
8. *Frente Unido,* No. 6 (September 30, 1965), p. 3.
9. *El Espectador,* July 7, 1965.
10. "Movimiento Obrero Estudiantil," June 7, III Congress (s.f.); pamphlet published in Bogotá in 1966, p. 5.
11. *Ibid.,* p. 20, passim.
12. *Frente Unido,* I, No. 10 (October 28, 1965), p. 8.
13. Camilo Torres Restrepo, "Message to the Non-Aligned," September 16, 1965.

CHAPTER 12

1. Jorge M. Cottier, O.P., "The Attraction of Communism" in the magazine *Concilium,* No. 3, March 1965, pp. 85, 86.
2. *Voz Proletariana,* No. 80.
3. *Ibid.,* February 24, 1966.
4. *Frente Unido,* I, No. 2 (Bogotá), September 2, 1965.
5. Diego Montaña Cuéllar, "Camilo Prometeo encadenado," *Voz Proletaria* (Bogotá), March 3, 1966, p. 4.
6. "El Diálogo de la Epoca" in Maria Gozzini, *Introducción al Diálogo* (Buenos Aires, 1965), p. 57.
7. *Ibid.,* Lucio Lombardo Radice, "Un Marxista ante Hechos Nuevos," pp. 78, 86.
8. *Ibid.,* Luciano Gruppi, "El PCI y los Católicos," p. 151.
9. *Ibid.,* Alberto Cecchi, "Perspectivas de Posibles Entendimientos," p. 186.
10. *Ibid.,* Ruggero Orfei, "No enemigos, sino hermanos separados," p. 161.
11. *Biblioteca de Autores Christianos,* "Mater et Magister," p. 239.

CHAPTER 13

1. *El Tiempo,* June 21, 1962.
2. *El Tiempo,* June 21, 1962.
3. *El Espectador,* June 20, 1962. Note, Camilo had held his position since March of 1959.

4. *El Catolicismo,* edition which circulated June 29, 1962. See also *El Tiempo* of the same date.
5. Jorge Child, "Leña y Fuego," article published in *Vanguardia* of M.R.L., June 28, 1962.
6. Camilo Torres Restrepo, "Critica y Autocritica," *El Espectador,* November 27, 1964.
7. *El Tiempo,* "El Verdadero Caso de Camilo Torres" (editorial), February 20, 1966.
8. Miguel Hernández, *Cancionero y Romancero de Ausencias* (Lautaro, Buenos Aires, 1958), p. 84.
9. Camilo Torres Restrepo, "Mensaje a los Estudiantes," November 25, 1965.
10. *Ibid.*
11. Jorge Zalamea, *Antecedentes Históricos de la Revolución Cubana* (Ediciones Sur América, Bogotá, 1961), p. 139.
12. Camilo Torres Restrepo, "Conferencia en la Universidad INNCA de Colombia," September 21, 1965.
13. Alvaro Mendoza Diez, *La revolución de los profesionales e intelectuales en Latinoamérica* (Mexico, 1962), p. 92, passim.
14. In *Frente Unido,* October 21, 1965.

CHAPTER 14

1. Otto Morales Benítez, *Planeamientos Sociales* (Imprenta Nacional, 1960), p. 124.
2. Guillermo Camacho Enriques, *Derecho del Trabajo,* Vol. I (Temis, Bogotá, 1961), p. 57, passim; also *El Pensaminento social de Rafael Uribe,* Biblioteca del ministerio del Trabajo, Vol. VI, 1960.
3. Otto Morales Benítez, *op. cit.,* p. 127.
4. *Frente Unido,* I, No. 5 (Bogotá), September 23, 1965, p. 1.

CHAPTER 15

1. *La Gaceta,* January-February 1966, p. 16.
2. Cf. *Hora-Cero.* Testimonios Revolucionarios de América Latina, No. 1, June-July 1967. Mexico.
3. *Ibid.,* p. 102.
4. *Churuco:* meat of a monkey which abounds in these regions.
5. *Frente Unido,* I, No. 3 (September 9, 1965), p. 1.
6. *El Tiempo,* September 10, 1965.
7. *Frente Unido,* I, No. 7 (October 7, 1965), p. 1.
8. Statement of General César A. Cabrera, Commanding General of the

Armed Forces, *El Vespertino,* No. 765 (January 7, 1967), p. 11; *La Patria,* January 8, 1967.

9. Colonel Alvaro Valencia Tovar, statements published in *El Pais,* No. 5.974, January 8, 1967.
10. *El Espacio,* January 9, 1967.
11. *El Espectador,* No. 1 (January 11, 1967).
12. *El Tiempo,* December 1, 1967.
13. CIDOC *Informa,* Vol. 11, No. 17 (September 1, 1965), p. 246.
14. *El Siglo,* March 6, 1963, p. 3.
15. *El Espectador,* July 5, 1965.
16. Camilo Torres Restrepo, Personal Documents, No. 15. *Insurrection* is the clandestine organ of information of the Army of National Liberation.
17. *Idem.,* Personal Documents, No. 16. In the original there are blanks where proper names should be.
18. *Idem.,* Personal Documents, No. 17.

CHAPTER 16

1. *El Espectador,* Friday, February 18, 1966, p. 5-A.
2. *El Espacio, January* 7, 1966.
3. *El Siglo,* January 17, 1966.
4. *El Tiempo,* February 1, 1966.
5. *El Tiempo,* No. 18905, Wednesday, February 16, 1966, p. 1.
6. *El Vespertino,* No. 500, February 16, 1966.
7. *El Espacio,* No. 174, February 17, 1966.
8. *El Tiempo,* February 18, 1966.
9. *El Espacio,* Thursday, February 17, 1966, p. 1; *El Espectador,* Friday, February 18, 1966, p. 5-A.
10. *El Vespertino,* February 18, 1966, p. 7a.
11. *El Tiempo,* February 20, 1966.
12. *El Siglo,* Monday, January 17, 1966.
13. *Insurrection,* special number, March 1, 1966, p. 1, passim.
14. Campaign against the Army of National Liberation, Notebook No. 4, pp. 370-371.
15. *Ibid.*
16. *Ibid.,* Notebook No. 4, pp. 372-373. Note: The text of the previous documents was taken from the article of Professor Eduardo Umaña Luna, titled "Asi recuerdo a Camilo," in *Cromos,* No. 2574, Monday, February 20, 1967, p. 19.
17. Camilo Torres Restrepo, Personal Documents, No. 11.
18. Ministry of Government M-0162. Dispatch of the Minister. Camilo Torres Restrepo, Personal Documents, No. 12.

19. Commandant of the Fifth Brigade—Private. Camilo Torres Restrepo, Personal Documents, No. 13.
20. C. de C. No. 20.083.747, de Bogotá. *Frente Popular,* I, April 15, 1967, p. 3.

CHAPTER 17

1. *El Espectador,* February 18, 1966.
2. *El Siglo,* February 18, 1966.
3. *Ibid.*
4. *El Espacio,* February 19, 1966.
5. *El Signo,* February 19, 1966.
6. *Voz Proletaria,* February 24, 1966.
7. *El Vespertino,* February 17, 1966, p. 5.
8. *El Espectador,* February 17, 1966.
9. *El Siglo,* March 3, 1966.
10. *El Tiempo,* February 22, 1968.
11. *Voz Proletaria,* March 17, 1966.
12. *El Espacio,* February 19, 1966.
13. *El Espectador,* February 18, 1966.
14. *Ibid.*
15. *El Espacio,* February 17, 1966.
16. *Ibid.*
17. *Ibid.*
18. *Voz Proletaria,* March 3, 1966, p. 7.
19. *Voz Proletaria,* February 24, 1966, p. 3.
20. *El Tiempo,* February 18, 1966.
21. *El Siglo,* February 19, 1966.
22. *El Siglo,* February 20, 1966.
23. *Ibid.*
24. *El Espectador,* February 22, 1968.
25. *El Espacio,* February 19, 1966. In the same paper, on February 23, 1966, a priest whose name was omitted by request fully rejected the theses of Amaya.
26. *El Siglo,* February 26, 1966.
27. *El Espectador,* February 21, 1966.
28. *El Espectador,* February 18, 1966.
29. *El Espectador,* February 23, 1966.
30. *C.N.P. Repórter,* No. 12, March 1966, p. 34, passim.
31. *Gaceta Tercer Mundo,* Nos. 29-30, September-October 1966, p. 11.

CHAPTER 18.

1. Juan Marinello, *Meditación Americana* (Procyón, Buenos Aires, 1959), pp. 169, 170.
2. CIDOC, Sondeos No. 5, p. 325.
3. Rafael Maldonado Piedrahíta, *Conversaciones con un Sacerdote Colombiano* (Antares, Bogotá, 1957), p. 28.
4. *C.N.P. Repórter,* No. 10, September 1965, p. 16.